Sarah Fielding

Twayne's English Authors Series

Herbert Sussman, Editor

Northeastern University

TEAS 522

ILLUSTRATION FROM SARAH FIELDING'S
THE HISTORY OF OPHELIA, 1785 EDITION.
Reprinted by permission of the Syndics of Cambridge University Library.

Sarah Fielding

Linda Bree

University of Essex

Twayne Publishers
An Imprint of Simon & Schuster Macmillan
New York

Prentice Hall International
London • Mexico City • New Delhi • Singapore • Sydney • Toronto

Twayne's English Authors Series No. 522

Sarah Fielding
Linda Bree

Twayne Publishers
An Imprint of Simon & Schuster Macmillan
1633 Broadway
New York, New York 10019

Library of Congress Cataloging-in-Publication Data

Bree, Linda.
    Sarah Fielding / Linda Bree.
        p.   cm.—(Twayne's English authors series ; no. 522)
    Includes bibliographical references and index.
    ISBN 0-8057-7051-8 (alk. paper)
    1. Fielding, Sarah, 1710–1768—Criticism and interpretation.
    2. Women and literature—England—History—18th century.   I. Title.
    II. Series : Twayne's English authors series ; TEAS 522.
    PR3459.F3Z58   1996
    823'.5—dc20   96-12872
                                                                                                        CIP

10 9 8 7 6 5 4 3 2 1

Printed in the United States of America

Contents

Preface

During the course of my research for this study, I have often found myself having to explain—to librarians, academics, students, friends, and relatives—who Sarah Fielding was. On each occasion I have found it easiest to answer, "the sister of Henry Fielding"; I have then added hastily—and with increasing confidence as my researches developed—"but she is also a significant writer in her own right." I have felt guilty in seeming to collude with the view of Sarah Fielding prevalent for 200 years after her death that the most significant thing about her was her relationship to one of the two great canonical novelists of the 18th century (and, indeed, that the second most significant thing about her was her relationship to the other: she was a close friend of Samuel Richardson); but I have comforted myself with the thought that much of my ambivalence about the value of being sister to Henry Fielding was probably shared by Sarah herself. She might never have become a writer at all if it had not been for Henry's active encouragement of her talents, and his knowledge of the publishing and reading world of 1740s and 1750s England clearly benefited her literary career. But his published comments about her work, while always intended to be complimentary, strongly suggest that he had a much more limited idea of both her general capability, and her aims in writing fiction, than her fiction itself demonstrates. Moreover, his ever-growing reputation has inevitably obscured Sarah's achievements, to the extent that her first—and highly successful—novel, *The Adventures of David Simple*, was for a long time chiefly sought out because Henry provided a Preface to the second edition. When critics of the canon noticed Sarah Fielding's work at all, it was either to learn more about Henry (Arnold Needham's 1943 Ph.D. thesis, "The Life and Works of Sarah Fielding," openly declares that one of its intentions is to throw "many an interesting sidelight . . . on her brother") or to dissect the style and content of Sarah's fictions as an inevitably unsatisfactory patchwork of qualities directly derived from her brother and her friend.

The purpose of this first full-length study of Sarah Fielding's life and work is to focus on Sarah Fielding, not as a sister or friend of the literary great but in her own right as a prominent writer and scholar, whose work influenced many of her readers as well as other writers. It is a timely project. Recent criticism has thankfully moved away from the idea that the work of the canonical novelists represents the sum total of all that is significant, interesting, or influential about 18th-century fiction. Feminist and historicist scholarship offers new perspectives on the role of the woman writer in the 18th century and on the ways in which 18th-century audiences reacted to the kind of didactic fiction with which many novelists—women and men—were closely concerned. Research into the culture and contexts of mid-18th-century fiction has revealed a complicated network of collaboration and mutual influence in which Sarah Fielding played an important part. Over the past 30 years, a number of Ph.D. students have concentrated on Sarah Fielding, and her work has been considered afresh in surveys of 18th-century fiction. New information continues to come to light about the circumstances of her life. Finally, the works themselves are becoming widely available once more. New editions of *David Simple*, *Volume the Last*, and *The Governess* were published by Oxford University Press in the late 1960s, and *David Simple*, with *Volume the Last*, has been available in paperback since 1987. Facsimile editions of several of Fielding's works were published in the early 1970s; *The Cry* was reproduced, with a scholarly introduction, in 1986; a critical edition of *The Lives of Cleopatra and Octavia* was issued in 1994; a facsimile edition of *The History of Ophelia* will be published in 1997. It is now possible for undergraduates and general readers—as well as scholars with access to specialist academic libraries—to read what Sarah Fielding actually wrote. She can once again be appreciated—as she was in her own lifetime—as a radical, original, and entertaining writer, whose works challenged the reader with serious issues of morality and ethics in action.

The conventions of feminine modesty and literary anonymity that operated in mid-18th-century England make it difficult, even now, to be sure that all Sarah Fielding's literary work has been identified. Her name is on the title page of one of her works, her translation of Xenophon's *Memoirs of Socrates* (1762), and affixed to the dedication of another, *The Lives of Cleopatra and Octavia* (1757). Most of her other fiction is clearly labeled "By the Author of David Simple," so authorship is not in doubt. There are, however, outstanding problems of attribution in minor works. I have assumed, with most other scholars, that she was author of Leonora's letter to Horatio, in Henry Fielding's *Joseph Andrews* (1742), and of Anna Boleyn's narrative in "A Journey from This World to the Next," in Henry's *Miscellanies* (1743); both provide interesting evidence of Fielding's writing before *David Simple*, and of the habits of collaboration developing among her circle. She also contributed some letters and articles to her brother's journals in the late 1740s, but it is impossible, at this distance, to determine which. She has been claimed as the author of a wide variety of novels, including *Leonora* (1745), *The Ladies Drawing Room* (1745), Sarah Scott's *The History of Cornelia* (1750), Charlotte Lennox's *The Female Quixote* (1752), Jane Collier's *The Art of Ingeniously Tormenting* (1753), *Memoirs of Sir Charles Goodville and His Family* (1753), and *The History of Betty Barnes*; most of these are surmises of Lady Mary Wortley Montagu, who was living abroad during the years of Sarah Fielding's literary career, and all may be discounted.

There is, however, at least one text that remains a matter of genuine doubt. *Histories of Some of the Penitents in the Magdalen House* was published anonymously in 1760, partly to publicize a charitable scheme for fallen women organized by, among others, Samuel Richardson and Fielding's half brother Sir John Fielding. One of Sarah Fielding's friends, Catherine Talbot, wrote that she did not know the author of this "very pretty book" but thought the writing "at least a very good likeness of Mrs. Fielding"; and it has since often been suggested that Fielding was indeed the author. I am not convinced. Although she would have been kindly disposed toward the Magdalen House scheme, there is no evidence that she used her writing skills for the purpose of supporting this, or any other, venture. The subject of fallen women is one in which—in striking contrast to many of her contemporaries—Fielding shows little interest in the rest of her fiction; in the late 1750s she was living in Bath (a long way from the Magdalen House in London) and working hard on a number of other literary schemes, including her translation of Xenophon, while coping with bouts of serious illness; some correspondence from this period that has recently come to light does not mention the *Penitents* project. For these and other reasons, I do not think Fielding is the author of *Histories of Some of the Penitents in the Magdalen House*, and I have not included it in this study; but the evidence is not conclusive, and further work may yield other opinions.

I am grateful to many people who have helped me during the preparation of this book. Particular thanks are due to Isobel Grundy, who read an early draft of my biographical chapter, and to Clive T. Probyn, who advised on my text at a later stage. I would also like to thank Martin C. Battestin, Rev. Patrick Birt, Judith Hawley, Bernard Jones, John Reeves, Betty Rizzo, Ms. J. M. Baillie of Leicestershire Record Office, Suzanne Edward of Salisbury Cathedral Library, Linda Matthews of Wiltshire Library and Museums Service, and the staffs of Cambridge University

Library and the British Library. I am especially grateful to Carolyn
Powell and Hoang-My Dunkle of the Huntington Library, who were
prompt and diligent in following up queries that were on occasion vague
in the extreme. Herbert Sussman, my academic editor at Twayne, has
been unfailingly patient and supportive, even in response to my requests
for more time. And finally, I must record my gratitude, as ever, to my
husband, Bill Bree, who has been a tower of strength, both in encouraging me to pursue my research and in advising me when to stop.

Chronology

1710   Sarah Fielding born 8 November at East Stour, Dorset, England, the fourth child and third daughter of Colonel Edmund Fielding and Sarah Gould Fielding.

1718   Sarah Gould Fielding dies 14 April. The East Stour estate left for the benefit of the children. Colonel Fielding remarries.

1719   Sarah Fielding and her sisters removed from East Stour by their grandmother Lady Gould in protest at Colonel and Mrs. Fielding's behavior and entered at Mrs. Mary Rookes's boarding school in Salisbury.

1722   Lord Chancellor awards Lady Gould custody of Sarah and her sisters: they are to remain with Mrs. Rooke during term time and spend their holidays with Lady Gould.

1733   Lady Gould dies. Sarah Fielding probably moves back to East Stour with her sisters.

1739   The East Stour estate sold. Sarah Fielding possibly moves to Bath.

1741   Edmund (now General) Fielding dies.

1742   Sarah Fielding's letter "from Leonora to Horatio" included in Henry Fielding's *Joseph Andrews*.

1743   Sarah Fielding's narrative of Anna Boleyn included in "A Journey from This World to the Next" in Henry Fielding's *Miscellanies*.

1744   *The Adventures of David Simple*; second edition published with Henry Fielding's "Preface" in place of Sarah Fielding's "Advertisement." Sarah Fielding goes to live with Henry Fielding in London after the death of his wife.

1747   *Familiar Letters Between the Characters in David Simple and Others*. Henry Fielding remarries; Sarah Fielding goes to live with her sisters—Catharine, Beatrice, and Ursula—in Westminster.

1749 *The Governess, or Little Female Academy* (January), print-
       ed by Samuel Richardson, by now a close friend of
       Sarah Fielding. *Remarks on Clarissa* (January). Sarah
       Fielding planning a "Book upon Education" (never
       published) and *The Lives of Cleopatra and Octavia.*

1750–51 Sarah Fielding's three sisters die. Sarah Fielding remains
         in London, lodging with close friend Jane Collier.

1751 Sarah Fielding sued for debt (March). Henry Fielding's
       Amelia published.

1753 *David Simple: Volume the Last.* Jane Collier's *The Art of
       Ingeniously Tormenting* published.

1754 *The Cry* (March), possibly written in collaboration with
       Jane Collier. Henry Fielding dies in Lisbon in October.
       Sarah Fielding in Bath for her health.

1754–55 Jane Collier dies. Sarah Fielding settles in Bathwick, on
         the outskirts of Bath, near Sarah Scott and Lady
         Barbara Montagu in Batheaston.

1757 *The Lives of Cleopatra and Octavia* (May).

1758 Sarah Fielding working with James Harris on a memoir
       of Henry Fielding, to be affixed to a new collected edi-
       tion of his work (the memoir was never published).
       Sarah Fielding working on a translation from Greek of
       Xenophon's *Memoirs of Socrates.*

1759 *The History of the Countess of Dellwyn* (March).

1760 *The History of Ophelia* (March). Sarah Fielding moves to
       Walcot.

1761 Publication of Sarah Fielding's Xenophon translation
       delayed because of her ill health. Richardson dies 4
       July.

1762 *Xenophon's Memoirs of Socrates, with the Defence of Socrates
       Before His Judges* (January).

1764 Ralph Allen dies, leaving Sarah Fielding £100.

1765 Lady Bab Montagu dies, leaving Sarah Fielding an
       annuity of £10, and £10 to rent a garden plot.

1766 Sarah Fielding leaves Walcot and moves into lodgings
       with or near Sarah Scott.

1767 Plans made by Elizabeth Montagu and Sarah Scott for Sarah Fielding to join Scott and others in an all-female retreat at Hitcham.

1768 Sarah Fielding dies 9 April in Bath. Buried at Charlcombe.

Chapter One

"A Woman of Singular Energy, Learning, and Ability"[1]

No full-length biography of Sarah Fielding has been written, for the simple reason that relatively little is known about long stretches of her life.[2] We do not know what she looked like, since there is no extant portrait. Even the memorial set up after her death records inaccurate details about her age and her family. However, Sarah Fielding has received more attention from literary historians and critics than have most other 18th-century women writers because of her close link with the two most prominent novelists of her time. Henry Fielding was her brother and Samuel Richardson her close friend; proliferating scholarship in the areas of their life and work has uncovered details about Sarah. More recently, new investigations into the mutually supportive circle of intellectual women of the mid-18th-century, including the sisters Elizabeth Montagu and Sarah Scott, have begun to offer a new perspective on Sarah Fielding in her mature years. Then, in 1993, some of Sarah Fielding's own correspondence was published for the first time. As a result, many aspects of her life are finally emerging from obscurity.

Sarah Fielding was born on 8 November 1710. Her father, Edmund, was a soldier who had seen active service in the wars against France and had been praised for his bravery at the Battle of Blenheim; by 1710 he was colonel of a regiment and in November had just returned from an unfruitful posting to Lisbon. Her mother—also Sarah—was the daughter of Sir Henry "Judge" Gould, a wealthy lawyer with a large country estate, Sharpham Park in Somerset.

The Fieldings (or Feildings, or Ffieldings as they variously spelled their name) were an old-established family with high-ranking connections; they were headed by the Earls of Denbigh and Desmond, who themselves claimed to be related to the Hapsburgs. There was a family tradition of gaining social or economic advancement through marriage: Edmund Fielding's great-great-grandfather William Fielding had become the first Earl of Denbigh in 1622 as a result of his marriage to the sister of the Duke of Buckingham, James I's favorite. It was a tradition that Edmund Fielding followed in his marriage to Sarah Gould, which took place in 1706, possibly following an elopement.

Judge Gould's strong-minded wife, Lady Gould, later stated that their daughter had married "contrary to their good liking";[3] and though Edmund claimed that there had been a perfect reconciliation between himself and his in-laws, tensions clearly remained. While Sarah Gould Fielding was returning to Sharpham regularly to give birth to her children—Henry in 1707, Catharine in 1708, Ursula in 1709—Judge Gould was attempting to establish financial security for his daughter and her children independently of Edmund. Judge Gould initiated the purchase of a handsome farm at East Stour in Dorset for £4,750 and installed the family in it.

Unfortunately, he died in 1710 before the purchase was completed and before he could confirm that he intended the farm to be a gift to his daughter. Under the terms of his will, only £3,000 was to be devoted to his daughter and her children; far from receiving the handsome legacy he may have hoped for, Edmund had to pay £1,750 even to complete the purchase of the farm. The resulting complexity of shared legal ownership of the East Stour property was almost bound to cause trouble in the future.

Sarah was the first of the Fielding children to be born at East Stour; after her came Anne—the only one of the children not to survive childhood—in 1713, Beatrice in 1714, and Edmund in 1716. But as the family grew, financial problems also increased. Some of these were undoubtedly the result of misfortune: Colonel Fielding's regiment was disbanded in 1712, and he was left on half pay for several years. It may not have been his fault that rents from the estate—which should have provided the family with a steady income—were very low, but evidence suggests that his financial judgment was unreliable at best. In 1716 he was fleeced of £500 in gambling at cards; in 1720 he lost a considerable amount in the South Sea Bubble. However, he was adept at borrowing—small sums from neighbors and larger sums from relatives and friends, including £700 from Mrs. Katherine Cottington, Lady Gould's sister, and £600 from the colonel's own housekeeper. As a result, during Sarah's early childhood the family somehow continued to live the relatively luxurious life to which the country gentry of the early 18th century were accustomed.

This period of Sarah's life came to an abrupt end. In 1718, when she was seven years old, her mother, Sarah Gould Fielding, died. The colonel left his six small children at East Stour in the care of their grandmother and great-aunt and went to London, where within a few months he married again. His new wife was Anne Rapha, a widow and—to the horror of Lady Gould—a Roman Catholic. The arrival of the newly married couple at East Stour in May 1719 provoked family tension into open warfare. The colonel and his new wife attempted to establish a family routine, but the children, encouraged by Lady Gould and Mrs. Cottington, were resentful and refractory. As a result, they were punished, possibly by being beaten or being denied food. By August 1719 Lady Gould had had enough: leaving Henry with his father, she removed the four little girls and baby Edmund to her own house in Salisbury and entered the girls at Mrs. Mary Rookes's boarding school in the Cathedral Close there.

Clearly Lady Gould was attempting to provide a stable environment and education for her grandchildren, away from the (as she saw it) pernicious influence of a feckless father and an infidel stepmother. To some extent she may have succeeded. The syllabus at Mrs. Rookes's school was conventional enough, covering only the limited range of subjects thought appropriate for young ladies of the period: "to work and read and write and to talk French and Dance and be brought up as Gentlewomen."[4] It would not have provided much intellectual stimulation for an intelligent child like Sarah. But there is no evidence that she was unhappy at the school; indeed, her children's book, *The Governess*, presents an affectionate account of just such a school, where a group of little girls are able to find companionship, guidance, and tranquillity away from turbulent home lives. The presence of a Mrs. Rooke or Rookes on the subscription lists of Sarah's books as late as 1762 suggests that Sarah's own "governess" remained in touch long after her schooldays were over.[5]

Lady Gould, it should be noted, was the widow of a senior law officer; and she was very angry with the situation in which her daughter's children found themselves. Probably in response to a suggestion that the children should be returned to their father, she lodged a formal complaint against the colonel in Chancery. First, she complained about his treatment of the children. Colonel Fielding and his new wife, she claimed, had been unjust and inhumane; further, they had attempted to corrupt the children by encouraging them into Catholicism. The colonel, Lady Gould alleged, "'has openly commended the manner of education of young persons in monasterys'" (Battestins, 20)—a serious charge in the early years of George I's reign, when Jacobite sympathizers still stealthily drank toasts to the ousted Stuart Catholic "king over the water."

Lady Gould's second allegation was also a serious one: she claimed that the colonel was cheating the children of their birthright. Under the terms of Judge Gould's will, on Sarah Gould Fielding's death her £3,000 share in the East Stour estate descended to her children. Lady Gould pointed out that since April 1718 the colonel had continued to collect the whole of the rents and profits of the farm himself; moreover, he had recently sold property, including East Stour land, and had kept (or, more to the point, spent) the whole of the proceeds.

The colonel denied any intention to corrupt the children, and he argued that the income from the East Stour estate had at least been devoted to their upkeep—a robust, if undeniably mean-minded, line of defense. By now this was a full-scale family row being carried on in the public courts. Members of the Fielding household, relatives, and neighbors were taking sides, brought forward as witnesses for the colonel or for Lady Gould. The situation was further complicated by the fact that the colonel was now fathering a second family. It is impossible to doubt the sincerity of Lady Gould's outrage or of her loyalty to her grandchildren; she was clearly at no pains to hide her extreme dislike of her son-in-law, his behavior, and his principles. The impact on the children at the center of such a quarrel must have been devastating.

In April 1721 Henry ran away from Eton, where his father had placed him, and effectively declared his allegiance to his grandmother and sisters by turning up at Lady Gould's house. The colonel demanded that all his children be sent back to him, on the grounds that he could give them a better start in life than their grandmother could. He wanted Henry back at Eton and the girls introduced to "'the acquaintance of some noble family, as might be much to their advantage'" (Battestins, 35). His protests were ignored. Mrs. Rookes refused to give the girls up, even when the colonel sent a servant to claim them; Lady Gould would not admit the servant into her house.

In 1722 the Lord Chancellor judged against the colonel on all counts. Sarah and her sisters were ordered to remain with Mrs. Rookes and to spend their school holidays with Lady Gould. Colonel Fielding, therefore, now ceased being a father to Sarah in any meaningful sense of the word.[6] She was 11 years old.

From this point onward, Sarah's life, no longer the subject of public legal wrangles, becomes more difficult to trace. She probably remained in Salisbury with her sisters during the rest of her school days—though she was not one of the "four G[rand] children of the Lady Golds" inoculated against smallpox in Salisbury in 1723[7]—and then continued to live with Lady Gould. The scene of Sarah's adolescent and early adult years, therefore, was Salisbury, which in the 1720s and 1730s was a lively city of about 7,000 inhabitants. Daniel Defoe wrote, at about this time, "The people of Salisbury are gay and rich, and have a flourishing trade; and there is a great deal of good manners and good company among them; I mean, among the citizens, besides what is found among the gentlemen."[8] Culturally and intellectually, Salisbury was surprisingly well endowed. Nearby neighbors in the beautiful and historic Cathedral Close even provided Sarah with a circle of intellectual people her own age: young men and women whose company and conversation compensated for any deficiencies of Mrs. Rookes's syllabus.

Strong loyalties developed among the members of this group, and the friendships that were then formed endured for decades. The group included Jane Collier, who would later share lodgings with Sarah and collaborate with her on at least one literary venture; Jane's sister Margaret, who joined Henry and Sarah Fielding's joint household in the mid-1740s as governess to Henry's children; Jane and Margaret's brother Arthur, who later tutored Sarah in Latin and Greek; and James Harris, classicist and grammarian, who, more than 30 years after they grew up together, assisted Sarah with her translation of Xenophon. John Hoadly, youngest son of the Bishop of Salisbury, was another friend from this period; after Sarah's death in 1768 it was he who arranged for a plaque to be placed in Bath Abbey in her memory.

Salisbury had an Assembly Room, and there were regular dances and concerts. By 1730 Sarah's brother Henry was writing verses in praise of the three beautiful Cradock sisters of Salisbury, one of whom he married in 1734. These were the years when Sarah and her sisters would themselves have been on the marriage market. Congenial and compatible young men were clearly available, and according to Arthur Collier, all four of the Fielding girls "had Parts above the common Run."[9] And yet none of them—and neither of the Collier sisters, for that matter—married. Given the wary (not to say jaundiced) comments about the institution of marriage that appear in later work by both Jane Collier and Sarah Fielding, it is possible that this group of young women chose not to marry. Probably, however, they were simply not rich enough to attract husbands from their own class. The Fieldings, and even the Colliers (whose father was a clergyman), would count themselves as "gentry," but their rank was not high enough to compensate for their lack of dowry. One of the very few matters that Lady Gould and Colonel Fielding agreed on, throughout their quarrel, was the importance of trying to ensure the girls a suitable marriage portion. Lady Gould's own wealth would go to her son; and, although Colonel Fielding was at times a very wealthy man, he continued to lose his money as fast as he gained it. As a result, the Fielding girls could be sure of nothing more than their sixth share of the East Stour estate: a few hundred pounds at best. Young men of their own class would expect a better dowry than that: when James Harris married, his wife brought him a dowry of £3,000 (as well as aristocratic connections). In an irony all too familiar to unfortunate gentlewomen in the 18th century, Sarah Fielding's one real hope of material security was from marriage, and yet she was too poor to attract a suitable husband.

Lady Gould died in 1733. The Fielding sisters may have continued to live in her house in Salisbury for a year or more afterward, but then they probably returned to live at East Stour, where Henry—now making a name for himself as a dramatist in London—and his wife joined them during the summer months. Ownership of the farm was the one reassurance that the Fieldings could still count themselves "gentry"—Henry insisted on being addressed as "Esquire" on the strength of his sixth share—but they must all have realized that this property was only a temporary home. As soon as the youngest, Edmund, reached his majority, in 1737, the farm and land were sold to provide income to live on.[10]

The sale yielded six shares of no more than £260 each. Shortly afterward, the colonel made a last attempt to bolster the uncertain prospects of Sarah and her sisters. Promoted to lieutenant general and a widower again, he applied in 1740 for the vacant governorship of Jersey (he had previously been acting governor), partly to "'lay the foundation of a secure provision for my 4 daughters'" (Battestins, 299). But his application failed, and his own financial misfortunes reached crisis point when he was declared bankrupt. Just before he died the following year, in debtors' prison, he married a woman said to be a servant. She declared he had died intestate and that he was worth less than £5.[11] There was no legacy to his children.

The Fieldings had better hopes from the estate of General Fielding's brother George, who died in 1738, leaving part of his fortune to his brother's offspring: this promised Sarah at least £20 a year. However, the will was contested and was not settled until 1749, by which time Henry at least had sold his interest in it for ready capital; since Sarah never mentions this source of income, she probably did the same.[12]

We do not know where Sarah lived, or with whom, or what she did with her time, between 1739 and 1744. There is a local tradition that by

1739 she was living in Bath, in a cottage on Church Lane provided by Ralph Allen, the philanthropist who was later one of her most generous benefactors (Peach, 32). None of the sparse evidence from this period contradicts this tradition. She was in close touch with her brother Henry and almost certainly became involved in at least two of his literary ventures of the early 1740s: she is the likely author of the letter from Leonora in *Joseph Andrews* (1742)[13] and of the narrative of Anna Boleyn in "A Journey from This World to the Next," which forms part of *Miscellanies* (1743).

In 1744, however, Sarah sought publication in her own right, with her own first full-length novel, *The Adventures of David Simple*. Again, brother and sister collaborated: Henry had seen part of the text in draft, and the novel was published by Henry's publisher, Andrew Millar. *David Simple*, however, was Sarah's project; and the Advertisement that she wrote for the first edition, the earliest direct expression now extant of her thoughts and opinions, is a personal and revealing statement repaying detailed consideration:

> THE following Moral Romance (or whatever Title the Reader shall please to give it) is the Work of a Woman and her first Essay; which, to the good-natured and candid Reader will, it is hoped, be a sufficient Apology for the many Inaccuracies he will find in the Style, and other Faults of the Composition.
>
> PERHAPS the best Excuse that can be made for a Woman's venturing to write at all, is that which really produced this Book: Distress in her Circumstances: which she could not so well remove by any other Means in her Power.
>
> IF it should meet with Success, it will be the only Good Fortune she ever has known; but as she is very sensible, That must chiefly depend upon the Entertainment the World will find in the Book itself, and not upon what she can say in the Preface, either to move their Compassion or bespeak their Good-will, she will detain them from it no longer.[14]

On the surface, this Advertisement has much in common with other prefaces and introductions by female writers of the time, including the emphasis on female modesty and humility, the air of special pleading that accepted the premise that female writers should be judged by less stringent standards than male, the suggestion that a gentlewoman publishing a book had to defend her actions, and the acknowledgment that personal misfortune provided one of the few valid justifications for female authorship. These were not merely rhetorical devices: they reflected views that were widely accepted in the mid-18th century, particularly among the aristocracy and gentry, the class to which the Fieldings still tenuously belonged. They provide a strong reminder of Sarah's temerity in undertaking a venture of this sort.

Women had been among the writers of prose fiction since the genre had begun to be popular. Some—Jane Barker, for instance, whose moral tales and romances had found an audience during the time of Sarah's childhood—had pioneered the use of fiction for moral teaching. Barker contributed to a steady increase in the number of novels by women in the early years of the 18th century, which reached a peak in about 1725. But between 1725 and the early 1740s the number of novels published by women declined; one recent study has identified none at all between 1737 and 1743 and only one woman novelist writing before 1737 who published anything later.[15] It has been recognized that *Pamela* (1740) and *Joseph Andrews* (1742) represented a new impetus for the novel as a literary genre. It is equally true that *David Simple* represents a fresh beginning for women writers.

It is impossible to be certain as to why the number of novels by women had diminished so markedly since the early years of the century; but it may well have had something to do with the fact that female modesty and respectability were growing increasingly important, and many female writers of the distant and immediate past had contributed to making the profession of writing anything but respectable for a lady.[16] Aphra Behn in the late 17th century, Delariviere Manley and Eliza Haywood in the 18th, had been scandalous in their personal reputations as well as in the content of their fictions. Clearly Sarah did not want to be considered as a member of a group that included women such as Behn, Manley, and Haywood.[17] Indeed, throughout her fiction, a body of work notable for wide-ranging references to other writers, she rarely, if ever, cites any female writer. Her route into the writing of fiction for publication was a result of collaboration with, and encouragement from, her novelist brother rather than an ambition to build on the achievements of women writers of the past.

It was Sarah's decision to publish her fiction, rather than simply to write, that was likely to provoke most offense; this is evident from the reaction of Lady Mary Wortley Montagu. Lady Mary was a distant relative of the Fieldings and a compulsive writer herself, but she published little—and that anonymously. She followed Sarah's literary career with a kind of appalled concern. Commenting on Sarah's having published novels (and giving her credit—if that is the right word—for several that were not hers, including Charlotte Lennox's *The Female Quixote* [1752]), Lady Mary wrote: "[I] heartily pity her, constrained by her circumstances to seek her bread by a method I do not doubt she despises."[18]

And yet Sarah's Advertisement does not indicate disdain for her work; it is as much assertion as apology. It is, after all, a personal "Advertisement." It makes a point of declaring that the author is female (complete anonymity would not have been unusual for the time). And the terms of the declaration can be read as a combination of honest self-assessment and shrewd judgment of a new and growing market for didactic fiction by a modest female moralist. Sarah's views—on marriage, on the position of women in society, and on the responsibilities of civic humanism—were often provocative, even radical; the stance of female conformism was in this context a useful strategy.

The Advertisement's acknowledgment of the author's carelessness about detail might read as modesty, but it is also honest and is endorsed by Sarah's later propensity to delegate the more mundane aspects of preparing her texts for publication whenever possible. In 1759, for example, she sent the manuscript of *The Countess of Dellwyn* to Richardson, with the request: "pray be not scrupulous to alter any Expressions you deslike [sic], but if this should do you any hurt, and you are overloaded with other business I will trust it to your nephew" (*Correspondence*, 149).

Her willingness to allow her readers to determine what kind of work she had produced contains a similar ambivalence: overtly an expression of authorial deference, it yet carries a suggestion of innovation—like her brother, Sarah avoids using the conventional term "novel" for her work—while also offering a calculated (and commercially desirable) flattery of the reader. Even her moving admission that "IF it [her book] should meet with Success, it will be the only Good Fortune she ever has known" is immediately followed by the elegant and ironic withdrawal of authorial self in favor of the reader and the text. Confession of vulnerability is here as much a matter of marketing as of revelation.

Overall, the Advertisement is a curious mix of humility and confidence. It strongly suggests that, after all, Sarah Fielding's opinion of the status of the woman writer of fiction was not so disdainful as Lady Mary suspected. In the letter that guesses Sarah's likely attitude, Lady Mary also quotes Henry, who had apparently once declared that he had had no choice "but to be a hackney writer or a hackney coachman." The option of being a hackney coachman—or indeed taking on any other trade or profession—was not open to Henry's sisters, but of these four gifted

women only Sarah, as far as we know, made successful efforts to earn an
income; only Sarah became a writer for a public audience. Her decision
was surely as much a reflection of belief in her own abilities as of financial necessity.

Self-confidence on Sarah's part was justified. *David Simple* was a great
success, and a second edition was called for within two months. Now,
however, the Advertisement was dropped, and in its place appeared a
Preface from brother Henry. Henry had become a controversial literary
figure long before 1744, and accusations concerning his political writing
had led him to declare that he would no longer publish his work anonymously. It was rumored, however, that he had written *David Simple*, as
well as other, more inflammatory works, and much of the Preface
rehearses his assertions of good faith—and his theories of fiction—rather
than anything directly concerning the novel or its author. Yet the Preface
does provide some useful biographical information about Sarah as she
reemerges from obscurity. For example, by making the limited extent of
his contribution to *David Simple* clear, Henry establishes the extent to
which his sister wrote the novel independently:

> In Reality, two or three Hints which arose on the reading it, and some lit-
> tle Direction as to the Conduct of the second Volume, much the greater
> Part of which I never saw till in Print, were all the Aid she received from
> me. Indeed I believe there are few Books in the World so absolutely the
> Author's own as this. (5)

His subsequent comments, which seem to the modern reader to lay a
quite unnecessary stress on Sarah's "grammatical and other Errors in
Style in the first Impression, which my Absence from Town prevented
my correcting" (it is one thing for Sarah to acknowledge this herself and
quite another for her brother to point it out), suggest that Henry considered himself mentor rather than collaborator. But he goes on to praise
the novel in considerable and knowledgable detail and concludes by
turning his critical comments into a graceful compliment:

> The true Reason why some have been backward in giving this Book its
> just Praise, and why others have sought after some more known and
> experienced Author for it, is, I apprehend, no other than an Astonish-
> ment how one so young, and, in Appearance, so unacquainted with the
> World, should know so much both of the better and worse Part, as is
> here exemplified: But, in reality, a very little Knowledge of the World
> will afford an Observer, moderately accurate, sufficient Instances of Evil;

and a short Communication with her own Heart, will leave the Author of this Book very little to seek abroad of all the Good which is to be found in Human Nature. (8)

The Preface as a whole presents a clear image of a young, inexperienced, under-educated woman, "unacquainted with the World" but gifted in "the greatest, noblest, and rarest of all the Talents which constitute a Genius": "a vast Penetration into human Nature, a deep and profound Discernment of all the Mazes, Windings and Labyrinths, which perplex the Heart of Man" (5). Allowing for a certain amount of literary license on the part of a man well aware of the power of "puffing"—the young, inexperienced Sarah Fielding was 33 when the Preface was written, for example—there is no reason entirely to discount this first of the few descriptions of Sarah's personality that survive.

If Sarah was inexperienced in the ways of the world in 1744, she soon experienced a style of living very different from anything she had known. When Henry's wife Charlotte died in October, Sarah came to London to act as her brother's housekeeper and remained with him for the next three years. The London setting of *David Simple* strongly suggests that Sarah already knew the capital well, perhaps as a regular visitor to her brother or even her father. Now she would be at the center of things, not only in terms of the literary marketplace but also of political events in the years of the Jacobite rebellion and of intense in-fighting among politicians of all persuasions (in which Henry was himself closely involved).

Henry's house, in Old Boswell Court, near Lincoln's Inn Fields, was a luxurious one, and Henry was a gregarious man. Furthermore, Sarah had achieved some fame in her own right as a result of the success of *David Simple*. She developed her own circle of friends among the gentry and even the aristocracy: in March 1745 the Countess of Pomfret recorded in her diary that "Mrs. Boothby brought Mrs. Fielding here."[19] But Sarah was also an object of interest for those who visited Henry. One young man, Joseph Warton, wrote excitedly to his brother in October 1746:

> I wish you had been with me last week, when I spent two evenings with Fielding and his sister, who wrote David Simple, and you may guess I was very well entertained. The lady indeed retir'd pretty soon, but Russell and I sat up with the poet till one or two in the morning, and were inexpressibly diverted.[20]

The relationship between Henry and Sarah Fielding was now at its closest. It has even been suggested that brother and sister might have shared an incestuous relationship, or at least been sexually attracted to each other, at this time.[21] But the sexual tension that undoubtedly existed in the Fielding household probably arose from the more prosaic fact of Henry's developing liaison with his cook-maid Mary Daniel. This affair was unlikely to have been approved of by Sarah, who frequently writes of the foolishness of gentlemen who become prey to their servants' physical charms. The echoes, which the whole episode must have prompted, of the general's behavior before his death would have added to the siblings' difficulties. When Mary Daniel became pregnant in 1747, Henry braved public ridicule (which was considerable), married her, and moved to a more discreet location in Twickenham. Sarah did not accompany them.

She was living with her sisters on Duke Street, Westminster, when Ursula wrote to an old Salisbury friend, Mrs. John Barker, on 25 October 1748. The lively tone of the letter suggests that the life may well have been congenial:

> All the sisterhood desire much love to you. Kitty is at work, Sally is puzzling about it and about it. Bea playing on her fiddle, and Patty scribbling. (*Correspondence*, 182)

Sarah's "puzzling about it and about it" is a reference to Alexander Pope's satire on false pedantry, addressed to the Goddess of Dullness:

> For thee we dim the eyes and stuff the head
> With all such reading as was never read:
> For thee explain a thing till all men doubt it
> And write about it, Goddess, and about it
> > *Dunciad*, 4.250–52

As Ursula's letter makes clear, Sarah's sisters not only shared her habit of literary allusion and her ironic sense of humor but also relished (and expected their acquaintance to relish) the aptness of the allusion to Sarah as a puzzling pedant. Arthur Collier, describing his early memories of the Fielding girls, said that even then "Sally was the scholar" (Balderston, 79). If Sarah was guilty of "grammatical and other Errors in Style," as Henry had suggested in his Preface to *David Simple*, this was not a sign of general lack of intelligence or application. Her habits of study were a defining characteristic among her friends. As references and citations in her fiction make clear, she became formidably well educated in British literature. She was familiar not only with Shakespeare (whom she, like many others of her time, saw as the greatest poet and dramatist of all) but also with Spenser, Ben Johnson, and Dryden, as well as the more recent poems and plays of Alexander Pope, Sir Richard Steele, and George Lillo. Her tastes were catholic: she studied a variety of literary theorists and philosophers, French as well as English, but she also developed, and publicly defended,[22] a lively and unfashionable interest in fairy tales.

By 1748 Sarah had acquired a new literary friend in Samuel Richardson, whom she had probably met shortly after she moved to London in 1744. The rivalry between Henry Fielding and Samuel Richardson was already well established. Henry had ridiculed Richardson's phenomenally successful novel *Pamela* (1740) by publishing a cruel parody, *Shamela* (1741), and the two men disagreed on a wide range of literary and ethical issues. It may have been disapproval of the growing association between his sister and his literary rival that prompted Henry's (at best) tactless remarks in his Preface to Sarah's second literary work, *Familiar Letters Between the Characters in David Simple* (1747) on the limitations of the epistolary style (a style widely associated with Richardson and that Sarah had used for her book): "sure no one will contend, that the epistolary Style is in general the most proper to a Novelist, or that it hath been used by the best Writers of this Kind."

Within a year of her departure from her brother's house Sarah had developed a close social and professional relationship with Richardson. He not only printed her third book, *The Governess, or Little Female Academy* (1749), but clearly influenced its contents. When Jane Collier—now living in London and working with her old friend Sarah Fielding—wrote to consult Richardson on whether or not corporal punishment should be mentioned in the novel, she concluded:

> I trust that you will do what you like best; for Mrs. Fielding desired you would determine upon it; and if you would still have it altered, then be so kind as to put in what you would have, and Miss [sic] Fielding will be perfectly satisfied with it.[23]

Jane Collier and Sarah Fielding were by now accepted as part of Richardson's intimate circle of friends and even "resided occasionally" at his house at Parson's Green (Barbauld, I.clxi–clxii).[24] Certainly Richardson did not feel restrained from giving Sarah the benefit of his low opinion of her brother. Richardson's view of Henry did not mellow as the years passed. In 1752 he wrote to Lady Bradshaigh:

I have not been able to read any more than the first volume of Amelia.
Poor Fielding! I could not help telling his sister, that I was equally surprised at and concerned for his continued lowness. Had your brother, said
I, been born in a stable, or been a runner at a sponging-house, we should
have thought him a genius, and wished he had had the advantage of a
liberal education, and of being admitted into good company; but it is
beyond my conception, that a man of family, and who had some learning,
and who really is a writer, should descend so excessively low, in all his
pieces. (Barbauld, 6.151)[25]

Sarah's own literary principles were in some respects similar to those of
her brother (though when Sarah produced a version of the story of
Amelia in her own novel *The Countess of Dellwyn*, Richardson printed it
without any recorded concern about its excessive lowness), but she
admired Richardson as a writer and moralist, as well as a friend and
adviser. In 1749 she published a pamphlet on Richardson's new novel,
Clarissa. *Clarissa* was the publishing sensation of the late 1740s, and the
central relationship between Lovelace and Clarissa in particular attracted controversy; the aim of Sarah's *Remarks on Clarissa* seems to have been
partly to celebrate the novel as a literary achievement and partly to
defend its morality (and its author) against criticism.

By 1749 Sarah Fielding, as she entered her 40th year, had established
herself in London, living with her sisters and publishing a regular stream
of literary work. The commercial and critical success that *David Simple*
had achieved, and the subsequent success of *Familiar Letters* (which had
been published by subscription and was therefore particularly remunerative for the author) and *The Governess*, had surely assisted in alleviating
the "distress in circumstances" that she had recorded in 1744. The growing range of her work indicates that commercial criteria were by now not
her only guiding principles: by 1749 she had written a novel, an epistolary miscellany, a school story for girls, and a pamphlet of literary criticism. It is also likely that she had contributed to more than one of Henry
Fielding's magazine ventures: if she was the author of the Letter from
"Honoria Hunter" in *The Jacobite's Journal*, as has been plausibly suggested,[26] she had even begun, tentatively, to write about the public, political
world. Her literary plans in 1749 included more new ventures, including
a "Book upon Education" (Barbauld, 2.63), which would advise parents
and teachers on methods of educating children, and a volume of fictional autobiography, *The Lives of Cleopatra and Octavia*.[27]

But in 1750–51 Sarah Fielding's life changed dramatically once
more, when her three sisters died within seven months of one another,

probably in one of the fever epidemics that regularly swept London. This must have been a terrible blow to Sarah, and a major cause both of the hiatus in her literary output at the beginning of the 1750s and of the mood of her next published work, *David Simple: Volume the Last* (1753). While the "Book upon Education" was abandoned and *The Lives of Cleopatra and Octavia* shelved, Sarah took up the characters of her first literary success and delineated, in stark and simple prose, the destruction of a paradise of mutual family love and support.

During this period Sarah owed much to the continuing loyalty of her Salisbury friends, particularly Jane Collier, with whom she was living in 1751.[28] Most of the old Salisbury set were by now either living in London or visiting it on a regular basis, and most were involved in literary activity. The intellectual stimulation of Sarah's adolescent years was to some extent re-created, as is shown in a letter from John Upton, writing in 1753 to update James Harris in Salisbury on the activities of "'our acquaintance'":

> Mrs. Fielding has just published a 3d volume of David Simple; the world thinks it a meer 3d volume and not a new story, and thus the book stops with the booksellers. She should, I told her, have changed the title; for Novelty is the charm of the present age. Jenny Collier has almost printed her art of Teizing, Richardson has near finished another novel [*Sir Charles Grandison*] on his old plan of letter writing . . . our friend the Dr. [Arthur Collier] has written a large book, being a scheme to provide for clergyman's widows . . . I much like [Henry] Fielding's schemes for providing for the Middlesex poor, but I am afraid will meet with the fate of other schemes. (*Correspondence*, xxxiii–xxxiv)[29]

Jane Collier's "art of Teizing" was *The Art of Ingeniously Tormenting* (1753), an extraordinary piece of ironic prose that completely subverts the form and content of a conduct book. Detailed advice is given on how to be thoroughly unpleasant to others in a variety of roles, including mistress of servants, wife, husband, teacher, and friend. The book is concerned with many of the subjects already discussed in Sarah Fielding's novels, including the peculiarly unfortunate position of the impoverished gentlewoman ("Let her be well-born and well educated," the narrator advises a lady thinking of taking a companion; "The more acquisitions she has, the greater field will you have for insolence, and the pleasure of mortifying her"[30]). In many respects it offers a nightmare version of the "friendship" theme of the original *David Simple* and a pointed commentary on the emotional climate that created *Volume the Last*.

Jane Collier may have assisted Sarah Fielding in her next work, *The Cry* (1754). Collaboration was clearly congenial to Sarah, and the similarities in theme between her previous work and Jane Collier's provide support for the theory that they wrote *The Cry* together. The book itself, however, is different from anything else written by either, or indeed anyone else of the period: it was in fact so original a combination of genres and discourses that few readers were able to appreciate its strengths, and no second edition was called for.

Sarah's efforts to resume her literary career after the death of her sisters received a double setback in 1754–55. In June 1754 Henry, seriously ill, set off for Portugal too late to gain any benefit from the change of climate: he died in October in Lisbon. Sometime between mid-1754 and late 1755—there is no evidence of exact time and place—Jane Collier also died.

Jane Collier had been Sarah's closest friend. They had known each other from childhood and had shared their domestic and social life as well as their literary interests. The importance of Jane's death to Sarah cannot be overestimated. Henry's death, too, must have affected her deeply, although a certain amount of disillusion might have been complicating Sarah's relationship with Henry by the early 1750s. Throughout his life Henry earned large sums of money, in both his literary and his legal career, but like his father he squandered money as quickly as he acquired it; certainly little of Henry's growing income went to alleviating Sarah's continuing money worries, and she might have been resentful. Much has been made of the regular occurrence of close brother-sister relationships in Sarah Fielding's early fiction (for example, Battestins, 9–10); *The Cry* presents a noticeably less optimistic picture of such relationships. The chief characters include a family of two brothers and a sister. The elder brother, after making money out of his share of a joint inheritance, refuses to share his wealth, or even his affections, with his siblings while the younger brother, more faithful to his sister and her interests, turns out to be morally unreliable.

In 1754 it was Jane Collier, not Sarah Fielding, who went to Gravesend to see Henry and his family on their way to Lisbon (and who received from Henry a rare edition of Horace "'as a Memorial [however poor] of the highest Esteem for an Understanding more than Female, mixed with virtues almost more than human'" [Battestins, 584]). Sarah, however, may simply have been too ill to go. She had been visiting Bath regularly for some years to take the waters. Now she moved to the Bath area on a permanent basis for the sake of her health.

She did not entirely lose her links with London. There are records of several visits to the capital during the last 14 years of her life. Some indicate ongoing connections with the depleted Fielding family, including Sarah's half brother John (son of Edmund Fielding and the reviled Anne Rapha), who had worked closely with Henry as a magistrate and who took responsibility for Henry's widow and children. Sarah's other main link with London, of course, was Richardson. Their friendship continued to be close, stimulated by their mutual grief over the death of Jane Collier ("Don't you miss our dear Jenny Collier more and more?—I do," Richardson wrote to Sarah at the end of 1756 [*Correspondence*, 132]) and their admiration for each other as writers. Richardson's high opinion of Sarah's abilities resulted in one of the most complimentary judgments ever made about her work. He wrote to her that he had been rereading *Familiar Letters*:

> What a knowledge of the human heart! Well might a critical judge of writing say, as he did to me, that your late brother's knowledge of it was not (fine writer as he was) comparable to your's. His was but as the knowledge of the outside of a clock-work machine, while your's was that of all the finer springs and movements of the inside. (*Correspondence*, 132)[31]

The "critical judge of writing" was probably Samuel Johnson; Johnson's later, more famous comparison of Richardson and Fielding as writers is couched in similar terms, suggesting that Johnson was recycling a favorite metaphor or that Boswell misremembered the names. In light of the currency that the Richardson-Fielding comparison has since achieved, it is worth pointing out that a judgment often seen to encapsulate important differences between the aims and style of Richardson and Henry Fielding may have originated in comparison of brother and sister and that Richardson saw Sarah's strengths as being in those areas that later critics have identified with Richardson himself.

Richardson continued to assist Sarah in practical ways. He was ready to advise on producing and marketing her work, suggesting, for example, that further efforts should be made to boost flagging sales of *The Cry*: "Suppose you make Ferdinand as worthy of his mistress at last, as he was at first; and by the help of a few cancellings, publish a second edition of it? I cannot bear that a piece which has so much merit and novelty of design in it, should slide into oblivion" (*Correspondence*, 135). And he lent her money more than once. They continued to correspond until shortly before Richardson's death in 1761 and to meet when Sarah visited London or

Richardson visited Bath. On one occasion Sarah wrote to tell Richardson how sorry she was that she had missed him, though she had only been in town for two days; her subsequent comments provide revealing evidence of the particular appeal of Richardson's gregarious household to a woman now finding that independence could easily slide into isolation:

> My love to Mrs. Richardson, and all who have the happiness to be under your roof.
>   To live in a family where there is but one heart, and . . . to have a place in that enlarged single heart, is such a state of happiness as I cannot hear of without feeling the utmost pleasure. (*Correspondence*, 130)

Richardson had connections in Bath, including his brother-in-law, the printer James Leake. Mindful of Sarah's possible loneliness in the early days of her life in the Bath area, he frequently asked her to undertake commissions or make contact with his acquaintances: for example, to seek out a particular shopkeeper: "[she deserves a better station] and when you have a vacant half hour . . . talk to her of me" (*Correspondence*, 132).

But in fact Sarah needed little help in forming acquaintances in Bath. She had been familiar with the city for years; *Familiar Letters* contains a firsthand account of the social rituals associated with "taking the waters." Ralph Allen, by now a firm friend, lived just outside the city at Prior Park; contemporary accounts confirm that she was a frequent visitor there.[32] Furthermore, the author of *David Simple* was herself something of a celebrity. The novelist Frances Sheridan, living temporarily in Bath in the late 1750s, visited Sarah frequently and recorded that her "company was much courted" (Lefanu, 95).

Sarah, however, did not relish public acknowledgment of her identity. "Why did you not tell Lady Bradshaigh, when you saw her at good Mrs. Bowden's, that you were my much esteemed Sally Fielding, the author of *David Simple?*" Richardson chided her in 1756 (*Correspondence*, 31). In fact she chose not to participate much in the public life of Bath: "I am told that the Bath is very full this Season, but I only know it by hear-say, for I have no Inclination to go amongst them only when my perticular [sic] friends come," she wrote in 1758 (*Correspondence*, 144).

In the middle of the 18th century, Bath was the most fashionable spa in England, attracting large numbers of people as temporary or permanent residents; in 1749 there was accommodation for some 12,000 tourists.[33] Many of these were from the aristocracy and gentry—it was from this group that Sarah's "perticular friends" came—but Bath was also a magnet for the less genteel and the downright criminal. Tobias Smollett's vivid satire of Bath social life, in *The Expedition of Humphry Clinker* (1771), presents a picture of a crowded and noisy city that was "the very centre of racket and dissipation."[34] Smollett also emphasizes the physical disruptions caused by the city's rapid expansion: the Assembly Rooms, the Royal Crescent, and Milsom Street were all under construction in Sarah Fielding's time. Her decision to stand aside from the social life of the city is an understandable one.

She had at least one opportunity to leave Bath completely, and take up paid employment, in 1755: Mrs. Dewes wrote to her friend Richardson that she had met Sarah in Bath, liked her very much, "and wish[ed] for her to be a Mrs. Teachum to Mary" (Barbauld, 4.109). Mrs. Teachum was the name of the benevolent schoolmistress in Sarah's *The Governess*; Mrs. Dewes was offering Sarah the position of governess to her daughter. But Sarah clearly preferred to live quietly in her lodgings at Bathwick, continuing to visit and be visited by old friends and spending much of her time on her own literary interests.

During the late 1750s, in particular, her literary output was substantial. *The Lives of Cleopatra and Octavia* finally appeared in 1757, *The History of the Countess of Dellwyn* was published in 1759, and *The History of Ophelia* appeared in 1760. All three were written with an eye to income: when Sarah wrote to tell Richardson that she had sold the manuscript of *The Countess of Dellwyn* for 60 guineas, with a further 40 guineas should the novel enter a second edition, she had to confess that only if the second edition was required would she be able to repay Richardson the 10 guineas she owed him (*Correspondence*, 148–49).

Other literary ventures were undertaken for noncommercial motives. Chief among them was the preparation of a memoir of Henry, to be affixed to a collected edition of his work. This was a collaborative project with her old friend James Harris, and both considered the memoir a labor of love as much as of obligation, though Harris hoped it would also provide income for Sarah. Harris—a nationally known figure for his book on grammar, *Hermes* (1751)—wrote the memoir, with the assistance of notes from Sarah; and Sarah, in contrast to her previous habit of delegating the practical aspects of publication, took responsibility for negotiations with the publisher. Accordingly, Sarah was highly embarrassed when she had to report to Harris, at least four years after the memoir had first been projected, that Henry's collected works "are going to be published without it, and another long Essay *weighing* heavily in every Sense will be published instead of it" (*Correspondence*, 172).[35]

Sarah was furious in defense of both Henry and the general, writing "you never saw such a shocking Creature as [the new essay] had made of my Brother, and not only of him but of his Father too" (*Correspondence*, 172). But she was also worried that Harris would think she had neglected her own responsibilities. She was particularly sensitive because Harris was at this time giving her substantial assistance on another, much more ambitious project: her translation from Greek of Xenophon's *Memoirs of Socrates*.

Sarah had learned French at Mrs. Rookes's boarding school. She came to read the language with ease and later provided her own translations for the passages of French philosophy and criticism that appeared in her work. But in adulthood she also became proficient in the classical languages. Hester Thrale wrote that Arthur Collier had described Sarah as "an able Scholar both in the Latin language and the Greek"; he had "taught her with prodigious Assiduity" and had "held the Book while she has repeated a Thousand lines at a Time without missing one" (Balderston, 78). Collier was convinced that Sarah's growing competence in the classics had soured her relationship with her brother. Recalling Collier's remarks, Thrale wrote that

> while she only read English Books, and made English Verses it seems, he [Henry] fondled her Fancy, & encourag'd her Genius, but as soon [as] he perceived She once read Virgil, farewell to Fondness, the Author's jealousy was become stronger than the Brother's Affection, and he saw her further progress in literature not without pleasure only—but with Pain. (Balderston, 78)

The veracity of this account is undermined to some extent by the fact that strong antipathy existed between Arthur Collier and Henry Fielding during the late 1740s, the period of time probably referred to here; but the attitute imputed to Henry is consistent with the view of Sarah that he presents in the Preface to *David Simple* and with the distinctly unappealing nature of the learned female as a figure in his own fiction.[36] It may well have contributed to a cooling of the relationship between Henry and Sarah in Henry's last years.[37]

If Henry did criticize Sarah for seeking classical learning, he would simply have been expressing the conventional views of his time. Even those progressive men who insisted that knowledge of history should form part of a woman's education made it clear, as Sir Richard Steele (one of Sarah's favorite authors) did, that they should "read the *Greek* and *Roman* histories in the best translations."[38] The author of *The Art of Knowing Women* (1730) spoke for many when he declared himself "fully convinced that *Learning* in *Women* is nothing but an extravagant *Self-Conceit*, upheld by a *lively Imagination*."[39] Classical learning was the most prestigious area of male education in the 18th century—indeed, it provided "a code of culture, a privileged discourse"[40] upon which the public and political world depended; but for that very reason it was regarded as entirely inappropriate for women, whose lives were led in the private and domestic sphere. Women skilled in Greek and Latin found themselves regarded as unfeminine, not to say unnatural. Sarah's friend Elizabeth Carter, who published a competent translation of *The Works of Epictetus* in 1758, was frequently faced with accusations of unwomanly behavior; Samuel Johnson defended her (and indulged his own prejudices at the same time) by reassuring critics that she "could make a pudding as well as translate Epictetus."[41] In successfully gaining a classical education despite opposition from close relatives, as well as the more general disapproval of society, "Sally the Scholar" reveals herself as a woman with not only a considerable degree of intelligence and application but also tenacity and a strong streak of intellectual radicalism.

These qualities were also evident in her decision, made in the late 1750s and probably influenced by the publication of Carter's *Epictetus*, to undertake a translation of Xenophon's *Memoirs of Socrates* for publication. She had never been overawed by displays of male learning, as her flippant reference to a *"hic, haec, hoc* man" whom she had once met at dinner makes clear (*Correspondence*, 123); but she had also been quick to criticize "those Women who, having pick'd up a few scraps of Horace, immediately imagine themselves fraught with all knowledge" (*Correspondence*, 125). She was determined that her translation of Xenophon would be respectable by the standards of classical—that is, male—scholarship. She wrote openly to Harris of her feelings:

> I have attempted an Undertaking in which I am very unwilling to expose myself, for tho I think it no shame to be ignorant of what I have never been taught, yet to publish abroad Ignorance together with a pretence of Knowledge is deservedly contemptible. (*Correspondence*, 159–60)

Memoirs was an appropriate choice of text. It includes large numbers of dialogues and anecdotes on moral topics that had already occupied Sarah in her own fiction: the nature of friendship, the importance of knowledge, the desire for liberty rather than slavery. Most interesting of all, perhaps, was the emphasis on reason over passion, self-discipline over self-indulgence. As a modern editor of *Memoirs* has pointed out, "The emphasis throughout is practical, prudential and result-oriented. Thus, self-discipline is important not just for itself, but because it enables a person not to be distracted by his appetites from doing his duty."[42]

Xenophon was widely admired as an author in the 18th century, and his style was seen to have a "peculiar simplicity, brevity & point."[43] Translating this style was not an easy task. When Fielding wanted help on particularly complex passages, she turned to Harris. "It has always been my maxim," she wrote, "to have the least fear of Redicule [sic] where real Knowledge dwells" (*Correspondence*, 141). Harris had already shown unusual enlightenment toward the idea that a woman could translate the classics by helping Carter with *Epictetus*, but he certainly would not have assisted even such an old friend as Sarah if he had believed she was not up to the task. As it was, he lent her his own copy of Xenophon and corresponded with her about problems in the text.

Fielding's pride in her achievement can be measured by the fact that *Memoirs of Socrates* is the only one of her works to carry her name—"Sarah Fielding"—on the title page. In *The Lives of Cleopatra and Octavia* (the only other of Fielding's texts to be concerned with a classical subject), the Dedication, to the Countess of Pomfret, was signed "S. Fielding"; her usual form of signature was "the Author of David Simple." Clearly Fielding wished the world to know her capabilities in the area of the classics. She must have been gratified by the favorable reception given to the work. *Monthly Review*, having pointed to "the difficulty of preserving, in translation, that elegant simplicity which is [Xenophon's] distinguishing excellence," handsomely acknowledged that Mrs. Fielding "executed her task in a manner that does her honour."[44]

Memoirs of Socrates was published by subscription,[45] and the subscription list provides testimony to the longstanding loyalties of Fielding's friends: it includes Ralph Allen, Dr. Arthur Collier, James Harris, Dr. John Hoadly, Samuel Richardson, and Mrs. Rooke. But some of this group did not form part of Fielding's circle for much longer. Within a year Richardson was dead; Ralph Allen died in 1764. Harris, elected a member of Parliament in 1760, spent much more of his time in London, and Sarah's declining health increasingly restricted her ability to travel out of the Bath area. From 1762, Sarah became more and more dependent on a network of female friendships she had been forming since the early 1750s. She became associated with the circle of intellectual women including not only Elizabeth Carter and her friend Catherine Talbot but also the sisters Elizabeth Montagu and Sarah Scott, and Scott's friend Mrs. Cutts. All of these names also appear on the subscription list for *Memoirs of Socrates*. These women became her most significant companions in the closing years of her life.

This was a different kind of friendship from earlier associations with like-minded contemporaries—and not only in the sense that, for the first time, Sarah Fielding was part of an exclusively female circle. Carter, Montagu, and Scott were all intellectuals—Carter formidably so—and all published writers; but they were all younger than Sarah, all financially better off, and all (despite the seemingly interminable sore throats and headaches recorded in their letters) in relatively robust health.[46] In these circumstances it was inevitable that their relationship with Sarah, developing at a late stage in her life, would veer toward that of patron to dependent. Carter and Talbot in particular had followed Sarah's career with interest from the publication of *David Simple*; the intellectual achievements and aspirations of the whole group provided matters of common interest with Sarah. However, although they must often have conversed with her on intellectual topics, there is little evidence of it in extant letters. Montagu's praise of *Memoirs of Socrates*, and of Fielding's "genius," which, she wrote in 1762, "points to the Portico & Academick Groves" (MO 5787), is a rare exception. Their preoccupations with Fielding revolve chiefly around her material well-being. Their attitude to her, though increasingly affectionate as the years went by, was protective rather than appreciative.[47]

In 1754 Talbot wrote to Carter that "Mrs. Fielding is a favourite with us all."[48] In her last extant letter Sarah Fielding wrote to Montagu, "Tell what tales you please to Mrs. Carter, I know you will not so far deviate from truth as to tell her that I dont love and esteem her" (*Correspondence*, 175). Montagu and Scott were even closer to Sarah. Scott in particular, having settled in another Bath suburb, Batheaston, with her friend Lady Barbara Montagu (always known as Lady Bab), saw Sarah regularly.

Montagu and Scott were both on visiting terms with Sarah by the mid-1750s, but initially, at least, Montagu does not seem to have been particularly impressed. She wrote to her sister that she had been calling on Sarah, who was

> impatient to get to Bath Easton where she intends to reside. I said all I could to divert her from ye scheme for tho she is a good sort of Woman I think you & Lady Bab will not want her in a long summers day nor a long winters evening. How is ones time taxed by civility and humanity & real & artificial devoirs? I grow savage in my disposition tho social & affable in my manners, & I felt for you & Lady Bab the hours of leisure & retirement she wd rob you of. (MO 5766)

Montagu was protective of her sister's privacy. Perhaps at this time Scott and Lady Barbara were living and working alone—later a small group of women, including a Miss Arnold as well as Mrs. Cutts, formed part of their menage—and any addition might have been seen as unwelcome. Or Sarah Fielding may already have been exhibiting signs of the loneliness, depression, or dullness that afflicted her in her later years. Whatever the reason, the coolness is clear.

Montagu's reservations, however, did not inhibit any of the women from developing their friendship. Sarah Fielding did not go to live at Batheaston, but she did settle at nearby Bathwick. She remained on ever closer terms with Scott and by extension, though rather more distantly (in terms of both location and social status), with Montagu.

The Montagu-Scott correspondence provides almost the only information we have about Sarah Fielding in the last years of her life and offers a clear, if partial, account of her mature personality and preoccupations. Apparently Sarah was often "low" in spirits. She lived in a retired way "by choice" but was evidently grateful for congenial company and companionship. Montagu was frequently amused by her unworldliness. Commenting on the imminent publication of *The Lives of Cleopatra and Octavia* in 1757, she feared (with some justification) that Sarah would distort the story:

> [A]s she is a virtuous maiden she will make Octavia the more agreeable of ye two which will give History ye lye & make Anthony appear a greater fool than ever he appeard. (MO 5766)

And later, when Carter wrote of having dined with Sarah, Montagu could not resist the humor of the situation:

> So you went to dine with Mrs. Fielding, a very pretty fancy! You might as well have dined with Duke Humphrey. Did she luxuriously feast you with a chapter of Epictetus? I hope her maid Sarah considered the grosser appetite of hunger, or you might come ill off, for I dare say poor Fielding never thinks of dinner till it is time to eat it.[49]

Sarah had become "poor Fielding" in the correspondence of her friends long before this example from 1766. The phrase referred both to Sarah's poverty and to her increasing ill health.

Poverty had dogged Sarah all her life. Even in the late 1740s, when she was making a good income from her writing, she was not financially secure; in March 1751 she was being sued for recovery of an unspecified debt (Battestins, 509). On that occasion a loan or gift of £9 from Henry helped, and her money worries must have increased after his death. Sarah was never destitute—she continued to employ a maid, for example—and she was not inclined to live lavishly, but her income, apart from what she could earn by her novels, depended almost entirely on charity and accumulated in very small sums. Sir John Fielding provided her with something, but it may have been no more than £10 a year on a regular basis.[50] James Harris's friends assisted her in purchasing "for half the usual price" a life interest in a little cottage in Walcot, another village in the environs of Bath, where she moved in 1760 (*Correspondence*, 156). Ralph Allen provided occasional presents and left her £100 in his will in 1764—a gesture that prompted the caustic comment from Montagu, "It was a great pity Mr Allen did not leave poor Mrs. Fielding a decent maintenance for life, sixty pound a year added to what she enjoys had made her happy" (MO 3155). Montagu herself offered practical assistance: presents over the years included home-fed chickens, partridges, potted beef, and "2 dozen bottles of raisin wine" (MO 5829, 5832); she also sent money gifts and regularized these into an annuity of £10 a year in 1767. When Lady Bab died in 1765, she left Sarah £10 a year, together with £10 for the rent of garden ground while she lived at Walcot.[51]

The only sizable sums Sarah received were those she earned from her literary work. During her Bath years these included about £150 for *The Lives of Cleopatra and Octavia* and slightly more for *Memoirs of Socrates* (both published by subscription), 60 guineas for *The Countess of Dellwyn*, and probably a similar sum for *Ophelia*. The poor sales of *The Countess of Dellwyn* meant that her earning capacity per novel was reduced from the £110 she had been paid for *David Simple*, but she was still earning well in comparison to others: Scott, for example, an experienced novelist, historian, and translator, was paid about 30 guineas for her novel *Millenium Hall* in 1762.

Sarah's decision to cease writing for publication after 1762—which must have had a catastrophic effect on her finances—could only have been due to worsening health. The nature of her health problems remains obscure, but she was having bouts of illness as early as the 1740s; in the early 1750s she wrote to Richardson that she had been overcome by the dampness of the weather: "I am as weak as a Feather every thing strikes me down" (*Correspondence*, 127); in 1755 she records one particularly severe attack by reminding Richardson of a recent visit to his house

from whence, Monday se'nnight, I ran away, being frightened with a
pain in my stomach, which put me in mind of an old story of a lady,
whose friend said she was very rude and uncivil to go a visiting to her
friend, and die whilst she was there. (*Correspondence*, 130)

There is some indication of a revival of good health—and a correspond-
ing increase in literary industry—in the late 1750s, but by 1760 illness
was seriously impeding her translation of Xenophon: "I have been so
much confined with Illness since the beginning of the Spring as has put
me backward in my Translation, but am now endeavouring to make up
that loss; yet who can recover lost time!" she wrote to Harris
(*Correspondence*, 156). Even when the translation was finished, she was
forced to make arrangements for it to be published in Bath, "for I could
not undertake a journey to London" (*Correspondence*, 169).[52]

The Montagu-Scott correspondence contains many references to
Sarah Fielding's worsening health. "I am very sorry Mrs Fielding is so ill"
(MO 5821); "she seems to want the waters very much . . . and I could
not see her gradually sinking into non existence for the want of them"
(MO 5319); and "Poor Fielding is in a very weak low way . . . she much
wants revival, but I fear is too far worn to receive any great amendment"
(MO 5321) are examples from 1765 and 1766.

Early in 1766 Sarah Fielding joined Scott in Bath, to take the waters,
and declared she was not going back to Walcot, where she had been feeling "too lonely." Scott's letter to her sister on the subject reveals the isolated nature of Fielding's existence by this stage of her life:

> I wou'd have had her come last monday, but she had affairs to settle; of
> what nature I can not guess, as she has no rent rolls or Bonds to look
> over, nor even a Band box of ribbons to sort; from Papers of consequence
> or the frippery of ornament I imagine no one clearer, but I find she does
> not intend returning any more to the house she is now in . . . but what
> she intends to do, or where to fix, we are totally ignorant. (MO 5319)

Scott looked forward to spending some time with Sarah but acknowledged, "It will be the sober certainty of waking bliss; none of that intoxicating joy which is easier felt than explained or accounted for" (MO
5319).[53] On another occasion Carter, while praising Sarah as "a friendly
and good woman," commented that "she is not a lively companion"[54]:
evidently Sarah was no longer considered a vivacious woman.

By the mid-1760s, Sarah's activities were more limited than before,
but she was still in touch with Henry's daughter Harriet, who sent her

a "favor" on her wedding day in August 1766. Scott wrote that the gift had given pleasure but that Sarah was also relieved at Harriet's tact: "as she married without her Uncle's knowledge, it was well judged not to acquaint her Aunt with it sooner: it made the offence less to him" (MO 5337). Clearly there were still tensions within the Fielding family. Harriet's death four months later must have been a further sorrow to Sarah.

Sarah was ill again in 1767. Her last extant letter bears witness, by the unsteadiness of her handwriting as much as by the humility of her sentiments, to her general frailty. It is devoted to thanking Mrs. Montagu for her generosity: "My poor useless Love . . . comes joyfully from a very true Heart, when thus pleasingly invited. — Take from me the fame of any thing I ever wrote, if any fame is due, whilst you cannot withdraw your own approbation I am well contented" (*Correspondence*, 175). It is very apparent from this letter that fame from her writing *had* been important to Sarah; however, she could no longer afford the luxury of independence.

By November 1767 Montagu was writing to Carter that "Poor Mrs. Fielding is declining very fast" (MO 3211), and from this point Montagu and Scott both took great care to make the close of Sarah's life as easy as possible. They were planning a *Millenium Hall*-type female establishment, to be based at a house at Hitcham owned by a relative of Montagu and Scott. For a while it seemed that Sarah would be able to join the venture "as a Guest," and it was understood that the short time remaining of her life could not be more happily spent than sitting in quiet conversation with Scott and Mrs. Cutts. Montagu was enthusiastic about the scheme, well aware of the fact that by this time Sarah had become dependent on Scott, whom she was seeing every day: "I could not enjoy Hitcham if it was to cost that good Woman all her happiness, & whatever deprived her of you wd do so; therefore she must not be left out" (MO 5873). In the circumstances, Montagu herself was prepared to contribute the difference between what Sarah could pay and the real costs involved, and she thought she could safely do this because "my friend Fielding is too much of a Bel esprit to know a little of ye ordinary affairs of life . . . we can cheat her as to knowledge of ye expences & let her imagine her present income equal to it" (MO 5873). Montagu was sensitive to the peculiar poignancy of Sarah's circumstances, which were so much more straitened than her birth and upbringing, and even her own efforts, had led her to expect: "it can never be pleasant to one as ill provided with money as Fielding . . . to feel a dependance upon another for what humanly speaking, she ought to have of her own, it is better she shd not be made sensible of it" (MO 5873).

This was a kind and generous gesture; but Sarah's sun did not set pleasantly at Hitcham as Montagu had hoped. The most Sarah's friends could do was to see that the doctor was paid for his services in attending her in her final illness (though his "generosity" diminished the expense [MO 5881]). On 9 April 1768—with Montagu still writing to Scott about the need for Sir John Fielding to pay money he had promised his half sister—Sarah Fielding died at Bath at the age of 57. Five days later she was buried at nearby Charlcombe, in the church where her brother Henry had married the fascinating Miss Cradock from Salisbury.

If her comments in *The History of Ophelia* are to be believed, Sarah was skeptical of epitaphs. " 'The Writer collects together all the Virtues, Graces, and Accomplishments, that are scattered among Mankind, and when these are all blended together with all the Elegance he is Master of, he applies them to any one who, at his Death, wants that memorial of his Goodness, which his Life has not testified,'" Lord Dorchester informs the novel's naive heroine. There is therefore a certain irony about the tablet that Sarah's friend Dr. John Hoadly arranged to be mounted in the west porch of Bath Abbey, as "a deficient Memorial of her Virtues and Accomplishments." Deficient it certainly is, since it calls Sarah's father Henry, describes Sarah as his second daughter, and gives the year of her birth as 1714. But the tribute that follows is more accurate. Candor—which in the 18th century meant freedom from malice—and freedom from affectation may be conventional feminine virtues, but both qualities are reflected in Sarah's letters and fiction. The reference to her piety is also valid: moral teaching in her fiction is consistently backed by an unobtrusive, but firmly held, set of religious principles. And the tribute, while emphasizing her virtuous character, does acknowledge both her scholarly achievements and the influence of her writing on other women. In this, at least, it seems an appropriate memorial:

> Her unaffected Manners, candid Mind,
> Her Heart benevolent, and Soul resign'd,
> Were more her Praise than all she knew or thought,
> Though Athens' Wisdom to her Sex she taught.

Chapter Two

A Moral Romance:
The Adventures of David Simple

Novels are either exceedingly useful or dangerous, according to the Nature of their Composition: For the Reader, under the Notion of Entertainment, comes open and unguarded to them; our good Humor disposes us to be affected . . . the Impression strikes deeply, and has a lasting good or bad Influence upon the Mind and Temper, in Proportion as the Images are more or less pure and just.

So wrote a literary commentator in *London Magazine* in January 1743.[1] His argument reflects the doubts felt by many in mid-18th-century England about the novel as a hybrid literary form, whose equivocal influence was reaching far more widely across the population than most earlier literature; and it draws attention to a resulting reliance on the responsibility of fiction writers for the moral and emotional effects of their work on their readership. It was a responsibility that many writers of the time willingly assumed. Later in the century Clara Reeve defined the novel as "a picture of real life and manners, and of the times in which it is written";[2] but this definition encompasses only part of what earlier writers intended by their use of the novel form. The same claim appears time and again in prefaces and dedications to early and mid-century novels: "the design of [Novels] in general is . . . to profit and delight the reader"; "to convey Delight with Instruction is, or ought to be the grand Aim of all who write."[3] These claims were sometimes conventional, or even tongue-in-cheek, involving little more than the affixing of some trite moral tag to a cheerfully amoral tale. But for many novelists they were a genuine attempt to establish the legitimacy of prose fiction as a literary form, by laying claim to a respectable pedigree for prose fiction alongside the "higher" literary forms of epic and tragedy (the idea of combining instruction and entertainment stemmed from the principles of Horace, who had written that poets should aim at "combining the giving of pleasure with some useful precepts for life"[4]) and by asserting the particular capacity of novels to display moral principles in action to a wide readership. Nowadays the presence of overt moral instruction in much 18th-century fiction is often regarded with distaste; but the fact that prose fiction gained massively in popularity precisely at the time when it was establishing its moral credentials in this way strongly suggests that didactic fiction was welcomed by large numbers of people with money to buy (or hire) and leisure to read.[5]

So when Sarah Fielding claimed in the Advertisement to *The Adventures of David Simple* that her work was a "moral romance," she was making it clear at the outset that her book was not merely a story, or a series of stories, that set out to entertain but that it would also contain instructive information and advice—and signaling an approach that would have had a positive appeal to potential readers.

Her emphasis on fiction's didactic function was particularly appropriate to validating the serious intentions of the woman novelist. Women's role in 18th-century society was limited, but it did involve responsibility for the provision of guidance on morals and conduct, particularly within the family: the extension of such "feminine" functions to the public sphere of novel writing was congenial to women and acceptable to readers, male and female, who wanted to be taught how to live in the contemporary world.[6]

As Henry Fielding pointed out in the Preface to the second edition, *David Simple* consists of "a Series of separate Adventures detached from, and independent of each other, yet all tending to one great end . . . the Perfection or Impurity of Friendship."[7] The separate adventures are linked by the continuing presence, and developing experience, of David Simple himself. His story is "simple" enough. It begins when his younger brother, Daniel, attempts to cheat him out of his modest inheritance. Although the plot eventually fails, David's disappointment in his early experience of human nature spurs him "to take a Journey through *London* . . . to seek out one capable of being a real Friend" (27). In the course of his journey (which traces a line roughly east to west, from the City to Fleet Street to the Strand to Westminster) he meets, and learns the histories and characters of, a variety of men and women. He deliberately seeks out rich and poor, gentry and tradesfolk, the leisured and the preoccupied, the indolent and the obsessive. On most occasions he discovers, sooner or later, that the hoped-for friend falls short of his ideal. There is, however, some virtue in the world—though it exists largely unrecognized by the majority. David's quest is eventually successful, and at the end of the novel he settles down with four "real Friend[s]": Camilla, who becomes his wife, her father, her brother Valentine, and Valentine's bride, Cynthia.

The action of *David Simple* is episodic: David meets someone, spends a little time in his or her company, hears his or her story, makes a tentative judgment, is hopeful or disillusioned, and passes on. Unity—at least the kind of formal unity that Ian Watt called the "interpenetration of plot, character, and emergent moral theme"[8]—is not important to Fielding. Even the tone of the discourse varies as the text moves between realistic accounts of day-to-day life, satirical set pieces, the heightened drama of romance, and the dream narrative of fable and fairy tale.

To a large extent, *David Simple* is concerned with studies of character. None of the characters, however, is intended to represent the rounded, often inconsistent, occasionally self-contradictory type of personality that actually exists in real life (and in some fiction); all are rather, in some way or another, personifications of moral or ethical characteristics. This approach to characterization was a common one throughout the 18th century: Fanny Burney described it aptly when she wrote that her aim was "to draw characters from nature, though not from life" (*Evelina*, 7). But the balance between "nature" and "life" in Fielding's characters, like Burney's, differs significantly. Many of the characters are little more than walking representations of particular philosophical principles: the principle is described, and they show it in action. In such instances, complexity only arises from the juxtaposition of contrasting exempla: for instance, the obvious comparison between Spatter, who speaks evil about people while doing good, and Varnish, who praises everyone while feeling nothing for them. Cynthia and Camilla, however, although they, too, exist within moral parameters defined for them, and although their characters and experiences are juxtaposed, have a relatively autonomous existence in developing relationships and experiencing events not directly stemming from their prescribed moral stance. Fielding deploys "nature"/"life" scale with great skill, and in one instance she uses it to create a genuine psychological shock, when the Atheist, who is introduced late in the novel as a two-dimensional figure along the lines of Spatter or Varnish, turns out to be David's erring brother, Daniel, morally and psychologically diminished after a career of vice.

David himself is a character of more moral complexity than his name might suggest. In Samuel Johnson's *Dictionary of the English Language* (1755), "simple" is given three definitions: (1) plain, undesigning, sincere; (2) single, not complicated; (3) not wise, not cunning. Clearly the predominant definition of the "Simple" in "David Simple" is the first, but as David's story progresses Fielding is alert to the difficulties a "plain, undesigning, sincere" view of life can cause. Moreover, there are occasions when the negative implications of the third definition—simplicity in the sense of foolishness—are also relevant to David's actions and reactions.[9]

In literary terms David's simplicity is reminiscent of two characters created by Henry Fielding in the years preceding *David Simple*: Parson Adams ("A Character of perfect Simplicity"[10]) in *Joseph Andrews* (1742) and Heartfree in *Jonathan Wild* (1743). But the general character of the innocent abroad clearly descends from Don Quixote, an earlier naive hero with an impossible quest. Between 1700 and 1750, 18 or 19 new editions of *Don Quixote* were published in England; according to Jerry Beasley, Cervantes's novel is "crucially important . . . to any understanding of the age's tastes in fiction" (Beasley, 10). Comparison between David's "adventures" in London in the 1740s and those of a "simple" knight in 16th-century rural Spain forms part of Fielding's satiric scheme; one of David's main functions is to provide a focus for the clash between idealism and reality in a contemporary world very different from that of Cervantes.

It is important, for this purpose, that David is male. It was unusual but by no means unprecedented in the 1740s for a woman to write a novel with a male protagonist. In 1727, for example, the popular writer Mary Davys had created Sir John Galliard as a young gentleman learning about life in London. Her purpose is satiric; her title—*The Accomplished Rake, or Modern Fine Gentleman*—speaks for itself.[11] As both Davys and Fielding found, a male protagonist was essential to the presentation of satiric scenes of contemporary London life. David Simple, as a man, has access to public spaces: he visits hotels and coffee shops; he wanders alone round 'Change and St. James's Park, places where women would have had to be chaperoned. He changes his lodgings at will. If he hears the sound of weeping in the next room, he can walk in and ask what is wrong. If he decides to give his money away, nobody has the power to stop him. If he wishes to indulge his quixotic impulse to spend his time traveling "through the whole world, rather than not meet with a real Friend" (27), he can.[12]

And yet, as a comparison with Davys's Sir John makes clear, there are many ways in which David Simple is a very "unmasculine" 18th-century hero. Sir John's sphere of activity extends much farther than David's. As well as going to inns and coffee houses, he frequents gambling dens and bagnios. He is the victim of physical attacks (including a deliberately administered bout of the pox and a firebomb), and he is provoked into defending his honor with his sword. Sir John's experiences are typical of other fictional heroes in 1740s and 1750s London, such as Tobias Smollett's Roderick Random and Peregrine Pickle, and Henry Fielding's Tom Jones.[13] Even Joseph Andrews—perhaps David's nearest fictional equivalent: a more innocent and vulnerable figure than Sir John Galliard, and of more equivocal social status even than Smollett's protagonists—leads a robust existence in the metropolis, including defending himself against sexual harassment from his amorous employer.

Against this David seems a sedate hero indeed. The nearest he gets to a gambling den is a series of genteel whist parties, which he "soon tired of" (80). He never has to defend himself against physical attack, even from lusty women. And his unruliness of passion consists chiefly of quickly passing resentment. It is David's brother, Daniel, who embodies the assertive male characteristics so typical in other heroes of the period. Daniel is combative; he has habits of gambling, drinking and whoring, rioting away thousands of pounds on "Women and Sots" (25), and making drunken advances to Cynthia (180). If—as seems very possible—the David-Daniel relationship formed a model for Henry Fielding's later unbrotherly brothers Tom Jones and Blifil, Henry's further redistribution of characteristics is significant: it is, after all, Tom who is prone to drinking and whoring, and Blifil who is not only abstemious of liquor but fails to find even the adorable Sophia Western attractive. For Sarah Fielding drinking and womanizing, far from being the natural characteristics of an innocent and naive young man, were symptoms of serious moral faults. Daniel's final reported litany of villainy—an astonishing series of attempts to cheat people out of their money and morals—ends in horror: he dies in mental and physical decrepitude, in the agonies of atheism and, though still a young man, with "all the Infirmities and Diseases incident to old Age" (290).

David's peculiar mix of characteristics arises partly from the multiplicity of functions he has in the novel. He is the innocent youth whose lack of familiarity with a corrupt world provides a specific focus for satire on contemporary life; he is also a natural benefactor whose generosity and faith in human nature provide providential relief for other victims of society, as well as an instrument of poetic justice. The vulnerability of the innocent and the generosity of the benefactor are combined in David's sensitivity and emotional empathy with the joys and sorrows of the people he encounters; both are expressions of the emotional cult of sensibility that swept mid-18th-century England. Although he urges moderation, restraint, and reason, David is himself a "man of feeling," consistently favoring the emotional over the logical. By contrast, the limitations of the logical approach are delineated in the unattractive character of Orgeuil, who has "'fixed in his Mind, what he ought to do in all cases in Life, and is not to be moved to go beyond it.'"[14] Specifically this is related to lack of sensibility: Orgeuil "'makes no allowance for the smallest Frailties'" and abandons any unfortunates who do not follow his advice, "'as he thinks they have no reasonable claim to anything further from him'" (73).[15]

The cult of sensibility as a literary phenomenon embodies real and urgent 18th-century social concerns, in particular deeply felt suspicion of the commercial and capitalist principles perceived increasingly to dominate human relations and society's structures. It is no coincidence that David, the son of an industrious tradesman, himself opts out of a productive in favor of a leisured life.[16] Commerce has no time for such nonproductive qualities as charity, generosity, and benevolence. "Sentiment," as Janet Todd points out in her study of 18th-century sensibility, "is a surplus in the economy with no exchange value" (Todd 1986, 97). In 18th-century society, *David Simple* argues, both old-style patronage and an idealized version of feudalism, involving mutual ties of the well- and lowly born, are anachronisms; in their place commercial principles are dominant. Charity and benevolence are rejected in favor of strict accounts of profit and loss.

The "even-handed" logic of contractual principles, reduced to its essence, merely justifies outright selfishness, the specific reverse of David's ideal of true friendship. The stories of David and his brother, Daniel, and of Camilla and her stepmother, Livia, aptly illustrate this. Instead of accepting his fair share of his father's estate, Daniel burns the old man's will and suborns the servants to witness a new one in his favor, virtually cutting out his mother and brother altogether, and all "from a Desire of engrossing to myself all my Father was worth" (291). Asked why she has deliberately destroyed a family into which she married with the goodwill of all the family members, the only excuse Livia can give— as her husband, Camilla's father, later reports to Camilla—is that "she thought her *Interest* and yours was incompatible; for the more I did for you, the less she could have for herself" (300).

The actions of the selfish are destructive to personal relationships, and this tendency is exacerbated by the inevitable attempts of selfish individuals to hide their true motives. Discovery of hypocrisy is at the heart of many of David's disappointments. He meets people with great hopes that they are what they profess to be, and the disappointment when they prove to be the reverse is severe. Significantly, David is debilitated by such discoveries. Early in the novel, when outwitted and insulted by Daniel, David makes no effort to defend his own position. As he sits alone in his room brooding over the quarrel (which Daniel has manufactured to get rid of him), "every Moment seemed an Age." He was "sometimes ready to blame himself," feeling that if a quarrel has occurred it must be his fault; when he hears that Daniel has gone out to dinner without inquiring after him, "he had hardly Strength enough left to go any farther"; and once he has somehow got out of the house, "he wandered up and down till he was quite weary and faint" (18–19). Even with new friends, David's reactions are the reverse of the combative and confrontational: when he can no longer make excuses for Spatter, "he went out, without taking Leave or any Notice of him, in order to take a new Lodging"; when he hears that Spatter has been ridiculing him behind his back, his anger is transient, "for Rage never lasted above two Minutes with him"; and soon "he was glad to hear an Account, which did not make *Spatter* so black as, by his last Conversation, he began to suspect him" (96–98).

Above all, David is genuinely both surprised and distressed at the wickedness of mankind. David himself is good-natured, gentle, and kind; none of these characteristics equips him to understand, let alone interact with or influence, the contemporary world. His inability to grasp the motivation for Daniel's behavior is matched by his reluctance to accept the corruption of the people whom he meets on his travels through London. He tries for as long as possible to discount his worries about the principles of the superficially attractive Spatter, "as he loved to excuse every body till he found something very bad in them" (98). He is benevolent by instinct but makes no attempt to try to convert others to his point of view. When faced with outright hostility, cruelty, or tragedy—as he is with Isabelle toward the end of the novel—he is likely to be helpless (250, 255).

David's goodness and simplicity marginalize him from the workaday world of 18th-century London and align his position much more closely with that of women, who are also marginalized from that world. It was widely believed at this time that it was women, rather than men, who reacted with their emotions, had a monopoly on qualities such as pity and selflessness, and were vulnerable to physical weakness; in this novel such qualities are part of the sensitivity and sensibility that David represents.

It is also significant, in this context, that of the "real Friend[s]" David makes, the two most important—Cynthia and Camilla—are female.

Fielding makes oblique comment, through the effects of David's "femi-
nized" qualities, about the powerlessness of femininity. But through the
lengthy interpolated life histories of Cynthia and Camilla, and the short-
er histories of other young women, such as Nanny Johnson (who loses
David's love, succumbing instead to the seduction of material wealth
promoted by her father), Fielding deals directly, and critically, with the
position of women in the contemporary world.

There are, unusually, two heroines in *David Simple*. More unusually
still, they are presented as very different, but equally sympathetic,
young women. Janet Todd, surveying mid-18th-century fiction by
women, writes, "Many of the heroines of the feminine novel were inter-
changeable . . . all beautiful because immaculate and undifferentiated in
their bodies which spoke purely of their minds' purity"; if women in fiction are differentiated at all, it is in the most simplistic way possible:
one is "good" and one is "bad" (Todd 1989, 141).[17] It is true that
women in 18th-century fiction often appear to be little more than
objects of male desire or symbols of an ideal. In *David Simple* this is
emphatically not the case. Cynthia and Camilla are both "good" in a
broad sense, but neither is perfect (both are specifically shown to have
at least minor moral failings), and they differ from each other both in
their ethical principles and in their actions and reactions. When Henry
Fielding wished to emphasize his sister's technical skill, he focused his
comments on Cynthia and Camilla: "the lively Spirit of the former, and
the gentle Softness of the latter, breathe through every Sentence which
drops from either of them" (8). What Henry did not add—did he really not notice it?—was that in telling their stories in their own words,
the two women provide convincing accounts of the almost insuperable
difficulties, in 18th-century society, of a virtuous gentlewoman in
adversity.

Cynthia tells her story first. She has been a sensitive and intelligent
child and therefore immediately at odds with the social expectations of
her situation as the daughter of an ambitious middle-class family:

> "I loved reading, and had a great Desire of attaining Knowledge; but
> whenever I asked Questions of any kind whatsoever, I was always told,
> *such Things were not proper for Girls of my Age to know*: If I was pleased with
> any Book above the most silly Story or Romance, it was taken from me.
> For *Miss must not enquire too far into things, it would turn her Brain; she had
> better mind her Needle-work, and such Things as were useful for Women; reading
> and poring on Books, would never get me a Husband*." (101)

The cruelest aspect of her family's attitude—the assertion that such advice is for Cynthia's own good—does not blind her to the fact that she is being denied the "Learning" she craves simply because she is female (a fact made more obvious by the insistence that her brother, who "'had a perfect Aversion to the very Sight of a Book'" was required to learn, until it literally killed him).

What was useful for a woman was solely what would get her a husband: a girl was seen to have no other purpose or function in life. Intellectual attainment was not only wasteful but incompatible with being a wife and ripe matter for ridicule, as Cynthia's more conventional (and infinitely less appealing) sisters do not fail to point out: "*'undoubtedly her Husband will be mightily pleased, when he wants his Dinner, to find she has been all the Morning diverting herself with Reading, and forgot to order any'*" (108). Cynthia's growing reputation for "Wit" is held against her, even though it is allied with more acceptable feminine virtues, such as consideration for a bashful cousin and sincere friendship for a young lady who lives locally.[18] Her unconventional views develop into open conflict with patriarchal values when her father presents her with a potential husband. Her suitor woos her with a bald statement of principles that must have formed the subtext for many romantic proposals in the 18th century (and since):

> "*I have seen you two or three times, altho' you did not know it; I like your Person, hear you have had a sober Education, think it time to have an Heir to my Estate, and am willing, if you consent to it, to make you my Wife . . . I shall expect nothing from you, but that you will retire into the Country with me, and take care of my Family. I must inform you, I shall desire to have every thing in Order.*" (109)

Cynthia replies tartly that she "'had no Ambition to be his *Upper Servant*'" and then laughs in his face. Both actions are, in her circumstances, extremely unwise.

The irony of the situation is that Cynthia's comment is to a large extent also a statement of fact. Under 18th-century British law a wife had no identity separately from that of her husband: she had no access to money—even her dowry—unless a specific contract was drawn up to provide her with some financial security; she had no rights even to her children, should her husband take them from her. Moreover, these stringent legal principles were backed up by even more powerful and pervasive beliefs based on biblical requirements for a wife to obey her husband. The injustice such laws and customs created for the woman in marriage had not gone unnoticed by earlier women writers. "Wife and servant are the same / But only differ in the name," Lady Mary Chudleigh had written in 1710.[19] The early feminist Mary Astell had gone further: "he may call himself her Slave a few days, but it is only in order to make her his all the rest of his Life."[20] But Mary Astell had a reputation for eccentricity; while in fiction even the courtesan Roxana was not entirely serious in her assertion that life as a mistress was preferable to life as a wife because "a Wife is look'd upon as but an Upper-Servant, a Mistress is a Sovereign."[21] Society was not yet ready to welcome the challenge to traditional thinking that such radical women posed.

Extraordinarily in this context, Cynthia's attitude is presented by Fielding as both logical and understandable. But at the same time it is an unacceptable position for Cynthia to adopt because it cuts through the polite fictions upon which the whole structure of society depends. The subsequent anger of her father lays bare the power nexus that lay at the heart of the 18th-century family. His weapons, inevitably, are economic: he cuts Cynthia out of his will and thereby leaves her, on his death, destitute.

This plight of genteel female destitution was not exclusive to fictional heroines of the time, nor did it depend on young women conspiring in their own downfall by inappropriate exercise of wit. By the time *David Simple* was written, the unprotected gentlewoman was beginning to be recognized as a genuine casualty of 18th-century constructions of the family. As the aptly named "T. Single" commented,

> Whilst the father lives the family makes a figure, when he dies, how soon do they fall to decay and she who lived like the daughter of a rich man, finds herself too soon reduced to the kindness of friends, not to say alms of relations, for support.[22]

Cynthia is indeed reduced to the "alms of relations." Her punishment for flouting the conventions of her society is a peculiarly fitting one: having rebelled against the idea of being a servant to a husband, she finds herself in the analogous—and even more powerless—position of "slave" to a distant relative. Her nominal position is that of "companion," which, as Cynthia points out, simply means that, like a wife, she receives no wages for her work. In fact she is totally at the mercy of her rich relative. Lady——is offered an opportunity, in the terms of David's philosophy, for benevolence, but she prefers the art of ingeniously tormenting, venting her envy and spite in the mental torture of a dependent who she believes can't answer back.

Cynthia, however, does not submit silently to her fate. Refusing to deny her intellectual skills—most notably her eloquence with language—she defends her own view of life, exposing the fashionable euphemisms behind which people hide selfish principles. She enlightens innocent David on a number of the less humane activities people enjoy, such as making a butt of others (106); she openly asserts that sensible women who marry fools for material gain "'prostitute themselves'" (109); she takes bitter relish in having been transformed overnight, because of her loss of fortune, from a "Wit" to a "Toad-eater." Once she has made the decision to escape from Lady ——, she seeks a confrontation with her former mistress to explain exactly why she is leaving.

Once freed from Lady ——, Cynthia exhibits a strength and independence refreshing in the novels of the period. Wit and intellect in a woman can after all, it seems, be positive characteristics outside a dependent situation. Cynthia travels a long journey, alone, in a coach with three men, adroitly handling the differing amorous situations that occur with all three.[23] She is, in fact, the only one of the four major characters in the novel to venture outside London: London is a "great Metropolis," of course, and David has made a conscious decision to restrict his search for a true friend to the city because "he had good Sense enough to know, that Mankind in their Natures are much the same every where" (27). Nevertheless, London is "home" to David, and he never ventures beyond its limits. The larger world outside is left to Cynthia.

In many respects, therefore, the intellectual female, Cynthia, is a stronger and more positive figure than the nominal hero, David. The same cannot be said of the other heroine, Camilla, whom David eventually marries. Camilla is in many ways a female version of David: "in my opinion," she tells him, "to live with any one we love, and find that every Action we do is pleasing to them, is the height of human Felicity" (137). The specifically feminine emphasis on duty and service with which she tempers David's philosophy of benevolence makes Camilla even less capable than he of dealing with life in the real world, even in the domestic environment. Although they are regarded in the novel as wholly virtuous, such principles, as Camilla's story demonstrates, leave their possessor dangerously vulnerable to the self-annihilation of victimhood. Camilla's soft and yielding temper—superficially much more acceptable to the family and society than Cynthia's rebelliousness—actually exacerbates her problems.

Camilla seeks to sublimate self in care for others and ends up a victim of the patriarchal structures she struggles to support, most particularly through her sense of duty to her father. Her philosophy plays into the hands of her stepmother, Livia, and this woman's determination to indulge her own desires. In these circumstances "My Father's House, which used to be my *Asylum* from all Cares, and the Comfort of my Life" is converted into "Torment," and (in an extraordinary image) her father is transformed in her imagination from her friend and protector to a ghost, "with a Face made grim with Death, and furious with some Perturbation of Spirit" (145).

Camilla, the dutifully submissive daughter, is physically as well as emotionally vulnerable, and the tensions of her situation climax, appallingly and appropriately, with a bodily blow: her father "suddenly sprung forward, and struck me" (153). Even the memory of this moment, in which the reciprocal duties of parent and child are so comprehensively negated, causes Camilla extreme physical distress: "her Voice faultered by degrees, till she was able to speak no more. . . . She trembled with the Agonies, the Remembrance of past Afflictions threw her into; and at last fainted away"; David "really thought she had been dead" (153–54). Camilla's internalization of the importance of family duty, and the conflicts raised in her by her father's rejection, brings her close to oblivion.

In the ideal family it is the responsibility of the brother to protect and advise the sister, the responsibility of the sister to care for and consider the interests of the brother.[24] But a close friendship between brother and sister, deliberately misconstrued by people who have no sympathy with such ideals, can bring imputations of incest—another nightmare version of the male-female relationships in the patriarchal family. The accusation of incest is hugely powerful because it is made in innuendo and is almost impossible to refute; it is particularly effective in destroying the reputation of the female involved. When Daniel Simple manipulated the law to get his brother, David, excluded from home, their uncle could discover the truth and put matters right. Livia's sexual accusations against Camilla and Valentine are infinitely more effective in excluding Camilla not only from the domestic surroundings that nurtured her but from the secondary support of the extended family, who are alienated by the enormity of her "dreadful sin."

Once Camilla is cast out from her father's house, her position is the more extreme because of the conventionality of her upbringing and behavior. Women like Camilla were explicitly brought up *not* to be able to survive without the male support of the father or husband; the problem of how those who did not marry, or whose fathers or husbands failed them, were to support themselves was one that occupied philosophers and novelists throughout the century.[25]

Penniless, and responsible for her sick brother, Camilla attempts to seek support in the only way a virtuous young lady knows: she seeks charity. But here she finds that the superficial expressions of benevolence from her father's peers hide a philosophy that has more to do with commercial contract than with noblesse oblige: "In short, I found I had nothing farther to expect from them, unless I would pay a Price I thought too dear for any thing they could do for me" (165–66). She learns enough to reduce her expectations, destroy her beauty to protect her chastity, and beg in the streets; but this time she is robbed by professional beggars who claim "*that street belonged to them*'" (168). She seeks to gain some income from sewing but has no money to buy her raw materials and no collateral or goodwill to back a loan.

Camilla concludes that "there is no Situation so deplorable, no Condition so much to be pitied, as that of a Gentlewoman in real Poverty." The privileges of the young lady, she discovers, can quickly become liabilities: "Birth, Family, and Education become Misfortunes, when we canot attain some means of supporting ourselves in the Station they throw us into." The very principles of the patriarchal family become weapons against the young woman who is excluded from its protection: "we must deserve our Distress, or our *great Relations* would support us" is the obvious conclusion to be drawn by a society looking for excuses not to feel responsible:

> In short, Persons who are so unfortunate as to be in this Situation, are in a World full of People, and yet are as solitary as if they were in the wildest Desart; no body will allow them to be of their Rank, nor admit them into their Community. (170)

At the very point that her landlady is threatening to throw Camilla and her sick brother out into the street—at a point of desolation analogous to that in which Defoe's Roxana decides she had better sell her sexual services than starve virtuously (*Roxana*, 27)—David comes to the rescue. But by emphasizing the unlikely nature of David's intervention (Camilla is "'sure he was some Angel, who had put on a human Form, to deliver her from . . . Distress'" [128] while Valentine declares that "'your Goodness has worked a Miracle on me'" [131]), the narrative makes it clear that relief from such suffering is not to be relied upon.

In the absence of a more than fortuitously effective hero, the overt moral guidance provided in the novel stems chiefly from the authoritative figure of the narrator. At the simplest level, the narrator acts as storyteller, mediating between the story told and the requirements of the readers: for example, "Mr *Orgeuil* was now quite exhausted with giving so many various Characters; and I think it full time to conclude this long Chapter" (67). The narrator does at least once assert the autonomy of the characters—"and I have often heard [David] say (for this History is all taken from his own mouth) . . ." (10)—but more frequently she refers to the characters in the novel as her puppets and considers them ironically at that: "And there for some time I will leave him to his own private Sufferings," she says of David early in the novel, "*lest it should be thought I am so ignorant of the World, as not to know the proper Time of forsaking people*" (20). With remarks such as this the narrator controls the text and at the same time flatters the reader—particularly the reader familiar with the scenes of domestic and public life in London, which occupy the major part of the novel—who relishes the satire and feels the force of the implied moral lesson.

The narrator is particularly prominent where scenes of sensibility are being enacted. In recording David's state of mind at realizing the awful fate from which he has saved Camilla, the narrator comments, "The *Raptures* David felt at that Moment . . . are not to be expressed; and can only be imagined by those People who are capable of the same Actions" (170). Remarks like this highlight the special nature of the experience of sensibility, but in addition they present a direct challenge to the sympathetic reader to experience David's emotional response for him- or herself. The bond thus forged between narrator, text, and reader is central to the communication of the "morals" of this moral romance.

Ultimately in *David Simple* the moral and ethical issues raised are far more important than the conventional trappings of the 18th-century fictional plot. Despite the fact that the narrative moves toward the double wedding of David and Camilla and Valentine and Cynthia, *David Simple* is not primarily a courtship novel; tendencies to see it as such distort what the novel is trying to achieve. Malcolm Kelsall criticizes, "Miss Fielding's inability to portray the courtship of David to which she has committed herself," and he even misinterprets the comments of one of Fielding's first readers to suggest that contemporaries saw that "when David says he wants a friend, what he really wants is a wife" (xiii–xiv). In fact, far from friendship's being regarded as a surrogate for romantic love, in this novel the reverse almost seems to be the case.

To begin with, Fielding's idea of courtship, in contrast to that of other male and female novelists of the period, involves mental as well as physical attraction: David is as interested in Camilla's opinions as in her beauty; Camilla and Cynthia marry "the only Men they could really like or esteem" (302)—hardly an expression of overwhelming passionate or romantic impulse. More radical still, although David proposes marriage both to Cynthia and to Camilla and is for a time betrothed to Nanny Johnson, courtship and its ramifications are of relatively minor interest: the stories of Camilla and Cynthia, which occupy a large part of the novel, are records of female experience that have almost nothing to do with romantic love. It is not surprising that, established as individuals with a strong ethical and moral life and some experience of the world, their courtships are described as low-key affairs. These are young women who, for the most part, have other things to think about than the attractions of young men.

By contrast, sexual desire is often portrayed by Fielding not as an aspect of romance but as a destructive passion, closely allied to other destructive passions involving loss of self-command, like greed and envy. The clearest example of this in the main part of the text is Camilla's father's "love" for Livia, a blindness that results in the surrender of his integrity, the alienation of his children, and the loss of his fortune.

Confusion over the function of romantic love in the novel is but one example of critics' propensity to consider *David Simple* a failure because it does not succeed in doing something that Fielding makes it quite clear is not her purpose. The novel's structure has puzzled many: one critic, for example, sees the novel in terms of blocks of narrative with no relationship to each other, which could therefore be presented in any order; he judges that the novel "begins to disintegrate at the end of the first episode."[26] Blocks of narrative do indeed exist, and there is some value in considering, for example, the David-Daniel story, David's satiric view of London, Cynthia's story, Camilla's story, Isabelle's story, and the story of Corinna and Sacharissa separately; but the overarching structure of *David Simple* operates through the rhythm of the connections within and between these various episodes. Variations on a theme begin to build up a comprehensive consideration of a particular phenomenon: for example, the experiences of Camilla and Cynthia, together with that of Nanny Johnson, and some more fleetingly described "histories," cumulatively present a critique of the position of the young gentlewomen in the contemporary world. Elsewhere situations, characters, and moral positions deliberately rehearse, or contrast with, each other. At its most basic, "pairs" of moral qualities exemplified through character illuminate the question, which Fielding addresses throughout, of what constitutes a workable and virtuous philosophy of life.

The "Isabelle" episode has been singled out as perhaps the most detached in the novel and has often been ignored altogether or dismissed as superfluous.[27] In fact this episode is one of the most interesting examples of Fielding's theme of friendship and of the extreme subtlety with which she moralizes the romance topos, retaining an emphasis on the romance as well as on the morality. The episode is, like Camilla's and Cynthia's narratives, an interpolated life history; but it is also a romance in a much more obvious sense than the rest of the novel, its tone and language instantly recognizable to readers of popular women writers—Haywood, Manley, Davys—of the period. By setting the episode in a romance world, ostensibly in France and with such exotic appurtenances as convent-bred heroines and titled suitors, Fielding allows herself a completely different kind of exploration of her main themes.

For Isabelle's world is in many respects a distorted, fantasy version of David's. Failure of friendship here is not a matter simply of disappointment in human nature, or changing one's lodgings, or leaving home; instead it involves poignards, poisons, and other forms of violent death. Friendship, however, is quite as important here as it is in the mundane world described in the rest of the novel. The quartet of David, Camilla, Cynthia, and Valentine—or at least recognizable fragments of their situations and concerns—reassemble in the form of Dumont, Isabelle, Dorimene, and the Marquis de Stainville. Within this framework, Fielding is able to explore various "what if" scenarios excluded from the rest of the novel. What if Cynthia's intellectual liveliness had been, like Dorimene's, without education and without restraint? What if Cynthia had married David when he asked her and had then given way to a passion for Valentine? What if Valentine and David had, like Stainville and Dumont, operated by a code by which men were obliged to fight over offenses to their honor? The answer to these "what ifs" is clear: disaster would ensue. The end of Isabelle's story is tragedy, with Dumont and Dorimene dead and the marquis in a monastery. Moreover, when Isabelle recounts her woeful tale to the parallel quartet in the day-to-day world, David's benevolence is entirely powerless: he has to admit that "'it is impossible for me to hope to afford her the least Consolation!'" (250). Isabelle will end her life isolated from society—and from any form of social friendship—in a nunnery.

The somber end of Isabelle's story provides a warning against considering the conclusion of the novel proper as a providential winding-up typical of much other 18th-century fiction. There is, of course, a certain amount of poetic justice in the closing chapters: Daniel dies, Livia dies, Camilla's father admits his faults. The great financial windfall, however, which in so many other novels of the period amply compensates the virtuous for the reverses they have previously suffered, is absent.[28] Livia has spent Camilla's and Valentine's inheritance. Valentine and Cynthia are finally able to marry, but with just enough to enable them to live in "a decent, though plain way" (302).

The gains in terms of moral improvement in the world of the novel are equally modest. David has converted no one from vice to virtue; in fact, he has made no attempt to change the society he has found so alien to his own ideals, having failed even to fulfill the secondary intention declared at the outset of his travels: "to assist all those who had been thrown into Misfortune by the ill Usage of others" (27). He has, however, succeeded in finding four "real Friend[s]"; and he has with them established a small community of like-minded people, who, "quite contrary to the rest of the World," make each other happy through "Tenderness and Benevolence, which alone can give any real Pleasure" (305). That modest personal achievement has to be enough. As Fielding makes clear in the novel's final words, she is now challenging the individual responsibility of the reader to act upon the moral of this very moral romance: "In short, it is this Tenderness and Benevolence, which alone can give any real Pleasure, and which I most sincerely wish to all my Readers" (305).

David Simple was an immediate success with the reading public, and there is evidence that it did provoke female readers, at least, to consider the philosophical and ethical issues that Fielding aired: the correspondence of Catherine Talbot and Elizabeth Carter, for example, reveals a genuine, if occasionally flippant, discussion about the nature of friendship and benevolence, based on their reading of "a book (David Simple by name)" (Pennington 1809, 1.61). Catherine Talbot had evidently lost no time in recommending the novel to her friends: in May 1744 Lady Grey wrote to tell her that "we follow'd your example, & amused ourselves upon the Road with David Simple, & it really did amuse me extreamly" (Battestins, 663). Lady Grey was not sure whether the book had been written by "Mr. or Mrs. Fielding,"[29] but the second edition resolved the confusion and established Sarah's independent reputation as a writer of moral fiction. Most of Fielding's later fiction was signed "By the Author of David Simple," and in the two hundred years since her death, she has remained most closely associated with this first published novel.

Chapter Three

Writing the Book of Nature:
Familiar Letters

Familiar Letters Between the Characters of David Simple and Others (1747) is a two-volume collection of 45 letters, two dialogues, and a moral allegory. It contains a wide variety of discourses, including long and short interpolated stories, at least one formal moral epistle, a fairy tale, fables, and original poems. It is also a collaborative text: Henry Fielding provided five letters and James Harris the two dialogues, "Much Ado" and "Fashion." In addition, there are numerous quotations, extracts, and poems from named and unnamed sources.[1]

It is perhaps easiest to begin to define what *Familiar Letters* is by establishing what it is not. First, it is not, despite the implications of its title, a sequel to *David Simple* in any recognizable sense: neither the situations nor the opinions of the characters from *David Simple* develop during the course of *Familiar Letters*. There is one overt thematic reference to the specific circumstances of the earlier novel, when a "Gentleman in Yorkshire" writes to tell David that he has been influenced by reading *David Simple* to set off himself in search of a true friend. The gentleman's search ends in repeated disappointment—"I was not so happy as to meet with even your Miss Johnson," he confesses plaintively (1.298)—and a contrast with David's good fortune is clearly intended. But after this one letter we hear no more of the Gentleman in Yorkshire, or of the friendship theme, which dominated *David Simple*. In the rest of *Familiar Letters*, the only real link with *David Simple* is that figures from the earlier novel—Camilla, Cynthia, Valentine, Spatter and Varnish, as well as David—all reappear, broadly in character, as writers and recipients of letters. Cynthia's strong principles and independent opinions give her contributions—witty comments on the social life of Bath and stringent judgments on the follies and deceptions of others—particular significance; her voice occasionally seems equivalent to that of an authoritative narrator, and when she gives her verdict, it is intended to be taken seriously. By contrast, David's "simplicity" seems a more ambiguous quality in *Familiar Letters* than in *David Simple*, and his helplessness is presented on some occasions as almost comic: for example, Camilla writes to Cynthia that David has been so affected at hearing one particular tale of woe that "I was forced to put him in Mind continually, that it was only a Scene of Imagination, to keep him from being melancholy" (2.156). But none of this is taking the story of David and his friends—or any exploration of the implications of their attitudes to life—forward. It is probably most significant that arguments about the merits and demerits of sequels are rehearsed in the Preface to *David Simple: Volume the Last* (1753)[2]: evidently Fielding and her friends considered *Volume the Last* the true sequel to *David Simple.*

Just as *Familiar Letters* is not a true sequel, so—as is already apparent—it is not a novel in any sense in which the term would have been understood in the 18th century. Indeed, this is made abundantly clear by the fact that one of the interpolated stories in the second volume is actually called "a Novel."[3] The text of *Familiar Letters* as a whole has no plot and little continuous characterization. Moreover, though a large proportion of the letters are ostensibly written by Cynthia, Camilla, David, and Valentine from *David Simple*, there are more than a dozen correspondents unconnected with the earlier novel or with any correspondent except the recipient of their own letter. In these circumstances, any internal coherence that the text maintains depends almost entirely upon a uniformity of moral viewpoint, which is (not unnaturally) most apparent in the sections of the book written by Sarah Fielding herself.

The basic narrative drive of *Familiar Letters*, in all its different manifestations, is the moral essay. This kind of discourse, often presented within or accompanying an illustrative tale or exemplum, was much more popular in the 18th century than it has been in the 20th. Joseph Addison and Richard Steele, in *The Tatler* (1709) and *The Spectator* (1712), gave wide circulation to moral essays and provided precedents for presenting moral didacticism within such literary contexts as character analysis, dramatized requests for and offers of advice, descriptions of social life, theoretical dialogues, fable, and allegory. *The Tatler* and *The Spectator* were read and reread, in selection and collection form, throughout the century, and their style and content were widely imitated—Eliza Haywood's *The Female Spectator*, for example, was being issued at the very time that Fielding was writing *Familiar Letters*. Fielding admired Steele as a writer and moralist; that she knew and respected *The Tatler* in particular is obvious from the frequent references to its contents in her own work.[4]

She was also influenced by Samuel Richardson, who had published his own *Familiar Letters* in 1739. Richardson's *Familiar Letters* is primarily an

instruction manual in the art of letter writing: it comprises a lengthy
series of specimen letters that could be copied by readers who found
themselves in the variety of ordinary and extraordinary situations he
imagines. Some of these situations—an aunt's advising her niece on matters to do with courtship, for example—involve both the assumption of a
moral stance and the exemplification of a moral position. Fielding's
Familiar Letters makes no pretense of offering specimen letters in stock
situations, but she might well have been encouraged, by Richardson's
example, to regard the letter form in particular as a medium for the provision of opinion and advice on moral subjects. Many of the exchanges of
letters in Fielding's *Familiar Letters*, with neither the purpose of instruction in the art of letter writing nor the drive of a novelistic plot to guide
them, find their justification purely in the airing of moral and ethical
issues.

It has been argued that Fielding's greatest literary strengths are in the
area of the moral essay (though this is often a backhanded compliment:
one critic complained, "As a novel writer [Fielding's] chief weakness was
letting her passion for moralizing and essay writing get out of hand"[5]).
But in *Familiar Letters* the combination of moral essay and epistolary
form seems an uncomfortable one. Richardson had moved on from his
Familiar Letters to full-blown epistolary fiction: *Pamela* (1740) had been
hugely successful, and Richardson was actually writing *Clarissa* at the
time Fielding was preparing her epistolary miscellany. Both these novels
revealed massive new possibilities for the use of letters in fiction. Yet
Fielding deliberately rejects many of the qualities Richardson demonstrates to be the strengths of writing in letters. The letters presented in
her text are rarely offered as documents of circumstantial composition,
and there is hardly any occasion in which letter writers express concern
about the position they find themselves in at the time of writing.[6] The
only suspense carried over from letter to letter occurs when an interpolated story is interrupted, and even here the breaks rarely occur at
moments of high tension. Moreover, only in the case of letters between
characters in *David Simple* is there any clear impression of a relationship
between writer and recipient (and even in these instances Fielding does
not develop the relationships established in the earlier novel). In letters
between other characters the individual circumstances of the writer and
recipient, and their reasons for writing to each other, are described in a
perfunctory way, if at all. For example, Lysimachus in Cambridge begins
his letter to Cratander in London by addressing the recipient as Sir and
expressing pleasure in being allowed to begin a correspondence with

him—and that is all the reader is given as context and introduction to a subsequent exchange of letters on miscellaneous subjects (2.1–28).

Most notable of all, perhaps, Fielding does not use the capacity of epistolary writing for self-revelation. Correspondents in *Familiar Letters* rarely write about themselves. Instead they recount stories that have been told to them (or told to other people who have passed them on). In this way the narrative is disconcertingly distanced from the reader of *Familiar Letters*. Even the letter writer is often at two removes from the action, and the reader of the book is thus left attempting to engage with a second- or third-hand tale.

But Fielding does deploy the potential of the epistolary form in other ways. Writing in letters allows her to present characters and actions as they appear to others as well as to themselves, and it enables a layered pattern of response and reflection, from primary and secondary recipients of tales, to be made available in its multiplicity to the reader. The reader of *Familiar Letters*, of course, is reading the letters at the same time as the recipient of the letter in the text. The reader's responses are therefore guided by those of the recipient, and in this way the reader does become implicated in the letters—though as commentator and judge of, rather than as participant in, the action.

In his Preface to *Familiar Letters*, Henry Fielding, after brusquely dismissing the epistolary form ("sure no one will contend that the epistolary Style is in general the most proper to a Novelist"[ix]), describes what he sees as his sister's main achievement: the skill with which "the Author . . . hath considered [the] Book of Nature." He expresses admiration of his sister's success in drawing true pictures of human nature, which contribute to the "Beauties" of the book (xiii, xiv). But he points out that *Familiar Letters* also has a didactic purpose, and as such it repays reflection. Specifically, he declares, *Familiar Letters* is calculated for the "Instruction and Improvement" of young ladies: "It is indeed a Glass, by which they may dress out their Minds, and adorn themselves with more becoming, as well as more lasting Graces, than that dancing-Master, the Manteau-Maker, or the Milliner can give them" (xx).

Henry recognizes his sister's didactic aims but fails to appreciate their scope. He overlooks the many occasions on which Fielding directs her recommendations for "Instruction and Improvement" to young (and old) men rather than simply to young women. Through a series of character portraits and commentaries on action and motivation, Fielding identifies the besetting sin of the male sex as that of pride, closely allied to selfishness—the continuing assertion of *"Self,* dear *Self,"* as Cynthia wearily puts it, after a particularly fruitless evening in male company (1.134). Fielding exposes the self-delusion of the ambitious, and the self-importance of the small-minded, man. Consistently, in the stories, anecdotes, and character sketches that make up the two volumes, she shows how men's pride and selfishness make life difficult for others, most often for the women who are married to them: Cyneas's wife, who dies of his neglect and cruelty once he has fallen in love with someone else (1.313); Leontia, who has the misfortune to be more intelligent than her husband and who as a result has to suffer his continual small-minded defense mechanisms of bullying and pomposity (2.119); Chloe, whose husband veers from one extreme to the other in his treatment of her, according to the opinions he borrows from his friends (2.32).

In story after story Fielding returns to the plight of married women, nearly all of whom are entirely in the power of unsatisfactory husbands. Almost the only exceptions are Cynthia and Camilla themselves; their happiness is presented as a stark contrast to the fate of most of their friends and acquaintances. Fielding is well aware of the injustice of frustrating the natural powers of intelligent women, particularly within marriage. As Cynthia comments, "It is a bold adventure to give another such power over us" (2.181). And yet nowhere is any real alternative to marriage offered. However inadequate their husbands, wives must learn to submit; however inequitable the married state, it offers the only chance of fulfillment for a young gentlewoman. Few women in these volumes choose to remain unmarried; even fewer are shown to have any autonomous economic and social power. Belinda, the heiress who uses her money to benefit the family of the man she has loved and lost (2.165), is a rare example of a comfortably off woman with no family commitments who is able to determine her own actions. Far more typical is Emilia, whose benevolent intentions are thwarted by her family's restrictions (1.250). The one story in the volumes that is presented overtly as a fairy tale is that in which a young woman is given the power to fulfill her own desires: after a series of disasters, and several years of unhappiness, she willingly gives up the power of choosing for herself and spends the rest of her life warning other unwary females not to seek such an equivocal gift (2.225–275).

If male faults are identified as pride and selfishness, women are seen as particularly susceptible to vanity and folly. Outward appearance, for example, is important to foolish women like Biddy, who "is called *Miss Biddy* every where; because she will not give up her Pretensions to Youth, nor part with her great Desire to make Conquests" (1.184), and

to Miss Brompton, an aging spinster who is delighted to have the opportunity to persecute a young woman who is even uglier than she is
(1.269). But although there are many faulty, and some downright bad,
women of all ages in these volumes—the worst perhaps being the predatory (and most inappropriately named) Clarissa, whose chief amusement
is to steal the husbands of her friends—Fielding's strictures on female
failings appear in the context of a generally sympathetic appraisal of the
difficulties young women have in achieving fulfillment in an often hostile environment. Since fulfillment, for Fielding, is most likely to take
place within a rationally based, affectionate marriage, courtship—the
main concern of several of the stories and anecdotes—is seen primarily as
a moral and social, rather than a romantic and sentimental, matter.

The heiress Isabinda argues that young men rather than young
women create most of the obstacles to rational and affectionate
courtship:

> "Civility they take for a modest Concealment of a Passion; Rudeness they
> construe into Love; if by Chance you look at them, you are eagerly
> desirous of engaging their Affection; and if by accident you overlook
> them, you are timorous lest they should engage yours." (1.73)

Isabinda's story, which occupies much of the first volume of *Familiar
Letters*, is that of an intelligent but self-willed and over-romantic girl
seeking love and marriage and unwilling to waste her time with cox-
combs.[7] Her opinions extend to a broader view on marriage choices for
gentlewomen in the mid-18th century:

> "I have often wished there were some bounds set to what Men call
> Encouragement, that it might not be thought a Crime in us to desire
> some little time for Consideration, before we put ourselves entirely in a
> Man's power; and that the Gentlemen would be so indulgent, as to allow
> us the Liberty to make a difference between drinking Tea, or sitting in
> Company every now and then an hour with a Man, and being married to
> him. If this is too much Indulgence to be granted us, they must proceed
> in calling every Woman, who is not stupid, a Coquette, and we must
> bear the Reproach as patiently as we can." (1.128)

The frustration experienced by lively and intelligent young women in
being branded coquettes—simply for being prepared with no view of
marriage to talk naturally to men—is a phenomenon that often recurs in
Fielding's fiction.[8] Isabinda's views are, unsurprisingly, approved of by

Cynthia, and they provide an interesting gloss on one of the most striking stories in the second volume that of Cleora, who on her father's
death is left with a much smaller fortune than she has expected and who
is encouraged by her mother to marry out of self-interest. Cleora's amatory adventure provides a graphic and detailed account of the ease with
which a young girl can marry a fortune if she puts her mind to it (which
was not, presumably, the kind of "Instruction" that Henry's Preface had
in mind). Cleora approaches courtship as a capitalist enterprise. Her
market is among the young male students of Oxford, and she sets her
sights on Celadon. "It was not long before I succeeded; for, as he was
naturally amorous and sincere, and I was young, handsome, and artful,
it was almost impossible I could fail" (2.81). However, Cleora's story
shows that marriage, even to a good man, does not lead to fulfillment if
it has been achieved under false pretenses. Ironically, it is when Cleora
begins to love her husband that she begins to feel remorse, while at the
same time her husband's artificially induced "love" evaporates. At the
point when Cleora tells her own story, she knows it will end unhappily:
she will soon die of grief, and Celadon will marry an honest and artless
woman whom he can really love.

Cleora's predicament—like that of the protagonists of other stories in
the volumes—can be considered with sympathy, if not with approval,
because the need for her to marry, and the difficulties inherent in her situation, are recognized. She is wrong to set out to ensnare a young man,
wrong to use art to enhance her marital prospects; but extenuating circumstances are given weight (especially since, in Cleora's case, these
include her mother's worldly advice). The issue, however, for Fielding is
primarily one of personal morality. Cleora takes responsibility for her
own actions only when she comes to recognize the force of honesty over
dishonesty—in particular the fact that, although she has not told an outright lie, she has certainly intended to deceive the man she married. She
accepts that she has done wrong and that she must therefore pay a price:
ironically, the price is higher because she is able to judge her own actions.
"'Reflection,'" she admits, "added to my Torments'" (2.86).

In Cleora's story and elsewhere, Fielding's depiction of young women
facing marriage choices differs from that of many other writers of the
time. In the Preface, Henry Fielding applauds the way in which his sister is able to reveal "the Mysteries, with which Men are perfectly unacquainted," in "the Conduct of Women, in that great and important
Business of their Lives, the Affair of Love" (xvi). Once again, Henry's
commentary—with its emphasis here on the differences between men

and women and the importance of love to the female sex—tends to obscure, rather than illuminate, his sister's achievements. In fact, Sarah Fielding's portrayal of young women in *Familiar Letters* demonstrates how rarely "the Affair of Love," in a romantic sense, *is* at the center of things. Ultimately, in *Familiar Letters* as in the rest of Fielding's fiction, the happiness or misery of young women is determined not by the standards of romantic love, which implicitly require a different code of behavior for men and women, but by moral standards that apply to men and women equally.

Within the pages of *Familiar Letters* are many issues and incidents that Fielding would treat more fully in her later work: for example, the story of two cousins who are brought up together and who fall in love with the same man (1.322–28) prefigures the tale of Cælia and Chloe in *The Governess*; and the incident in which a benevolent man burns himself out of his house and possessions (1.207) is expanded in *Volume the Last*. Nevertheless, Fielding found it difficult to fill two volumes with the material designed for *Familiar Letters*. Her supply of moral tales and epistolary dialogues on moral subjects—whether or not they involve the characters in *David Simple*—dries up by the middle of the second volume; much of the rest of the volume is filled by Henry Fielding's letters and James Harris's dialogues.

This makes the final text in *Familiar Letters*—a 40-page allegory, *A Vision*, written by Sarah herself—all the more extraordinary. It is quite unlike anything else in the book, and in form, if not in moral intention, quite unlike anything else she ever wrote. Taken as an entity, it is a highly concentrated, carefully patterned, and unexpectedly moving text.

The "plot" of *A Vision* is quite simple. The narrator falls asleep and dreams: "Methought I was conveyed into a large Plain, amongst such Multitudes of Men and Women, that I could have no other Idea, than that all Mankind were assembled together" (2.352). On this plain are four "prodigious large high Gates," ostentatiously labeled the Way to Wealth, Power, Pleasure and Virtue, respectively. The narrator follows each way in turn to see where it leads and what is offered to those who reach their destination.

So far the narrative promises a variation on the theme made popular by John Bunyan's *The Pilgrim's Progress* (1678/1684).[9] Like Bunyan, Fielding offers the metaphor of a journey on foot through difficult or deceptively easy terrain. The main obvious difference, at the outset, is that Fielding's scope, though clearly based on Christian principles, is largely secular: that is, her protagonist's companions are personifications of moral and ethical, rather than religious, states of being, and the purposes of the journey revolve around promises of fulfillment in this world rather than salvation in the next.

Almost no one in this narrative is as fair as he or she initially seems (or claims) to be. The narrator alone of all the multitudes on the plain is able to see behind the appearance to the reality of the tempting invitations on offer, and that is because she[10] is set apart from the others—"I was but a Spectator, and came with them only from Curiosity" (2.355)—in contrast to the rest, whose "Choice had been visibly fixed before by Inclination" (2.353). The narrator can see the selfishness, greed, and envy that lie behind the aims of her traveling companions in each of the four Ways (which allows Fielding opportunity for sharp satire on human behavior in general and the behavior of the ambitious world in particular). More importantly, she is able to understand the falsity of the delusions they follow and foster in order to obtain their desires.

The narrator is also able to read alternative messages beneath the labels on each of the gates: for "Wealth" she reads "Avarice," for "Power" she reads "Ambition," for "Pleasure" she reads "Disappointment," and for "Virtue" she reads "Pride" (3.352). As she travels to the various palaces, expectations may initially seem to be fulfilled, but the alternative messages soon demonstrate the significance of truth: at the Palace of Pleasure, for example, as Hope gives way to Certainty and the cup of Pleasure literally runs over, the narrator notices, just under the roof of the room, "a little ugly Monster called *Disappointment*," who soon attaches the whole of the company to himself by means of hooks buried in their bosoms—here is "the real Deity of the Place" (2.374–75).

The pattern of illusion and disillusion is cumulative, and the fourth Way provides a climax to the narrator's experience. This is the Way to Virtue, or rather to Pride, and here the metaphor, vivid throughout, becomes very grisly indeed. The palace is swarming with Pride's myriad offspring (many conceived by incestuous coupling with Pride's 5,000-year-old father, Folly). The fate of those who find their way here is explained by Deception, whose designated task is literally to affix "Pictures" to reality:

> "Know, that all these Pictures, through which you saw me put Screws, are hieroglyphical Representations of some Virtue or Faculty of the Mind, for example, that given me by *Indolence*, is a hope of Greatness of Mind; that by *Spiteful Criticism*, of Learning and Understanding; that by *false Ridicule*, of true Wit . . . I have the Power of screwing into the Bosoms of all who love and caress me, that Picture, of which they make choice. This

puts them to great Pain, but yet they are so eager to have it done, that they suffer it very patiently. Sometimes, when I meet with any small Seed of that Virtue only falsely represented, I am at great Trouble to root it out; but then the Reflection how much I impose on these Fools (who by cultivating and improving this Seed, might really possess what they suffer so much only to fancy they possess) doubly overpays my Labour, and I am ready to burst my Sides laughing." (2.385–86)

The moral principle here is in almost reductive harmony with Fielding's views elsewhere in *Familiar Letters*,[11] but personification makes the analysis shrewder and sharper than elsewhere, and the allegorical context gives it a dramatic and powerful significance.

In these circumstances the narrator of *A Vision* becomes involved in—is even compromised by—the narrative, in a way very unusual in Fielding's work. In the rest of *Familiar Letters*, layers of narrative distance the reader from the action; but here the action is unmediated, the story told directly to the reader in the first person. In the early part of her vision the narrator is isolated by virtue of the fact that she is the only one who can see past the deceptions and deceits all around her. As the story proceeds, however, it becomes ever clearer that the narrator is not a detached observer of human follies and foibles; instead she yearns to find something that is not deceitful, a Way of life that does not lead to disappointment and disillusion. She "had a great mind to stay" at the well-built and convenient Castle of Ease (2.369) but is urged to continue. She is initially taken in by the superficial strength of Virtue—"even to me, at first sight, [she] appeared of Bulk and Strength equal to the Task of supporting her Followers" (2.376). When she finally gives up her journey to the Court of Vanity, she is "melancholy that no palace was where I could wish to stay" (2.388).

The resulting sense of disillusion and disappointment at the ways of humankind appeals to the reader's emotional, rather than reasoning, responses and enhances the effect of the unexpected discovery of a fifth Way, which might after all offer happiness. In "a narrow winding lane" the narrator finds a group of people very different from those she has previously met, in that they are mutually supportive rather than mutually destructive. The difference is significant because mutual support is shown to achieve much more in terms of self-fulfillment for everyone concerned than do envy and selfishness: "every one helped his next neighbour as much as lay in his Power, which softened the Roughness of the Way, and made the most rugged Paths seem easy to us" (2.388). Patience guides them to "the most beautiful Prospect imaginable," and there lies the Castle of Benevolence. Unsurprisingly, it is a utopia very similar to that imagined by David Simple—a place where friendship, moderation, and duty are the guiding forces.

Fielding insists that this is a Christian utopia: "here Christianity was really taught and really practised" (2.390). But it is not Bunyan's Celestial City. In an instant the image dissolves: "alas! I awoke, and all the Vision vanished from my Eyes" (3.392). Fielding has to admit that her paradise of human benevolence and mutual love is a mirage, and the admission turns the moral allegory into something more than all the rest of the book could offer: a small but undeniable record of the tragedy of the human condition.

The slightly specious link Fielding drew between her first and second publishing ventures is one indication that with *Familiar Letters* she was determined to build on—not to say cash in on—the success of *David Simple*. Another indication is the form of publication she chose. *Familiar Letters* was the first of Fielding's books to be published by subscription.[12] This method of publication was a kind of midway option between old-style patronage and modern mass-market publishing: subscribers paid half the price of the book in advance (which funded the publication process) and the other half on receipt; the author made arrangements for printing and distribution and kept the profit. The system was first used with a reissue of *Paradise Lost* in 1688 and proved so successful with this and other high-profile publications that it was regularly used throughout the 18th century[13]—despite the suggestion that those who published their work by subscription were indulging in a rather questionable search for profit by a means "tainted with commercialism, involving an undignified touting of work."[14] Few novelists, and even fewer women writers, had published their work in this way before Fielding herself.[15] But the attractions of a financially remunerative project for a writer admitting the motivation of "Distress in her Circumstances"[16] are obvious, and she had an immediate example of the profits to be made from subscription publication, in her brother's *Miscellanies* (1743), which his publisher estimated might well have netted him about £650 (Battestins, 369).

In this context the harnessing of the famous name of David Simple to the new publication could only improve its chances of sale, especially if it could be brought out while the reputation of the earlier novel was still current. Fielding began work on *Familiar Letters* as soon as it was clear that *David Simple* was a success. However, its publication was delayed: an Advertisement in Henry Fielding's journal *The True Patriot*, 11–18 February 1746, announced that Sarah's

Friends were totally prevented by the late Public Confusion, to favour her
with their Interest, as they kindly intended; nor could she herself think it
decent to sollicit a private Subscription, in a Time of such Public Danger.
(Battestins, 414)

Whether the upheavals of "the late Public Confusion"—that is, the
events surrounding the Jacobite rebellion of late 1745—were indeed the
cause of delay or whether they were only an ingenious surrogate for a
sluggish level of subscriptions is a matter for conjecture; by the time
Familiar Letters was finally published in April 1747, however, it had
attracted the impressive number of 500 signatures, outstripping the 427
who had subscribed to Henry's *Miscellanies.* At a price of 10 shillings per
copy, *Familiar Letters* was a financial success.

Contemporary readers' reactions were mixed. Catherine Talbot, for
example, wrote to Elizabeth Carter that she found Fielding's insistent
moral standpoint "vexatious . . . proceeding from her inclination to support, I fancy, a false system, and deduce every variety of action from the
source of pride and vanity." But she also offered warm praise: "where she
[Fielding] writes naturally one loves and honours her extremely"
(Pennington 1809, 2.131). Samuel Richardson's admiration of the book
was unreserved: it was on rereading *Familiar Letters* that he commented
in a letter to Sarah:

What a knowledge of the human heart! Well might a critical judge of
writing say, as he did to me, that your late brother's knowledge of it was
not (fine writer as he was) comparable to your's. His was but the knowledge of the outside of a clockwork machine, while your's was that of all
the finer springs and movements of the inside. (*Correspondence,* 132)

Richardson, like Henry Fielding before him, was singling out Sarah's
sharp and accurate descriptions of the human heart—her skill in writing
the Book of Nature, to adapt the phrase used by Henry Fielding in his
Preface—rather than her moral and ethical teaching, for praise. But
didacticism was clearly a main purpose of *Familiar Letters*, as it had been
for *David Simple*, and Sarah Fielding's next venture—another new departure—was to be an even more overtly educational project.

Chapter Four

Conquering Giants: *The Governess,*
or Little Female Academy

Attitudes toward children were changing in the 18th century.[1] In 1693 John Locke's influential treatise *Some Thoughts Concerning Education* urged a new consideration of the needs and wishes of the child in the education process. Locke argued for the importance of education as a character-forming experience: "I think I may say, that of all the men we meet with, Nine Parts of Ten are what they are, Good or Evil, useful or not, by their Education. . . . The little, and almost insensible Impressions on our tender Infancies, have very important and lasting consequences."[2] Chief among the tools of such education, he argued, was appropriate reading. And yet he admitted that it was not easy to find "some pleasant Book suited to [the child's] capacity." He could recommend Aesop's fables ("which being Stories apt to delight and entertain a Child, may yet afford useful Reflections to a grown Man") but was then in some difficulty in suggesting anything other than parts of the Bible (*Thoughts,* 147.212).

In the 50 years following the publication of Locke's treatise, a small number of books for children were produced, but these were mostly religious in nature and gloomy in tone. Meanwhile, children continued to enjoy chapbook stories, such as "Jack the Giant Killer," and they colonized early novels for adults, especially *The Pilgrim's Progress, The Adventures of Robinson Crusoe* (1719), and *Gulliver's Travels* (1726).

Then in 1744 the printer and entrepreneur John Newbery published *A Little Pretty Pocket-Book,* "the use of which will infallibly make Tommy a good Boy and Polly a good Girl."[3] This was a commercial venture: in addition to the extravagant promise of the advertisement, Newbery even offered free gifts ("price of Book alone, *6d.,* with Ball or Pincushion, *8d.*"), and it paid off. He had identified a large and growing market for a new kind of literature for children: texts that were both educational and enjoyable.

Sarah Fielding's *The Governess* was published within five years of *A Little Pretty Pocket-Book* and to some extent followed Newbery's formula.

In many respects, however—in the coherence of its narrative, for example, and its intended audience of school-age children (*A Little Pretty
Pocket-Book* was chiefly aimed at toddlers)—*The Governess* was highly
original. It has recently been cited as "The first fiction specifically written to amuse children,"[4] and as a sustained fictional narrative designed
for the "Entertainment and Instruction of young Ladies in their
Education,"[5] it has no direct precedents in English literature.

Although Newbery's success of *A Little Pretty Pocket-Book* might have
given Fielding an idea for a profitable publishing venture, the writing of
a children's book was a project that she must have found particularly
congenial in the late 1740s. From 1744 to 1747 she was managing a
household of growing children, including her niece, Harriet.[6] Moreover,
the idea of writing a book of instruction and entertainment for girls represented an extension of the didactic purposes evident in *David Simple*
and *Familiar Letters*. Fielding would have been well aware of the widely
acknowledged need to improve educational standards for girls. One of
her favorite authors, Richard Steele, had even devoted an edition of *The
Spectator* to the subject. Steele had concluded:

> The general Mistake among us in Educating our Children is, That in our
> Daughters we take Care of their Persons and neglect their Minds; in our
> Sons, we are so intent upon adorning their Minds that we wholly neglect
> their Bodies. (Ross, 255)

These strictures may well have been in Fielding's mind in delineating the
frustrations of Cynthia and her brother in *David Simple*; certainly
Fielding's general attitude toward the education of girls and young
women is consistent with them. All her works, in some form or another,
are concerned with the education of women's minds; in *The Governess* she
found a way of directing her ideas at young girls. And here her combination of didacticism and radicalism is, at least implicitly, informed by
Steele's views: one of the most striking aspects of *The Governess* is the way
in which Locke's ideas, intended by him largely to apply to the education of boys, become principles of female education.

The title page of the first edition of the novel clearly describes the
work: *The Governess, or Little Female Academy. Being the History of Mrs.
Teachum and Her Nine Girls. With Their Nine Days Amusement*. The story
opens with a brief account of the background of Mrs. Teachum, who has
set up her school as a means of keeping herself after being widowed and
impoverished. This short introduction establishes that Mrs. Teachum is a

virtuous woman, an experienced parent substitute (she has herself been a mother), and a capable teacher. But the narrative proper begins in her absence, with a furious quarrel in which eight of her nine pupils participate; and the main part of the story concerns the ways in which, after the crisis of the quarrel and its aftermath, the girls, as a group, work toward their own improvement and happiness by encouraging one another, telling their own life histories, reflecting on their experiences at the school and during day visits, and commenting on stories, plays and letters, which they read to one another in their leisure time. As the novel progresses, reason, logic, and self-discipline triumph over inconsiderate and antisocial selfishness.

The Governess is not bound together by a linear plot. Instead the text has the patterns and rhythms of thematic repetition and variation. Moreover, a twofold narrative drive is created: the narrative encompasses each of the girls telling her own story in turn, until even the baby of the school, Polly Suckling, has had her moment of attention; and there is a gradual development of the group as a whole toward their goal of right reason and true happiness. Their comments on stories at the end of the volume, for example, are more reasoned and thoughtful than at the beginning, and they behave in a noticeably more humane and considerate way on their second visit to the local dairy than on their first.

It is difficult for us now to appreciate that in setting her story in a girls' school Fielding was being both innovative and radical. As Julia Briggs has pointed out, school would count as an exotic setting for 18th-century readers of *The Governess* (Avery and Briggs, 225). Fielding had herself attended a boarding school for girls, but that experience was unusual in the early 18th century. Locke (who did not much approve of public schooling even for boys) dismissed the idea of girls' schools out of hand, regarding as beneficial the "Retirement and Bashfulness" that the domestic environment encouraged (*Thoughts*, 70.129). Throughout the 18th century the idea of sending girls to school, although increasingly fashionable with the new middle class, was frowned upon by education theorists and moralists. Stories abounded of the ignorance (or worse) of teachers and the encouragement of idleness and vanity among pupils. In a society where it was widely acknowledged that the chief aim of a girl's life should be to get herself a husband and where learning was seen as a handicap rather than an advantage in this objective, even well-meaning teachers had to tread a very fine line between inculcating unwomanly knowledge and encouraging frivolity. Back in the 1670s Bathsua Makin, who ran a girls' boarding school at Tottenham High Cross, had accepted that education should enable girls "'to be meet helps to your Husbands'" but argued fiercely that her pupils should have something better to do than "'making Flowers of coloured Straw and building Houses of stained Paper.'"[7] The debate was still current as Fielding was writing *The Governess.*

And yet the setting suited Fielding's purpose very well. Not only was she personally familiar with such a school (and, from the evidence of the text at least, happy to remember her own schooldays),[8] but she was also aware, from her own experience, that such schools were likely to attract pupils who for one reason or another were unwanted at home. All the little girls at Mrs. Teachum's academy have been sent to school either because their guardians are abroad or dead or because they have been too disruptive for the family environment. Such children are likely to be, at least initially, unhappy, at odds with themselves and others; and they can clearly be seen as in need of moral and ethical guidance.

It is in the moral aspect of education, rather than the formal matter of subject-based knowledge, that Fielding is particularly interested. To some extent this, too, follows Locke's ideas: after describing what he thinks a tutor should be teaching a young pupil, he comments to his readers, "You will wonder, perhaps, that I put *Learning* last, especially if I tell you it is the least part" (*Thoughts*, 147.207). But Fielding is also asserting her own conviction that a firm grounding in moral principles is the basis of education.

It is appropriate, therefore, that *The Governess* is not much concerned with the girls' official lesson time. There is a settled school routine, involving formal lessons in the morning and the afternoon, daily prayers, and two visits to church on Sundays. A curriculum of "Reading, Writing, Working, and . . . all proper Forms of Behaviour" (1) also involves needlework and dancing (which included deportment and socially important skills, such as bowing and curtsying[9]). More unexpectedly, perhaps, the girls are instructed in gardening and are encouraged to undertake physical exercise.[10] But Fielding's main interest is in the girls' activities outside school hours, when, left to themselves and in an informal environment, they read, listen, talk, debate, play, and—initially, at least—squabble.[11]

Fielding's overriding moral message—and the overriding principle of Mrs Teachum's teaching philosophy—is stated in the novel's preface, addressed directly to "my young Readers":

The Design of the following Sheets is to prove to you, that Pride, Stubbornness, Malice, Envy, and, in short, all manner of Wickedness, is

the greatest Folly we can be possessed of . . . Love and Affection for each
other makes the Happiness of all Societies; and therefore Love and
Affection (if we would be happy) is what we should chiefly encourage and
cherish in our Minds. (xiii)

The subsequent account of nine days in the lives of the members of Mrs.
Teachum's academy enacts this twofold dictum: that the passions—that
is, all forms of uncontrolled emotional response—must be subdued, and
that the subduing of passions leads to personal happiness and content. It
is fitting, therefore, that this progress should begin with a quarrel, which
actually degenerates into a physical fight, over who should have sole possession of the finest of a basket of apples left by Mrs. Teachum to be
shared among her pupils.[12] The only girl who stands aside from the quarrel is the eldest pupil in the school, Jenny Peace. Her surname is significant, as it becomes her task to try to convince her fellow pupils of the
need to acknowledge their faults, participate in the restoration of harmony (which requires the cooperation of all the girls), and build on this
harmony to seek their individual moral improvement. She sets about her
task by reasoning with the next senior girl, Sukey Jennett, and by telling
the story of her own conversion to a sense of duty and virtue.

Despite their type names, each of the pupils is a girl with a distinct
personality and not simply an exemplification of a certain moral trait. In
Sukey, in particular, Fielding provides a psychologically convincing
description of temperamentally confused adolescence:

It is enough to make me mad! when I imagined myself so wise and so
sensible, to find out that I have been always a Fool. If I think a Moment
longer about it, I shall die with Grief and Shame. I must think myself in
the Right; and I will too. — But, as Miss *Jenny* says, I really am unhappy;
for I hate all my School-fellows: And yet I dare not do them any Mischief;
for my Mistress will punish me severely if I do. I should not so much
mind that neither: But then those I intend to hurt will triumph over me,
to see me punished for their sakes. In short, the more I reflect, the more
I am afraid Miss *Jenny* is in the Right; and yet it breaks my Heart to think
so. (16–17)

Having established through this detailed description of Sukey's unregen-
erate state of mind the acute misery of being at war with oneself,
Fielding is able to demonstrate quite naturally that the girls will be
much happier being at peace with themselves and one another: conquer-
ing self-indulgent passion in favor of mutual affection does indeed, in

these circumstances, lead to personal happiness. In a larger context the reductive implications of such a moral could not be avoided, but as presented here it is effective—well suited to, not to say comforting for, her audience of displaced children.

Elsewhere it soon becomes apparent that female happiness is achievable only through more limiting forms of self-denial than those demonstrated by Sukey Jennett after the quarrel over the apples. As Jenny Peace gives her account of the way in which she had herself earlier been reasoned by her mother into controlling her passions, her lessons emphasize the importance of duty and submissiveness in female education. When she and her brother quarreled, it was Jenny's responsibility to seek reconciliation (29); in the brother-sister relationship, "my good Mamma bid me remember how much my Brother's superior Strength might assist me in his being my Protector; and that I ought in return to use my utmost Endeavours to oblige him" (29–30). As far as daughterly duty is concerned, her mother acknowledged to her "that your Obedience to me will make you at least put on the Appearance of Chearfulness in my Sight: But you will deceive yourself, if you think that is performing your Duty; for if you would obey me as you ought, you must try heartily to root from your Mind all sorrow and Gloominess" (34–35). Jenny's example, then, is one that argues for happiness only through self-control, self-discipline and self-denial; throughout the book there is considerable emphasis on the importance of obedience to elders and superiors (teaching "the most exact Obedience" [245] is one of the chief aims of Mrs. Teachum's academy). It is no surprise to find that the final fable of the novel comes to the conclusion that the submissive, domestic female dove is the happiest of all birds (234–36).

Fielding here seems to be arguing in favor of the principles that would lead a woman to the kind of victimhood that caused Camilla so much suffering in *David Simple*. And yet this overt encouragement of female submissiveness is counterbalanced by arguments provided less explicitly but equally unmistakably by the narrative. Even the story of the dove is given an unexpected gloss when Mrs. Teachum declares its moral to be not the importance of the dove's submission to her mate (*"the Lord of my Desire"*) nor even protection of her brood (*"Ye tender Objects of my Care"*) but "'that Innocence of Mind, and Integrity of Heart, adorn the Female Character; and can alone produce your own Happiness, and diffuse it to all around you'" (235–36).[13]

In fact the novel as a whole makes a strong argument for autonomous female morality. It is, after all, concerned with a society that is both feminocentric and complete. Though Mrs. Teachum was educated by her clergyman husband, as a widow she is a figure of authority in her own right; while she employs a dancing master and a writing master, neither of them has any autonomous status, either in the school or in the narrative. A small number of male figures are described, or appear in inset tales, but they are marginal to the main action of the story (and are often figures of weakness or deceit).

More strikingly, perhaps—and particularly significant, given contemporary criticisms about girls' boarding schools—there is a marked absence in Mrs. Teachum's academy of preoccupation with education for courtship and marriage. Self-display—most in evidence during the visit to the school of Jenny Peace's former friends Lady Caroline and Lady Fanny Delun—is held up to outright ridicule (187). Moreover, in implicit contrast to the training in submissiveness that is seen as appropriate to future wives and mothers, the girls are specifically taught to make their own judgments about life and to learn from one another rather than simply deferring to the opinions of others, including Mrs. Teachum.

Despite the title of the novel, the "Governess" herself is by no means dominant in the more informal aspect of the educational process. She is prepared to exert her authority as teacher, and her "lively and commanding Eye . . . naturally created an Awe in all her little Scholars"; but she prefers to give the girls the opportunity to educate one another wherever possible, in the firm belief that example and experience provide more valuable lessons than precept, and she is pleased to "smile, and talk familiarly" (4) to her pupils as soon as they deserve it. Her action after the quarrel over the apple—first taking all the apples away and then inflicting "the most severe Punishment she had ever inflicted on any Misses, since she had kept a School"—is most unwelcome to her, and she admits her delight in seeing the girls reconciled afterward on their own initiative: "She herself had only waited a little while, to see if their Anger would subside, and Love take its place in their Bosoms, without her interfering again; for *that* she certainly should otherwise have done, to have brought about what Miss *Jenny* had so happily effected" (37). She allows her pupils to decide how to spend their leisure time and encourages them to go on visits without her supervision. Although she is keen to hear her pupils' personal histories, she is content to have these at second hand from Jenny so that the rest will not be inhibited from speaking openly about their past and present principles. As a result of this combination of discipline and trust, the girls are not denied moral guidance, but they are encouraged to rely on their own judgment both in their activities and in their opinions. Their chief obligations are developed toward one another: female friendship is clearly regarded as a valuable and important relationship that brings mutual benefit as well as pleasure.

It is female friendship that is the main subject of one of the stories inset into the main narrative. The Story of Cælia and Chloe is offered (fittingly) by Dolly Friendly for the entertainment of her fellow pupils.[14] Two orphan girls are brought up with their rich maiden aunt, Amanda. They are very alike, and their friendship is so rewarding that they live "perfectly happy in their own little Community" (86), rejecting all offers of marriage (despite the fact that this behavior has "got them the Name of Jilts" [87]), until an army officer, Sempronius, comes to make his addresses. Sempronius "in reality liked them both extremely" (89), and they like him; to help him make up his mind between them he asks each in turn whether her cousin has any faults. Chloe is tempted to lie about her cousin; Sempronius sees this as failing his test and rejects her, reaching an understanding with Cælia. At this point the story takes an unexpected turn. Chloe, full of remorse, falls ill and cannot recover until she and Cælia are reconciled; this problem can only be resolved by truth-telling between the two girls—Sempronius is dispatched back to his regiment, and even Amanda (rather like Mrs. Teachum) cannot interfere. The friendship between the two girls is shown to be strong enough in itself to bring about reconciliation, forgiveness, and recovery. The story ends with Cælia, Chloe, and Amanda all living happily with Sempronius, a "Family of Harmony and Peace" (101).

The tale of Cælia and Chloe is one of three lengthy narratives that the girls tell to one another in their arbor and the only one that is a broadly realistic account, offering the girls an example of behavior they might try to emulate. The other two, "The Story of the Cruel Giant Barbarico, the Good Giant Benefico, and the Pretty Little Dwarf Mignon" (41–57) and "The Princess Hebe" (122–77) are fairy tales, set long ago in distant lands inhabited by giants and wizards. Both have overt morals drawn out by Mrs. Teachum, and both have subtexts that offer a more radical proposition to their hearers.

Some recent commentators have criticized Fielding for failing to include a genuine element of fantasy in *The Governess*.[15] It is true that the girls are not encouraged to make up their own stories and that the fairy tales they hear are subject to a rigorous analysis by Mrs. Teachum, who highlights conventional moral applications of the tales. In her own time, however, Fielding's decision to include fairy tales at all, even in this slightly compromised way, shows her willingness to be radical in an area

known to be controversial in early education theory. The whole concept
of fantasy was an object of suspicion to two highly influential groups,
who were otherwise in the forefront of advanced thinking on children's
education in the 18th century: on the one hand, religious groups operat-
ing under the Puritan legacy saw little distinction between fantasy and
the sin of lying; on the other, the growing industrial and commercial
classes distrusted fantasy as an unproductive waste of time. At the same
time fantasy was further denigrated by its link with the folk tales of the
oral tradition; these age-old tales, with their trappings of giants and
magic, were rejected by those who saw their age as enlightened, in contrast to a primitive, ignorant past.[16]

Most of the fairy tales we know today—including *Cinderella*, *The
Sleeping Beauty*, and *Bluebeard*—were created in aristocratic French salons
in the late 17th century and became popular in Britain only as a result of
Charles Perrault's English edition of 1719. In contrast to older folk tales
they were consciously constructed literary narratives, informed by moral
principles specifically relevant to the 18th century; nevertheless, they
included fairies and fantasy and so were subject to many of the same criticisms as older creations of the imagination.

Fielding was herself a storyteller, and *The Governess* is all about the
process of telling stories, from animal fables to personal confessions; the
girls' histories are written down by Jenny Peace for Mrs. Teachum to read,
and at the end of the novel we are told that the actual narrative of the
whole has been reified as "the Story of Miss *Jenny Peace*'s reconciling all her
little Companions" (244) for the edification of future generations of pupils
at the school. Although Fielding often expresses distrust of the untram-
meled imagination, she did not extend her disapproval to fairy tales. In
fact, she had already declared her enthusiasm for such tales through
Cynthia's avowal, in *Familiar Letters*, that "I loved that kind of writing."
Cynthia's view is unpopular—she reports "the Sneers, Witticisms, Jokes,
that immediately flew round the Room" and the declaration of one lady
that she had forbidden all her servants suffering such books to enter her
house: "For . . . I have two little Girls, the eldest is about six years old;
and I would not for the World they should be even now so childish as to
read Fairy Tales."[17] Through Cynthia, Fielding offers a defense of the fairy
tale, on sound principles of literary precedent, including *The Odyssey* and
The Faerie Queene; she specifies only one criterion: that "in my opinion, a
good Moral attends it" (*Familiar Letters*, 2.222–24).

Mrs. Teachum, like Cynthia, approves of fairy stories on the basis of
their moral usefulness:

remember, that the Fairies, as I told Miss *Jenny* before of Giants and Magic, are only introduced by the Writers of those Tales, by way of Amusement to the Reader. For if the Story is well written, the common Course of Things would produce the same Incidents, without the Help of Fairies. (179)

In fact, the two fairy stories that are recounted in *The Governess* are lively tales, whose interest extends well beyond the moral messages Mrs. Teachum claims for them. "The Story of Barbarico and Benefico" concerns a land in which two giants, the cruel and the good, live a wary coexistence. Though the good Benefico is not powerful enough totally to defeat the evil Barbarico, he is often able to rescue potential victims. He has not, however, managed to rescue Mignon, a young man who has been enslaved by the cruel giant for most of his short life. Barbarico is an effective villain: he is introduced to the reader "taking most horrid Strides, rolling his ghastly Eyes around in quest of human Blood, and having his Breast tortured with inward Rage and Grief, that he had been so unhappy as to live One whole Day without some Act of Violence" (42), and his intended acts of cruelty to his prisoners are genuinely threatening. But he is betrayed by his own stupidity—an inevitable accompaniment, the tale demonstrates, of barbarism and cruelty. Mignon is thrown into a dungeon for his effort to help Fidus, Barbarico's latest prisoner. Unfortunately, the giant forgets to close the door leading from the dungeon to his treasure house, within which lie the means to the giant's own destruction. Mignon plucks up the courage to tie the magic fillet round the giant's neck, the giant is disempowered, and the captives are freed.

The whole tale concerns the nature of tyranny and the limitations of prudence in the face of brute force; the last scenes in particular, in which Benefico hacks off the unrepentant Barbarico's head and fastens it up on a pole for all to see, have a tantalizing political resonance when it is recalled that *The Governess* was published in the aftermath of the 1745 rebellion (when the same punishment was meted out to supporters of the ousted "tyrannical" royal House of Stuart). But it is moral rather than political subtexts that are recognized by Mrs. Teachum and her scholars. Naturally the little girls identify with Mignon, who, although an adult male, is "one of the least Men that was ever seen, tho' at the same time one of the prettiest" (48) and an obvious exemplar of powerlessness. Mrs. Teachum's interpretation of the main moral of the story— that patience will overcome sufferings in the end—is drawn from Mignon's experience and is appropriate advice in terms of the novel's stated allegiance to self-discipline and submission. But Mignon's success also depends on powers of endurance and the courage that enables him finally to outface and escape his oppressor—factors that would be apparent to Jenny Peace and her companions and to readers of *The Governess*.

The story of "Hebe" concerns a young princess exiled from her kingdom, having been forced to fly by the machinations of her uncle and aunt.[18] There are some similarities between Hebe and, say, Cinderella (from one of Perrault's fairy tales), particularly in the sense that the main forces of good and ill in the lives of both heroines are female. Hebe's domestic circle consists of her mother and the good fairy Sybella; the evil characters are headed by Hebe's aunt (the driving force behind the princess's exile), Sybella's wicked sister Brunetta, and Brunetta's chief agents, the "shepherdesses" Rozella and Florimel. The primary difference between the moral of "Hebe" and those of Perrault's fairy tales stems from Fielding's insistence on the possibility of female autonomy.[19] The moral force of stories like those of Cinderella and Sleeping Beauty resolves itself into the dictum that beauty and passive virtue will lead to marriage with a handsome prince, followed by a "happy ever after" existence as consort, wife, and mother. Hebe's journey to maturity is very different. Her important lessons concern the extent, and limits, of her moral strength: she must learn to take personal responsibility for her actions. The end of the story finds Hebe queen of her own kingdom once more, "seated, with universal Consent, on her Father's Throne; where she and her People were reciprocally happy, by her great Wisdom and Prudence" (176). There is not a handsome prince in sight: instead an educated woman has become capable of ruling a whole kingdom alone and making both her people and herself "happy ever after" in the process.

Mrs. Teachum's comments on "Hebe" do not point up this radical alternative to conventional female goals; she refers to the need to curb the passions and reiterates the argument that personal virtue promotes individual and general happiness. But as with "Barbarico and Benefico," Fielding is able to convey moral lessons more radical than those endorsed by the overtly authoritative voice of Mrs. Teachum. The conscious complexity of Fielding's narrative strategy is apparent from evidence of her working methods. In October 1748, Fielding's friend Jane Collier wrote to Samuel Richardson, who was printing the text, to respond on Fielding's behalf to his proposal that Fielding should be more explicit about the exact nature of the punishment that Mrs. Teachum inflicted on her pupils after the quarrel over the apple. Collier argued that *The Governess* was designed not so much for teachers as "for girls how to behave to each other, and to their teachers"; in this context it would be better not to be too specific, so that each reader could "think it to be the same that they themselves have suffered when they deserved it" (Barbauld, 2.63). Moreover, Fielding was opposed to corporal punishment in principle but planned to argue her case further in a "Book upon Education," which was conceived as a companion volume to *The Governess.* If it was made clear in *The Governess* that Mrs. Teachum was not in favor of "corporeal severities," Fielding might lose the chance of arguing the case in detail:

> whereas if she leaves this place as it is, all these aforesaid Thwackums' will say, upon the words, *severe punishments,* &c. "Aye, this Book upon Education will be worth reading, for I find the lady has a just notion of severities"; which they, of course, will suppose to be bodily; and, when they come to find the contrary, set forth in this future Book on Education, as the reason for it will be there set forth, they may happen to be convinced.
>
> And now, as to the other party, they will easily infer, that as no whipping is mentioned, no whipping is implied, and therefore they also are engaged in favour of this other book. (Barbauld, 2.63–64)

As far as is known, the book on education was never written. But the arguments in this letter reveal the extreme self-consciousness that lies behind the apparently artless narrative strategy of *The Governess.* The narrative in fact exists on several levels. It is not only a series of stories, bound together by the experiences of a small group of girls, for the education and entertainment of other such children, but also an account of a few days in the life of a school, describing the kind of education that Fielding saw as ideal in such an environment (despite her declaration that her book was primarily aimed at children, Fielding was well aware of its potential to provide "many a sly hint" to "governesses for their management of their scholars" [Barbauld, 2.62]). On yet another level, the book is itself a sort of textbook, particularly in those parts where Mrs. Teachum, or occasionally Jenny Peace and her fellow pupils, provide a commentary on the stories told.

The clearest example of *The Governess* as a textbook in its own right is the extended section of the story in which Jenny reads a play to her companions, who then, with their governess, comment on what they have read. The play *The Funeral* was enormously popular at the time,[20] and, quite apart from the fact that it was written by Richard Steele, it is easy to see why it appealed particularly to Fielding. The basic situation of an elderly man's falling in love with a younger woman who, when she becomes his second wife, alienates his family from him and spends his money; the importance of inheritance, and the ease with which a rightful heir can be ousted by an unscrupulous claimant; the emphasis on benevolence as one of the most important virtues for men and women; the destructiveness of the passions; the strong element of poetic justice in the play's resolution: all are subjects that Fielding dealt with at length elsewhere in her own work.

In *The Governess* the pupils read the play, and their experience is then analyzed for a number of more or less educational purposes. Their initial emotional reaction to the play gauges the girls' sensitivity and sensibility: they are able to demonstrate that they have feeling hearts. Their ability to remember what they have read then becomes an academic exercise: Mrs. Teachum's "'Design was to try the Memory and Attention'" of the girls (197). Then Mrs. Teachum picks out significant features of plot, theme, and characterization for particular note. Finally, she gives a short lecture on the general value of plays:

> "I have endeavoured, my little Dears, to shew you, as clearly as I can, not only what Moral is to be drawn from this Play, but what is to be sought for in all others; and where that Moral is not to be found, the Writer will have it to answer for, that he has been guilty of one of the worst of Evils; namely, That he has cloathed Vice on so beautiful a Dress, that, instead of deterring, it will allure and draw into its Snares the young and tender Mind. And I am sorry to say, that too many of our dramatic Performances are of this latter Cast; which is the Reason, that wise and prudent Parents and Governors in general discourage in very young People the reading of plays." (207–8)

This statement is interesting for several reasons. First, in allowing plays to be considered valuable and relevant literature for girls, even within the limits Mrs. Teachum sets, it demonstrates a point of view on Fielding's part that is unusually liberal for its time. Second, it shows Fielding entering the hotly contested debate on the subject of "mixed" characters, which troubled the minds of novelists and literary commentators throughout the 18th century—and entering the debate, seemingly, on the side of Richardson and Dr. Johnson rather than that of her brother Henry.[21] Third, it enacts one of the lessons that Fielding proposes as a central aim of *The Governess*—to teach young people that "the true Use of Books is to make you wiser and better" (vii)—and thus provides criteria for the way in which *The Governess* itself should be read.

The Governess was a success. Children loved it; Mrs. Teachum and her pupils were a strong formative influence on many women, and men, of the late 18th century.[22] One of the more extravagant tributes to the book came from Constantia Philips, who claimed in her autobiography that, if she had had an opportunity to read *The Governess* when she was a child, it might have saved her from later mistakes in life:

> [I]t were to be wished, the first Book that every young Lady in *England* would read, were that excellent Performance, lately published, called *The Governess*. . . . Prudence and Virtue need not then be taught them by a laborious Instruction; they would become pleasant and amusing, and as natural and habitual as all other youthful Impressions. (*Correspondence*, 183–84)

This may not have been an entirely welcome compliment, since "Con" Philips was a notorious woman (who elsewhere in her autobiography carried on a vigorous war of words against Henry Fielding), but it provides some indication of the way in which *The Governess* was seen in its own time. By 1768, the year of Fielding's death, the novel had reached its fifth edition in England and had appeared in Dublin and Leipzig; the "Barbarico and Benefico" story had also been published in Boston.[23]

Fielding's innovative idea of setting a book on female education in a female academy was taken up by many educationalists, including Ann Murry in *Mentoria, or the Young Lady's Instructor* (1778) and Mary Wollstonecraft in *Thoughts on the Education of Daughters* (1787). However, while Fielding's format became ever more popular, by the end of the 18th century her work itself was beginning to lose its influence. For progressive and radical political thinkers, the influence of Rousseau on education principles diverted thought from the lines Fielding had been pursuing; politically and morally, she must have seemed to them either unacceptably conformist or outdated, and writers such as Mary Wollstonecraft and Erasmus Darwin simply ignored *The Governess*.[24] The evangelicals were more actively hostile. The problem with *The Governess*, from their point of view, involved some of the very aspects of the novel that had earlier been perceived as its strengths. The appeal to children's imagination through fairy stories and to children's judgment through the reasoned teaching approach of Mrs. Teachum were both seen as aberrant, not to say sinful. The daily "public Prayers" conducted at the school (194), the two visits to church each Sunday, even the importance clearly placed by Jenny Peace on "my Duty to God" (35) were not enough: the novel was regarded as irreligious. Looked at in this light, the book's undeniable attractions for children became to the evangelicals clear evidence of temptation to sin, which had to be combatted.

Sarah Trimmer, writing in *The Guardian of Education* (1802), initially recommended *The Governess* to her readers. She commented that "much good is to be learned" from the book and that its author was "one of the best female scholars England has produced"; she concluded her remarks with the summary, "When such works as this cease to be admired and approved, we may regard it as a certain sign, that good morals and simplicity of manners, are banished from the system of English education, to make room for false philosophy and artificial refinement" (Grey, 72–73). However, Trimmer later recanted, and in her zeal to remove the iniquity of fairy stories from the eyes of corruptible children, condemned *The Governess* outright. An unfortunate spin-off of Fielding's novel *The Governess; or, Evening Amusements at a Boarding School*, published anonymously in 1800, probably aggravated her suspicions of the original: as F. J. Harvey Darton comments wryly, "Mrs. Trimmer is unlikely to have enjoyed the references to Mecca and Medina, or to chewing opium" (Darton, 97, 353).

Mary Sherwood, the prolific writer for children, was another who changed her initially commendatory view of *The Governess* in light of religious principle. Sherwood had enjoyed *The Governess* as a child, but as an adult she became convinced that it was a force for evil in the schoolroom. She was not content to condemn Fielding's novel; instead she rewrote it, "raising its low-keyed and reasonable tone to one of high-pitched religious exhortation, and altering the tales accordingly."[25] In 1820 she issued the new version of *The Governess* in her own name; in a grotesque parody of the willingness of Fielding's own circle to acknowledge joint literary endeavors, she thus virtually eclipsed Fielding's novel and its enlightened contribution to the entertainment and education of girls until Charlotte Yonge had the original republished in 1870.[26]

Although Sherwood wrote a long series of school stories of her own after 1820, none are quite so narrow-minded as her revision of Fielding's novel, "Sherwood having revised *The Governess* during her strongly Calvinistic period" (Cutt, 42). However, Fielding's own version of *The Governess* survived despite Sherwood's vigorous attempt to supersede the authority of the original Mrs. Teachum. On the flyleaf of the copy of the third edition of the novel held by Cambridge University Library is written: "To Miss Jane Russell. A reward for her attention at music. May 26, 1821."

Chapter Five

A Candid and Good-Natured Reader: *Remarks on Clarissa*

Published in three lengthy installments in December 1747 and April and December 1748, *Clarissa, or the History of a Young Lady* was Samuel Richardson's second novel. His first, *Pamela, or Virtue Rewarded* (1740), had been both popular and controversial: it had provoked many responses in the form of letters, pamphlets, and alternative narratives—the most famous being Henry Fielding's scabrous *Shamela*, which deconstructed the moral message Richardson intended, portraying the "vartue" of the heroine as the conscious falsehood of a calculating and amoral social climber.

Both *Pamela* and *Clarissa* are epistolary novels, of which Richardson claims to be the editor, not the author. In *Pamela*, however, the heroine is almost the sole "correspondent" and therefore the dominant narrative voice, while the story she tells is entirely her own; the reading public either agreed or disagreed with her view of herself—hence the terms "Pamelists" and "Anti-Pamelists," which were used to describe zealots in the two camps. *Clarissa* consists of a collection of letters from a disparate group of people, each involved in a different way with the main action of the narrative. As one critic has pointed out, "no single viewpoint provides an adequate key to *Clarissa*, and . . . all viewpoints alike are implicated in (even contaminated by) its conflicts."[1] The novel's early readers were puzzled. *Clarissa* was quite as controversial as *Pamela*, but fewer critics ventured into print to attack or defend Richardson's second novel: there were simply too many, and too many-sided, controversies involved.

Fielding's *Remarks on Clarissa*, a 56-page pamphlet published at the beginning of 1749, acknowledges the complexities of the novel, most strikingly by the obliquity of its own address. *Remarks* is cast in the form of an anonymous letter to the author; this letter describes a number of "Conversations" about the novel witnessed by the letter writer and encloses further exchanges by participants in those conversations. Though the letter writer confesses herself "the sincere Admirer of *Clarissa*," Fielding does not rely solely on her own evident enthusiasm for

Richardson's novel,[2] nor on an apologia for Richardson and his intentions. Instead, her arguments are intended to be "fairly deducible from the Story . . . by the candid and good-natured Reader" (56).[3] In the 18th century the word "candid" carried the meaning "free from bias; impartial."[4] By raising in debate form the main issues raised by the novel, and referring back to the text, she appeals to an ideal reader, both judicious and attentive, to make his or her own judgment independently of the author of *Clarissa*.

Bellario, one of the participants in the conversational debates and the author of one of the long letters that follow, is just such a reader: "Candor . . . was known to be one of the most distinguishing Marks of his Character, by all who have the Pleasure of his Acquaintance" (18). Bellario's "Conversion" from an initial position of skepticism to enthusiastic support of the novel reenacts the process of arriving at an ideal reading of the original novel: it strongly argues that the novel can only be judged in light of its achievement as a whole work, when "all the vast Building centres in the pointed View of the Author's grand Design" (41) or when "the Web is wove so strongly, every Part so much depending on and assisting each other, that to divide any of them, would be to destroy the whole" (50).

The pamphlet is actually structured to reproduce the experience of reading *Clarissa*. The three conversational debates take place on publication of the three installments of the novel and concern specific criticisms raised at each stage. Fielding would have witnessed conversations similar to those she records here; Jane Collier wrote to Richardson of a debate she had overheard in which "your sweet girl" was "most unmercifully condemned for not marrying Lovelace at St. Albans" (Barbauld, 2.66). Fielding was also being accurate in reproducing the generally adverse reactions of many early readers: "In the first Conversation I heard on this Subject, the whole Book was unanimously condemned, without the least Glimpse of Favour from any one present who sat in judgment on it" (4).

The letter writer—an "I" never openly identified as Fielding (the pamphlet was published anonymously) but broadly representing her view of the novel—makes no attempt to answer such wholesale condemnation. Even when more specific criticisms are made, the anonymity of the letter writer, and the debate format of much of the argument, does not allow complete closure, and Fielding takes full advantage of the opportunity to put her own gloss on the novel. She is, for example, very critical of Clarissa's family, particularly of Clarissa's mother. "Totally to justify Mrs. Harlowe was not attempted" (9), she reports. Fielding acknowledges the difficulties of Mrs. Harlowe's situation and allows the possibility that Richardson had intended Mrs. Harlowe to be seen as faulty. However, she could hardly have expected the author of *Clarissa* to endorse Bellario's considered description that Mrs. Harlowe's letters embodied "the broken timorous Spirit of Meekness tyrannised over"; or that when her husband "condescends to sign his much-valued Name, the dictatorial Spirit of an indulged tyrannic Disposition indites every arbitrary Command" (38). The emphasis on the Harlowes as a meek wife and a tyrannical husband, while not a complete distortion of Richardson's text, demonstrates that Fielding was keen to read in *Clarissa* a reinforcement of her own particular moral concerns.

Such concerns determine the scope of Fielding's discussion. She does not, for example, address the allegations of gratuitous licentiousness that were frequently made against *Clarissa*: there is no detailed comment on the crucial act of violation in the novel, the rape of Clarissa, and none at all on the famous fire scene, whose "warmth" was widely objected to. On the other hand, true and false friendship (46), example by contrast (48), and the importance of benevolence, on which Fielding has much to say in *Remarks*, were subjects that had already been explored in her own fiction. One of the interesting features of *Remarks* is that it acts as a reminder of the moral interests that Fielding and Richardson shared; indeed, there is evidence that contemporaries saw Richardson as building on Fielding's example. The anonymous author of a later pamphlet on Richardson's work saw his novels, including *Clarissa*, as also-rans in a field dominated by "the ingenious authoress of *David Simple*, perhaps the best moral romance that we have."[5]

It is Fielding's own belief in the destructive nature of unbridled passion that informs Bellario's opinion of Lovelace—that "the Author designed *Lovelace* should be impolite, in order to prove that indulged over-bearing Passions will trample under Foot every Bar that would stop them in their raging Course" (40). Fielding's reading of the novel allows little sympathy for Lovelace, and what was one of the main points of controversy among readers of *Clarissa*—whether Lovelace should be admired as well as condemned—is dismissed rather than answered. But Fielding's refusal to condone the actions of either Lovelace or the Harlowes enables her to concentrate her support and sympathy on Clarissa herself, both as embodying many of the conflicts endemic in 18th-century femininity and as providing an exemplary ideal. It is significant that Miss Gibson, whose enthusiasm for the novel as a whole is unshakable and who is presented as an attentive reader of the text

(Fielding refers to Miss Gibson's "usual Penetration" [14]), is the warmest defender of Clarissa.

Miss Gibson begins by admitting the premise that Clarissa, to be a worthwhile example of womanhood, must be capable of loving: "Love is the only Passion I should wish to see harboured in the gentle Bosom of a good Woman"; other passions, including ambitions, are rightly left to men (18). But from this conformist beginning, Miss Gibson goes on to differentiate the kind of love she claims for Clarissa from the love that characterizes other literary heroines. She caustically criticizes what one of the gentlemen praises as "the lovely *Emma*'s Passion for *Henry*" in Prior's famous poem (19) and even forces Bellario to admit that the kind of posturing passion he would approve of in a fantasy mistress would appall him if it were the real-life behavior of one of his daughters. Miss Gibson will admit no criticism of Clarissa, and appropriately she closes the pamphlet with a long summary of the action of the novel expressed through sympathetic identification with Clarissa's experiences.

But the first half of the pamphlet consists of the airing, discussion, and rebuttal of some of the more general complaints about *Clarissa*. The first complaint is the simplest: that it is too long. One gentleman "was certain he could tell the whole Story contained in the two first Volumes in a few Minutes" and, having proceeded to do so, asks "how is it possible for this Story, without being exceeding tedious to be spun out to two Volumes, containing each above 300 Pages?" (5). (Hester Thrale made the same point even more pithily about the novel as a whole: "There is no story. . . . A Man gets a Girl from her Parents—violates her Free Will, & She dies of a broken Heart. That is all the Story" [Keymer, 48].)

The counterarguments to this charge bring Fielding not only to Richardson's intentions in this particular novel but also into larger issues relating to the nature of fiction. Comparisons are immediately made between Richardson's "History of a Young Lady" and other, more traditional forms of history: Miss Gibson asks whether the gentleman's contention would lead him to choose an almanac as the best account of the kings of England, and another participant in the discussion, Mr. Johnson, points up the limitations of a one-paragraph summary (which he helpfully provides) of 20 volumes of the history of Rome. Mr. Johnson argues that some of the "chief Beauties" of any worthwhile history depend on its length: "for to that we owe the displaying so many various Characters, and the diving into the Motives of those great Mens Actions, who guided that extensive, powerful . . . Common-wealth" (6).

Even given the 18th-century perception of history as valuable chiefly for the moral lessons it can provide, the comparison between *Clarissa* and the history of Rome is an audacious one. It provokes laughter here, but the "Lady of the House (who has bred up three Sons and three Daughters, who do Honour to her Education of them)" supports Mr. Johnson:

> "I really think the penetrating into the Motives that actuate the Persons in a private Family, of much more general use to be known, than those concerning the Management of any Kingdom or Empire whatsoever: The latter, Princes, Governors, and Politicians only can be the better for, whilst every Parent, every Child, every Sister, and every Brother, are concerned in the former, and may take example by such who are in the same Situation with themselves." (7)

This is an extraordinary claim for the importance of that upstart genre, the novel—an importance that Fielding continues to buttress during the course of the pamphlet by introducing comparisons of various aspects of *Clarissa* with Shakespeare, Milton, and Homer. But the basis upon which Fielding places a high value on fiction is significant: it is not as entertainment but as instruction, not as diversion but as example. And so it follows that, for Fielding, the power of the novel comes from its exploration of character and motive, from which the reader may learn how to act in his or her own life. Hence—completing the process that gave rise to the debate—the length of *Clarissa* may be justifiable:

> "Tho' . . . there may be some Exuberances that might have been spared, as they stop the Progress of the Story . . . the scattered Observations have generally the Recommendation of Novelty to amuse the Curious, Depth to engage the Attention of the Considerate, and Sprightliness to entertain the Lively; and Story is considered by the Author, as he says in his Preface, but as the Vehicle to convey the more necessary Instruction." (8)

The nature of that "necessary Instruction" is expanded in Bellario's letter, which gives the considered views of this "candid and good-natured Reader." Bellario commends Richardson's conception of his characters and the technique that enables them to express themselves appropriately in their letters. In this discussion of "character," however, Bellario is using the same criterion that motivated Fielding in her own fiction: that is, the presentation of different moral facets of human nature—"the Obstinacy of old *Harlowe* . . . the Pride of the two old Batchelors . . . the over-bearing impetuous *James Harlowe*'s Envy . . . the two-fold Envy of *Arabella*" (36)—rather than the cluster of qualities that might be said to coexist in an individual personality. In consequence he praises Richardson, not for accurate observation of individual human beings but for his "picture of human Life" (35).

The picture metaphor is frequently repeated, claiming Richardson as a sort of verbal version of Hogarth, and associated images of drama also stress the calculated moral-tableau effect of the text's "moving tragick Scenes . . . all judiciously interspersed with Scenes of comic Humour" (45). The raw emotional power of these scenes draws in the reader—"we catch the Servant's silent Grief; our Words are choaked, and our Sensations grow too strong for Utterance" (44)—but this involvement is important not for its own sake but because it provides an index of the shared understanding of moral principle between author and attentive reader.

> Whoever can read her [Clarissa's] earnest Request to *Lovelace*, that she may not be exposed in a public Mad-house, on the Consideration that it might injure *him*, without being overwhelmed in Tears, I am certain has not in himself the Concord of sweet Sounds, and, must, as *Shakespeare* says, be fit for Treasons, Stratagems and Spoils.[6] (42)

Bellario rightly interprets the process of reading *Clarissa* as one of collusion between reader and author. In fact, Richardson had been encouraging reader involvement in his novel in a much more direct way even before its official publication, and the text of the novel was still developing in 1749. Richardson had actually finished a first draft several years previously[7] and had then redrafted the manuscript taking account of the opinions of close friends to whom he had circulated it. His decision to publish the text by installment enabled him to undertake further redrafting in light of readers' responses to the story as it unfolded. And even after that he was not satisfied: the second and third editions contained further amendments, chiefly intended, as he himself confessed, "to obviate, as I went along, tho' covertly, such Objections as I had heard."[8]

In these redrafts he undoubtedly made use of *Remarks on Clarissa*, especially since he was impressed with its arguments. Fielding presented him with a copy the day after publication (*Correspondence*, 123),[9] and he probably recommended it to his friend Edward Young; Young wrote to Richardson that he had circulated the pamphlet, which he had read "with great pleasure," to "five very proper hands" (Barbauld, 2.27–28). Four years later Richardson still felt highly enough of the pamphlet to send a copy of it, with a short pamphlet of his own, to Johannes Stinstra in Holland. Stinstra was "delighted" with *Remarks*, adding that "when the need arises to dispel similar objections, if perchance they turn up here, it will be easy to translate them into Dutch" (Slattery, 6.10).[10] Thus, for a work that by its nature was an ephemeral document, Fielding's pamphlet had considerable influence, becoming itself a part of the ever proliferating web of the *Clarissa* narrative.

Remarks was one of the earliest published comments on *Clarissa*. It has been seen as the "most ambitious defence of *Clarissa*," which "analyses the book's virtues in some detail and with a good deal of perspicacity" (Eaves and Kimpel, 292–93). Recent critics have pointed out that Fielding was the first to emphasize the importance of *Clarissa* as a whole rather than the sum of its parts[11] and have acknowledged that the analogies between the novel and Milton became a "critical commonplace" once Fielding had aired them (Keymer, 67). In what was in 1749 the male-dominated field of literary criticism, Fielding clearly made a confident and competent contribution. She wrote the pamphlet out of admiration for Richardson's achievement in *Clarissa*, but her arguments also show clear understanding of Richardson's technical achievements as well as the power of his presentation of moral principles in action.

Despite her appreciation of Richardson's multivocal epistolary fiction, Fielding was never prompted to copy it. Her single epistolary novel after 1749, *The History of Ophelia* (1760), is effectively a personal narrative from the sole correspondent. The spare, sober—and short—third-person narrative of the novel Fielding wrote after *Remarks*, *Volume the Last* could not have been more different from the techniques displayed in *Clarissa*. And yet *Volume the Last* is informed by the detailed consideration of the form and purpose of fiction that arose out of Fielding's defense of Richardson's novel. In particular, Richardson's insistence upon a tragic, rather than a comic, ending, as consistent both with real life and with true Christian exemplarity, helped to shape the final part of David Simple's story.

Chapter Six

Chains of Being:
David Simple: Volume the Last

Defending the tragic ending of *Clarissa*, Fielding wrote in *Remarks*:

> Rightly I think . . . is it observed, that what is called poetical justice is
> chimerical, or rather anti-providential justice; for God makes his Sun to
> shine alike on the Just and the Unjust. Why then should Men invent a
> kind of imaginary Justice, making the common Accidents of Life turn out
> favourable to the Virtuous only? Vain would be the Comforts spoken to
> the Virtuous in Affliction, in the sacred Writings, if Affliction could not
> be their lot. (49)

In *David Simple: Volume the Last* (1753), Fielding puts this theory into
practice. She returns to David Simple, shows "the common Accidents of
Life" stripping from him and his family all the material benefits of
income and property bestowed upon them during the course of *David
Simple*, and examines the effect of such loss on David and his virtuous
principles.

The preface to *Volume the Last*, written by "A female friend of the
author" (probably Jane Collier), suggests that this last chronicle of David
Simple was written with two purposes particularly in mind. The first is
openly didactic: "to exemplify the Behaviour of a Man endowed with
such a turn of Mind as *David Simple*, in the natural and common
Distresses of this World, to illustrate that well known Observation, that
'The Attainment of our Wishes is but too often the Beginning of our
Sorrows,'" and to show how "chearful Poverty may become almost the
Envy of many that are called the Rich and Great."[1] The second purpose
is realism: the reader is invited to compare the contents of the story with
what might happen in "real Life (which these kind of Writings intend to
represent)" (311). Fielding's rejection of the principles of "poetical
Justice," which governed most novels and romances of the time, is based
on the fact that such a doctrine flies in the face both of Christian morality and of real life.

As a story *Volume the Last* is straightforward enough, and it is sparely told, with no subplots, few digressions, and minimal allusion to myth or literature—except for the Bible. We are reintroduced to David Simple and the extended family of "real Friends" that he had established at the end of *David Simple*: his wife, Camilla; her father; her brother, Valentine; and Valentine's wife, Cynthia. Gradually, over a period of years, this small group of virtuous and well-meaning individuals lose the financial security they have relied upon for their future lives. David, as head of the family, becomes increasingly concerned for the future of those for whom he is responsible and increasingly reliant on the benevolence of others— a benevolence that, in contrast to his own in his prosperous days, is often promised but rarely performed. The community is first broken up when Valentine is offered employment in the West Indies and takes Cynthia with him. And then the deaths begin: several children born to both couples die; Camilla's father dies; news comes that Valentine has died in the West Indies. The Simple house is burned down and the last of their property destroyed. Camilla dies. Finally, David himself dies, leaving behind his one remaining child, Camilla, to be looked after by Cynthia, under the protection of a belatedly identified, truly benevolent man.

Each single event is little out of the ordinary—a natural misfortune arising from bad luck, or common human failings on the part of David and others; but cumulatively such repeated blows overwhelm David and his family in tragedy. Yet David retains throughout a capacity for happiness and contentment: not through insensitivity to the miseries he and his family undergo but through the mutual love that continues to underpin their lives. In this context, the openly declared Christian morality of the story focuses on David as a type of Christian hero. In his appreciation of the modest, natural things of life he is compared with the pre-Fall Adam (the simile is extended to Camilla as Eve and even to their small plot of land as the Garden of Eden); in his sorrows he is likened to Job. Each bereavement, therefore, is a test of his Christian virtue; not only does he pass each test, but he encourages his wife and children to follow his example. This Christian aspect to David's character is much more apparent in *Volume the Last* than in the earlier volumes in which he appears. But in each of the three books in the trilogy the "simplicity" of his nature is given a slightly different emphasis: in *David Simple* he is a benevolent innocent abroad; in *Familiar Letters* he is almost a figure of fun.

One critic of Fielding's work has condemned *Volume the Last* on the grounds that the "reversal of fortune" it depicts "has no relation to David's character" (Needham, 200). But many of the predicaments in which David finds himself arise as a direct result of his character, as established in all three volumes. What in prosperous times manifested themselves as positive characteristics—a feeling heart and a sympathetic mind—compound his problems in adversity; even his refusal to appear ill-mannered to others entangles him further in associations he would have done better to avoid.

Almost from the beginning of the novel David's judgment is overborne by others, to the detriment of himself and his family. His first serious setback comes when a distant relative makes a legal claim to the estates left to David by his uncle. David reasons that, despite the fact that he has justice on his side, "a tedious and expensive Law Suit" against "a young Fellow of a very large Fortune . . . very learned in all the Tricks of the Law" is likely to end badly, and "he should be much the least out of pocket, by giving up at once the whole Money" (318). This view is shown, by subsequent events (the estate is finally lost), to be accurate, and yet David is repeatedly talked into continuing with the lawsuit.

As his troubles increase so do a natural timidity and fear, and his virtuous and conscientious concern to protect his family hinders him from taking actions that might guarantee—but also risk harming—their happiness and security. In these circumstances he becomes virtually unable to act at all. His openness is increasingly compromised, even his natural optimism works against him, and he resorts to imposing on his own common sense: "*David* would not doubt the Friendship of a Man, who gave him the Pleasure of thinking, that, whatever Misfortune befel him, his eldest Son would, however, have an Education, and a good Prospect of being provided for" (350). It is not until those he loves best are dead that he regains something of his original integrity of purpose, and by then the world has proved too much for him. It is this opposition between David and his family on the one side and "the world" on the other that lies at the heart of the somber morality of *Volume the Last*.

It has been suggested that the novel enacts the crippling implications of the marginal position of women in 18th-century society.[2] But—unlike *David Simple*—*Volume the Last* is not really about the specific disadvantages of women: it is a woman, Cynthia, who is the strongest member of David's little family (by dispatching her to the West Indies, Fielding removes an important positive influence on David's decision making); and the fact that Cynthia and little Camilla alone survive at the end of the volume demonstrates that it is perhaps easier in their world for disadvantaged women than disadvantaged men to gain protection. In a real sense, David's problems in *Volume the Last* are specifically those of a man, disempowered by an all too credible series of misfortunes and misjudgments to the extent that he is unable to protect the extended family whose security and happiness depend on him.

Fielding's target, in fact, in *Volume the Last*, is nothing less than the structure of society itself—a society in which many members can only prosper through a system of patronage and dependence but in which true benevolence is replaced by selfishness and consequent cruelty to others. Even in *David Simple* benevolence is seen as a rare commodity; in *Volume the Last* it is swamped by the self-serving codes of gentlemen, lawyers, moneylenders, and others throughout England and as far away as the West Indies. This is a society that lives by the distinctly unbiblical creed "to him that hath shall be given."

The crucial point in David's reversal of fortune, therefore, occurs when he crosses the single most important dividing line in that society: that between self-sufficient and suppliant. David never abandons his own instinct for benevolence—as is apparent when, reduced to poverty in a tiny cottage, he yet spares some food and straw for a beggar—but once he is unable to support his own family without outside assistance, his plight is actually aggravated by the two people he comes to believe he can depend on as others once depended on him: Orgeuil and Ratcliff.

Ratcliff is David's first adviser, although he later becomes the less prominent of the two (because he deserts David first; in this novel "town" friends—Ratcliff lives in London and is concerned with David's London activities—prove their unreliability even more quickly than "country" ones). Ratcliff obtains influence over the family by his offer to be godfather and patron to David's eldest son. But there is an ominous aspect to his intentions from the beginning: because of him David's son is named not David, after his father, but Peter, after his godfather. Consistently thereafter, Ratcliff diverts David and his family from the course their judgment would otherwise lead them to take, and consistently his actions aim to divide, rather than reinforce the coherence of, David's family. He encourages them to continue with the lawsuit, though he knows that David faces ruin if the suit is lost. He requires young Peter to be educated at school, against his parents' wishes. He sends gifts of "a new Suit of Clothes, Hat, Stockings, Shoes, &c, for my God-son; and . . . a green Damask Sack, dirted but on one Side, which, turned, will make a Nightgown for Miss *Camilla*, and a Coat for little *Fanny*" (350).

Moreover, Ratcliff never fulfills his lavish promises of practical help. He offers to obtain for David, from "my Friend, the great Man" (348), a valuable sinecure with a generous income—and then takes it himself. He declares his intention of making young Peter his heir—until it becomes more convenient for him to promise his fortune elsewhere. All this is consistent with Ratcliff's underlying aim in offering David his friendship; what he really enjoys is not being benevolent but having a dependent.

He shares this motive with David's other potential benefactor, Orgeuil, though in many other respects Ratcliff and Orgeuil are contrasting figures. Ratcliff is a luxurious man who extrapolates, from his individual whims and wishes, a philosophical structure to suit himself; Orgeuil, by contrast, molds every fact to fit the theory by which he governs his life. Orgeuil first appeared in *David Simple* as a personification of human pride (orgeuil in French means pride), which Fielding interprets as reason without care or compassion; here the personification is fleshed out in satire as savage as anything Fielding's male contemporaries ever produced. For example,

> I must exonerate Mr. *Orgeuil* from having any Hand in the ill Usage of little *Cynthia*. He was generally in his Study, contemplating on his Rule of Rectitude, and exulting in the Beauties of Human Reason; that if any Man should be so mad as to blaspheme this his much reverenced Idol, he might be ready to do his Duty, and write an elaborate Rhapsody in its Justification. (353)

It seems extraordinary that Fielding, who so frequently praises the superiority of reason over passion, should reserve her harshest criticism for the operation of reason; but in Orgeuil reason itself becomes a servant of the passion of egotistic pride, and as such it is supremely destructive. In the Christian framework of the novel, Orgeuil is the idol worshiper: when his idol is not "the Beauties of Human Reason," it is himself, to the extent that late in the novel, when he is undergoing a serious illness, "instead of thinking on Death, he was diverting himself with being the Admiration of the Gods" (419). A wealthy man who could easily afford to support David and his family, he prefers to buttress his theories and keep his money. Unfortunately for David, "it was one of Mr. *Orgeuil's* most settled Maxims, that Man, by the Use of his own Reason alone, has a Power to prevent or heal any Misfortune" (357). The diametric opposition between such theorizing and the facts of life is made clear in the narrator's comment that Orgeuil's only liberality to David occurs

> in a Commodity, which it was impossible for his Family to feed on, namely, in Advice to practise what either his Disposition, or his Situation, rendered

impracticable. . . . Nay, he advised him to lead his Life back again, —to
unlend every Sum of Money he had lost by assisting the Unfortunate, —to
ungive every Benefaction his happier Days had enabled him to bestow, —
to unbuy every Comfort and Convenience with which he had pleased and
delighted his own Family . . . or if I may not be permitted to give to this
Part of his Conversation the Name of Advice, I cannot, with any Propriety,
think of a softer Appellation for it than Reproach. (356)

The "advice" of both Orgeuil and Ratcliff is anything other than help-
ful to David. Both, in their different ways, welcome the dependency of
others as a means of endorsing their own idea of their own importance.
They reproach, command, or demand to suit their own convenience; the
last thing on their minds is to benefit the increasingly needy David. The
actions of men such as Orgeuil and Ratcliff—and the agents and moneylenders whose interests are guided by them, and even to some extent the
farmer-tenants whose livelihood is at their mercy—combine to produce
a world very different from that envisaged by David. The links binding
David and his family are voluntarily and affectionately entered into, and
maintained by every member of the small community: it is "impossible
for any the least Link of the Society to be loosed without being strongly
perceived by all the rest" (341). But, as Fielding makes explicit, the vol-
untary links of mutual love are transformed by the Orgeuils and Ratcliffs
of the worldly world into chains binding a slave to a master: "Such
Dependance is Slavery, worse than working in the Gallies" (383).

If Orgeuil and Ratcliff had been the only villains of the novel,
Fielding's condemnation could have been seen as directed at a patriarchal society dominated entirely by male egotism. In fact, they are ably
supported—indeed, to a large extent led—by their wives, who amply
demonstrate that worldliness and selfishness are not exclusively masculine qualities. Mrs. Ratcliff appears only briefly in the novel; but her
instinct for divisiveness is shown to be quite as strong as that of her husband. Mrs. Orgeuil is more prominent. Her initial structural function
seems to be to provide symmetry: she exists to fail Camilla and Cynthia
as her husband fails David. But in many respects she represents an
advance on, rather than an analogy to, Orgeuil's iniquity. Whereas
Orgeuil lets David down through inaction and insensitivity, his wife's
actions are motivated by more active malevolence.

As the handsome wife of a wealthy man, the mistress of a large estate,
and the directress of the activities of her husband's tenants, Mrs. Orgeuil
is in a position to help those less fortunate than herself and ease the miseries of families like David's. But her relationship to David and his fam-

ily is soon dominated by the envy and hatred she feels for Cynthia, in particular, as a woman of greater understanding than herself. Mrs. Orgeuil's envy and hatred are powerful forces—significantly, she is the only character in the novel openly described as motivated by malevolence—which manifest themselves in a deliberate desire to harm the reputation or well-being of anyone whose existence challenges her own view of herself. Her chosen weapons are words, which she uses as tools of deceit. "Mrs. *Orgeuil* had an art, by dropping some Circumstances, and altering and adding others, of turning any Story to whatever Purpose she pleased" (408).

Mrs. Orgeuil clearly understands that the one who controls words can begin to control reality. Toward the end of the novel she recounts her version of the experiences of the Tilsons, a local family, as an object lesson (directed at her husband, whom she suspects—quite unjustly—of planning to give David money) of the ill effects of generosity: Mr. Tilson's foolish benevolence, she declares, has ruined his whole family. Mrs. Dunster, the farmer's wife, whose homely honesty is often compared with Mrs. Orgeuil's art and whose modest benevolence to David and his family provides a silent contrast to the Orgeuils' inaction, questions this version of events. Mrs. Dunster points out that Mr. Tilson's widow and daughters are all secure and happy (and, furthermore, that they continue to exercise real benevolence in the community). However, she is quickly crushed:

> "I tell you, Dame *Dunster*, being reduced from Forty thousand Pounds to Six, is certainly being utterly ruined; and when Mr. *Tilson* was living, notwithstanding he appeared happy and chearful, yet I doubt not (although he was too proud to own it) but he had many miserable Hours of Reflection, when he thought of his own Imprudence, or he must have been an insensible Brute." (407)

Mrs. Dunster's version is nearer the truth than Mrs. Orgeuil's, but it is Mrs. Orgeuil's version that prevails—not with her husband, who is too busy thinking about reason to listen to her, but with the farmer's wife: "Mrs. *Dunster*, who was a great Lover of Stories, greedily hearkened after every Word" (408). And so Mrs. Orgeuil poisons the minds of all about her by "telling Stories," in the euphemistic sense of telling lies.

It should be pointed out that Mrs. Orgeuil, despite her cruelty and malevolence—and despite her significant role in causing the destruction of David and his family—is (like her husband) essentially a comic, or rather a gloriously black-comic, character. Her exaggerated sensibilities, her ingenuity in misrepresentation, her role playing, and her cultivated stupidity combine to make a monstrous, and yet entirely credible, creation. One of the reasons that *Volume the Last*, despite its undeniably grim plot, is not depressing to read is the realization that David, the ultimate object of many of Mrs. Orgeuil's machinations, is protected by his virtuous simplicity from understanding almost all of her intrigues and stratagems.

But Mrs. Orgeuil is more successful with others. While Orgeuil is binding his dependents with the chains of slavery, Mrs. Orgeuil enchants hers by the beguiling appeal of her lying words.[3] Fielding comments that, had Mrs. Orgeuil succeeded in her plan to take charge of little Camilla on David's death, "she would have put on all the Charms of Good-humour (which she was capable, when she pleased, of doing in the highest Degree)" until the child had begun to trust her; only then would Mrs. Orgeuil have "proved the worst of Tyrants" (417–18).

Mrs. Orgeuil's lack of love and benevolence is often presented in direct contrast to the attitudes of David and his family. Her idea of emotional response is a display of exaggerated sensibility, and much of her contempt for David and Camilla, Valentine and Cynthia, finds its focus in the accusation that because they do not show their emotions they do not truly care for one another. When Valentine and Cynthia leave for the West Indies, Mrs. Orgeuil "delighted to relate what she called the insensible Behaviour of our Society . . . yet wilfully omitted publishing the Sorrow which *David* and *Camilla* could not forbear expressing as soon as they knew their Friends were out of the Reach of being hurt by their Tears" (339–40). At the time, "she should have been more affected (she said) than any one of them, if she had been to lose her favourite Cat" (339). The unconscious truth in Mrs. Orgeuil's comment is taken up later when her husband falls dangerously ill. Mrs. Orgeuil writes a hysterical letter of "uncontrolled" grief to an aristocratic friend and is so enthusiastic in her role as grieving widow that it clearly comes as something of a disappointment when Mr. Orgeuil recovers; but shortly afterward her lap dog dies, and Mrs. Orgeuil is able to lament his death "in full as pathetic Terms as she had before done the imagined Death of her Husband" (423).

David and his "little Family of Love" (372) are unable to negotiate with a world made up of Orgeuils and Ratcliffs on the only terms that would bring success to a suppliant. "In Theory no Man breathing knew better than *David* that the painting your Misery in the strongest Colours, is necessary to raise what is called Compassion in a proud

Mind" (356); but he cannot exaggerate and falsify—that is, make a story out of—his distress, and so he obtains no relief. When he seeks a loan from the steward Mr. Nichols, on the strength of a hopeful letter from Valentine in the West Indies, the difference in principle between the two men is clearly expressed by linguistic impasse: "'You don't talk our Language, sir,'" says David, trying in vain to explain the bonds of loyalty and affection that would ensure that Valentine shared his prosperity with David. "'I think I talk plain *English*,'" replies Nichols, "'and only want to know what Security I should have, should I advance any Monies?'" (369). The interview inevitably concludes to the advantage of the worldly man. Equally inevitably, the bargain in the short term cheats David and in the long term ruins him: the drunken bailiff unnecessarily called in to enforce the debt gets drunk and sets fire to David's house.

One of the most powerful motifs in this novel is the unreliability of language in the mouths of those whose interest is served by deception. Words and meanings are manipulated by powerful people for their own ideological purposes, justifying themselves and condemning others. As Ratcliff considers his own actions, "the Treachery that had a little before clearly appeared to be on the Side of his breaking his Word with *David Simple*, [he] suddenly, by some hocus-pocus Trick, conveyed quite to the other Side of the Question" (389); and as he considers David's, simplicity becomes naiveté becomes imprudence becomes deserving victimhood.

The propensity for words, concepts, and principles to be distorted and misinterpreted preoccupies the narrator of the tale from the beginning:

> to those, who mistake *bon-mots*, *insulting* Raillery, malicious Ridicule, and murtherous Slander for the *Attic* Salt of Society, I write not. Indeed, to such I *cannot* write, concerning *David* and his Company; as no Words are equal to the raising in such Minds, any true Image of the pleasures of our happy Society. (315)

While describing the misinterpretations and manipulations of the Orgeuils and Ratcliffs of the world, the narrator maintains that she, unlike the "storytellers" in the narrative, aims to tell the truth. She diligently points out where the truth lies between various versions of it and shows where mistake merges into deliberate misconstruction. Occasionally this stance leads to a level of complicity with her hero that Fielding had largely avoided in *David Simple*. Since David and his family are the only truth tellers in a world of falsehoods, the narrator has no real need to remain at a distance from them; in this most satiric of narratives, there is little or no satire at David's expense. Instead, the narrator openly sympathizes with him in his griefs, writes movingly herself of the pain of watching loved ones suffer and die (412, 415), and "Joyfully" imagines Mrs. Orgeuil's intended cruelty to little Camilla, "for it was not *Camilla*'s miserable fate" (418).

No word or concept is so clearly betrayed in this novel than the talisman of *David Simple*: that of the true friend. Orgeuil, Mrs. Orgeuil, and Ratcliff all regularly proclaim themselves "true Friends" to David and his family, but their claims are meaningless because they are inconsistent with their actions. With the Orgeuils as with Ratcliff, "in proportion as friendly Actions decreased, friendly Professions flowed the more largely" (319). It is a significant and moving moment when David, having tried to believe in the harmony of word and deed as long as possible, finally admits that the "true friendship" of the Orgeuils is illusion. He has already given up Ratcliff, and when Camilla dies and the Orgeuils have stood by and done nothing for her, David finally slips his chains:

> Mr. *Orgeuil* now, would he have given his whole Estate, had it not in his Power to make him amends for sending him home with empty Advice to do Impossibilities, and with the Stings of Unkindness in his Heart, when his House was a House of Distress and Sorrow. (414)

But in waking from this last illusion, there is nothing left for the simple man to do but to turn his face to the wall and die of a broken heart. When David is finally reunited with the last of his real friends, Cynthia, Fielding's narrative endorses their own distrust of words. "Neither shall their Conversation be repeated by me. It is sufficient to say, that they spoke the Words dictated by the Hearts of *Cynthia* and *David Simple*" (427).

It is unsurprising that a novel that privileges silence over words also rejects many of the trappings of other 18th-century fictions. At various points in the narrative it seems possible that David and his family will triumph over an uncaring world and return to prosperity, but such expectations are always dashed. Valentine's opportunity in the West Indies, for example—the source of many a fictional fortune—results in his death rather than his success. The novel remains consistent to the end, maintaining its defense of Christian fortitude and also its denial of poetic justice: David, Cynthia, and little Camilla are not corrupted by the corrupt world around them, but neither are their virtues rewarded with anything but a serene death, in David's case, and the merest hope of survival, in the cases of Cynthia and Camilla. The Ratcliffs and the

Orgeuils, and the many others like them, take all the earthly rewards for themselves.

When *Volume the Last* was published, the whole *David Simple* trilogy was reissued, and the nature of David's story was completely changed by its somber conclusion. But the transformation was not a success. *Familiar Letters* quickly fell into oblivion once more; *Volume the Last* had only a limited popularity. Lady Mary Wortley Montagu thought the character of Mrs. Orgeuil "well drawn, and . . . frequently to be met with," yet she deliberately misread the novel, claiming its moral as "the ill consequences of not providing against Casual losses, which happen to almost every body" (Halsband, 3.67). A more sympathetic friend thought the fault was, rather, in Fielding's publishing strategy: "The world think it a meer 3d volume and not a new story, and thus the book stops with the booksellers. She should, I told her, have changed the title; for Novelty is the charm of the present age" (*Correspondence*, xxxiv). The reissue of *David Simple* in the 1780s renewed its popularity and restored its autonomy: it appeared without either sequel. Most critics who sought out *Volume the Last* were unimpressed. "There is little to be said about *Volume the Last* of *David Simple* and—one is tempted to add—even less to be said for it" is a typical early-20th-century view (Needham, 200).

But thanks to the reissue of *Volume the Last* with *David Simple* by Oxford University Press in 1969, there has been a resurgence of interest in the sequel, increased understanding of its intentions, and increased appreciation of its achievement as a disturbing indictment of the principles of 18th-century society and an intensely powerful polemic on the destruction that occurs when words become separated from their meanings and actions from morality.[4]

Chapter Seven
"Free, and not Licentious": *The Cry*

In November 1753 Sarah Fielding signed a receipt for £50.10.00 as half-payment for "a Book written by me and to be printed in three Volumes in duodecimo, entituled [sic] *The Cry*" (*Correspondence*, xx). The fact that she required her publisher, Dodsley, to make himself responsible either to her "or to whomsoever I shall appoint" for the profits on the other half may indicate that the remaining share was to go to someone else,[1] and it has commonly been accepted that the novel was a collaborative venture between Sarah Fielding and Jane Collier.[2] The concept of multiple authorship was congenial within the Fielding-Collier circle, and this particular collaboration is likely enough: the two were close friends with personal and literary interests in common; they shared lodgings in the early 1750s; they wrote jointly authored letters to their friends;[3] they were both published authors, with a lively interest in each other's work;[4] and they were both enthusiastic supporters of didacticism and innovation in fiction—central concerns of *The Cry*.

In the absence of further external evidence of collaboration, however, the argument for Collier's participation hinges on an unsigned but clearly jointly authored Introduction to the novel, which emphasizes "our" intentions for the rest of the work.[5] Contemporaries, including some who might be expected to know of any joint authorship arrangements, such as Catherine Talbot, ascribed *The Cry* to "Mrs. Fielding" (Pennington 1809, 2.182–83);[6] some modern critics—notably Mary Anne Schofield in her introduction to the recent reprint of the novel—have done the same. Whether or not Collier participated in the project, there is nothing in *The Cry* that is incompatible with Fielding's other writings, and I, too, will assume her sole authorship for the purposes of this chapter.

The plot of the main narrative of the novel—Portia's story—is relatively simple. Portia has become acquainted, through her childhood friend Melantha, with a widower, Nicanor, and his three children: Oliver, the eldest son, and the twin brother and sister, Ferdinand and Cordelia. According to Melantha, Nicanor is an unfortunate man, Oliver "a young gentleman of great learning and wisdom," and the twins nothing more than "inoffensive and good-humor'd" (1.28). Portia's own judgment—and that of the reader—is very different. Portia instinctively dislikes Oliver, is drawn to Cordelia as a friend, and falls in love with Ferdinand. However, she is aware of considerable unhappiness in Nicanor's family. Nicanor, Ferdinand, and Cordelia are poor because Nicanor has spent Ferdinand and Cordelia's money as well as his own (he has squandered most of it on his mistress, Cylinda, who has since disappeared and whose influence on Nicanor is generally regarded as a main cause of the family's joint and several woes). As a result, the whole family is dependent on the generosity of Oliver, and Oliver's main enjoyment is in keeping his father, brother, and sister in a state of dependence on him.

Ferdinand eventually sails to the West Indies in hopes of making his fortune. In his absence, Oliver schemes to blacken his reputation; extraordinarily, when Ferdinand returns a wealthy man, he seems by his behavior to endorse his brother's accusations. Portia, who has kept faith with Ferdinand until his own actions demonstrate the contrary, is desolate. She rejects Ferdinand's offer of marriage but in her attempt to escape him falls into a near-fatal fever. Ferdinand, shocked at this turn of events, reveals that an "idle love of refinement" (3.258) had tempted him to try Portia's virtue by pretending to have lost his principles. Their misunderstanding unraveled, the two marry and take Nicanor and Cordelia to live with them; the scheming Oliver is left to the misery of marriage with Melantha.

Throughout her narrative, Portia insists on the importance of truth, and truth to self, assessed from experience and informed by reasoned judgment. Her own self-respect depends on her being true, not to her lover, but to her soundly based principles—even at the cost of considerable pain to herself. It is to provide Portia with the ultimate test of these principles that Fielding engineers the otherwise inexplicable plot twist of making Ferdinand declare, and act out, unlikely iniquities in front of Portia: she has trusted her own judgment and withstood reports that his "very principles are corruption" (3.186), but when she sees for herself the change in him she acknowledges her mistake and rejects his proposals of marriage. However "honorable" he may be in the eyes of the world (3.212), he is no longer worthy of her love.

This assertion of female self-respect above romantic love is a radical theme for a novel of the 1750s. But even more radical are the form and structure of the text as a whole, which consistently displace the main plot by commentaries, discussions, and debates. Although the novel begins with Melantha's description of Nicanor and his family, 200 pages later the themes of *The Cry* have been well aired, but the plot has not advanced; when it does finally get under way, there is considerably more interest in the psychological states of mind of the protagonists than in the events in which they become involved. Overall, *The Cry* is a very unusual text indeed. It has been variously described as "the most curious item with which the critic of Sarah Fielding will meet"[7] and "an innovative and wholly original prose work, a combination of allegory, philosophy . . . feminism, and social satire" (*Correspondence*, xxxiv)—the difference in nuance reflecting readers' varying responses to Fielding's wholly self-conscious strategy of innovation in form and content.

Fair warning is given of Fielding's intentions. Pointedly addressing her Introduction to "the candid reader" (1.1), whose mind must be receptive to new ideas, Fielding proceeds to discuss the instability of prose fiction as a form and the importance of continued experimentation: "stories and novels have flowed in such abundance for these last ten years, that we would wish, if possible, to strike a little out of a road already so much beaten" (1.8). The reader is first reassured that the "humour, character, moral, and every other proper requisite" of novels will be maintained and is then clearly told what *not* to expect in the novel itself: "we beg to inform our readers, that our intention in the following pages, is not to amuse them with a number of surprising incidents and adventures, but rather to paint the inward mind" (1.11). While fully aware of the attractions of the trappings of traditional romance, Fielding rejects them in favor of psychological exploration. "Thoroughly to unfold the labyrinths of the human mind" (1.14), she states, is her purpose. She adds that in order to fulfill this purpose—one that, however familiar it may have seemed to readers of Fielding's earlier fiction, was a clear declaration of war on most popular fiction of her time (including not only the traditional romances but also the currently popular *Tom Jones*)—"'tis necessary to assume a certain freedom in writing, not strictly perhaps within the limits prescribed by rules." Then she adds significantly, "Yet we desire only to be free, and not licentious" (1.14).[8]

The caveat is a crucial one, and it signals a process of negotiation and counterbalance that permeates the novel as a whole: throughout, innovation and experiment are first claimed as highly desirable and then countered by an appeal to tradition and precedent. For example, one of the reasons the formal "plot" is relatively unimportant in the novel as a whole is that the novel's dominant mode is not really narrative at all but something close to allegory: type figures, such as Una (Truth) and Duessa (Falsehood), debate ethical and philosophical issues with, and

respond to narrative events related by, "real" characters Portia and
Cylinda, in some symbolic environment seemingly outside the real-world
boundaries of time and place. And yet the undoubted originality of such
a methodology is explicitly denied by linking *The Cry* to literary precedent: Fielding claims for herself a legitimate place within mainstream literary tradition, citing an extraordinary range of writers—including
Virgil, Horace, Plutarch, Ariosto, Spenser, Shakespeare, and Milton—to
demonstrate that her novel is not, after all, "new." Here, as elsewhere in
The Cry, Fielding's determination to be "free, and not licentious,"
resolves itself into arguing in favor of newness and innovation—but
within the boundaries of convention and precedent. It proves, on occasion, a risky strategy and one calculated to create tension.

Such tension is immediately apparent in the structure of *The Cry*.
Ironically, the three-volume format—of which *The Cry* is an early example—was to dominate prose fiction in the 19th century and therefore
now seems conventional; but it was not common in the 1750s. and it
does not easily accommodate *The Cry*, which consists of five parts, presented in alternating dialogic and narrative modes. The first part largely
comprises discussion on the philosophic and ethical issues that are exemplified later, in which Portia argues her case against the negative voices
of the eponymous Cry, in the presence of Una; the second is a third-person narrative history of some of the "real-life" characters before Portia
met them; the third is dominated by philosophical debate, as the slow
advance of the main plot prompts new topics for discussion by Portia
and the Cry; the fourth is the personal history of Cylinda, who has
already appeared in the second part in a minor role; and the fifth comprises discussion about the nature of character and some hectic plotting
to allow the desired moral and narrative closure to be brought about.

The five-part structure suggests drama rather than fiction, and in
many respects *The Cry* is reminiscent of a play rather than a novel. This
blurring of genres is again intentional. Fielding declares in the
Introduction that the customary division of prose narrative into chapters is "a worn-out practice"; instead, since both the characters within
the text and the readers of it "shall constitute an audience to hear the
stories of those who shall be brought before them," the idea of scenes
and dramatic speeches, borrowed from the stage, will better give "life
and action to our history" (1.15–16). But the wary author is not prepared entirely to relinquish the authority of the fictional narrator,
informing the reader that "we have kept the privilege of being our own
chorus . . . to point out the behaviour of our actors . . . to express or

relate some things which are not proper to be spoken by our principal characters; or . . . to tell what we cannot prevail on any of our actors to tell our readers for us" (1.18).

The resulting text is a hybrid between dramatized discussion and narrative fiction, but analogies with drama are maintained throughout the novel. After the initial "Prologue" the narrator declares that there is "nothing to do but to draw up the curtain . . . to discover our chief personage on the stage" (1.25); and at the end of the novel, after the curtain is said to have fallen, an epilogue is provided, "to preserve the uniformity of our piece" (3.296). Sometimes comparisons with the stage are clearly intended as direct satire on the conventions of the contemporary London theater: in an allegorical novel, metaphor—in an inversion of its usual purposes—serves to remind the reader of its connection with the "real world" of 1750s England, which is otherwise only indirectly described.

Frequently, characters in the novel are given formal dramatic speeches or participate in dramatized discussion. Portia, whose name is taken from that of the heroine of *The Merchant of Venice*, argues for mercy over justice and actually quotes Shakespeare's famous speech on the subject. Cylinda expresses her repentance in a doubly dramatic way, declaiming, with overt reference to Shakespeare: "My life hath been . . . a tale told by an idiot, and my imagination a strutting player, full of sound and fury signifying nothing" (3.279). The underlying point is to reveal behavior as performance, and this way of looking at human action is organically connected to the novel's deeper concerns. In *The Cry*, where every form of human behavior is acting of a sort, the importance of harmony between intention and action, between inner self and outward appearance, is crucial. Overacting, for example, is a sure sign of moral inadequacy, as Portia points out:

> I should be very sorry if I could not be imposed on by a judicious actor, as that would imply a suspicion of mind which I abhor: but raving and ranting, however it may on the stage attain a thundering acclamation from the upper gallery, will never pass for sensibility of heart, except on those who have never experienced what that sensibility really is. (3.153)

Moreover, the play analogy is central to the nature and function of the Cry themselves. The Cry are a personification of "all those characters in human nature, who, tho' differing from each other, join in one common clamour against Truth and her adherents" (1.20), and this allegori-

cal role is amplified by its relationship to the metaphors of drama. The
Cry often act as a kind of Greek chorus, commenting on and responding
to the reported narrative of the main protagonists, Portia and Cylinda.
But this is not their only role. Often the Cry resemble the audience in
the theater rather than the players onstage: when the curtain falls at the
end of the novel, it leaves the Cry on one side and Una and Portia on the
other. The Cry's opinions, in contrast to the usual comments of the chorus in Greek drama, are noisy, thoughtless, and ignorant: they

> wanted nothing but the assistance of cat-calls with their shrill and pierc-
> ing notes, to express their dislike, in order to have been a true picture of a
> condemning playhouse audience. *Portia* several times in the midst of their
> noise and uproar, began to speak, but found it as impossible to gain
> attention, as the player doth when the multitude are resolute to hear
> nothing explained. (1.192–93)

Such descriptions add force to Fielding's satire not only of contemporary
playhouse audiences but, by extension, of public opinion in general—
including, possibly, those members of the public who have read *The Cry*
without due attention to its moral message.

The Cry are sometimes considered in terms even more hostile to
Portia than an audience that cat-calls an actor. They are often likened to
a hunt, "open'd on a new scent" (1.91) or "in full cry" against their prey
(3.200); and by the end of the novel, clamoring to claim sinners as their
own, they are a "gloomy crew" (3.278), indistinguishable from the
demons of hell. But in all their roles the members of the Cry are consistently abusive, jeering, and malicious; their opinions are consistently
negative as they pour scorn not only on the exercise of moral and ethical principles but even on the idea that serious discussion of such matters is worthwhile. They thus form a natural force of opposition to
Portia, and Fielding uses the combative discussions between the two
opposing points of view to raise the central concerns of the novel in theoretical form.

One such concern is the nature and extent of freedom allowed to
women in 18th-century society—a concern in which Portia's very
refusal to accept the conventional wisdom of the Cry is considered as
unwomanly. The Cry's acolyte, Melantha, "looked on a lover as one of
the necessities of life" (2.135); one of the main problems for Portia is
that the Cry insist on reducing her arguments—and the designated
scope of women's activities in general—to matters relating directly to

love, courtship, and marriage. It has recently been pointed out that many 18th-century guides to female behavior "in effect cordoned off women from the rougher and more 'real' world of problems and human confrontations reserved for men" (Hunter, 265). The aim of the Cry is to reduce all of Portia's motivation to the hopes and fears of loving and being loved. When Portia attempts to discuss questions of ethics and morality, the Cry accuse her of parroting Ferdinand's views and conclude that she "is most excessively in love with Ferdinand" (1.129). In this context, Portia's willingness openly to acknowledge her love confounds the Cry, offending their demands for female reticence and cheating their salacious interest in her emotional life. Portia's ready admission of love transgresses the code of acceptable female behavior in at least two ways: first, because she admits to loving a man before he has declared himself to her (an act of assertion currently being explored in a much less radical manner in Richardson's *Sir Charles Grandison* [1753–54]);[9] and, second, because her open declaration cuts through the suspense seen as an essential part of romance.

Moreover, Portia places love in the context of other matters important to her sense of self: for her, love is not a gratification of selfishness but "a sympathetic liking, excited by fancy, directed by judgment, and to which is join'd also a most sincere desire of the good and happiness of its object" (1.104). She has fallen in love with Ferdinand as a result of witnessing his kindness, good humor, knowledge of human nature, and general affability; her emotion is therefore rationally founded, and it does not conflict with her general moral and ethical well-being until her lover's behavior suggests that her opinion of him is radically at fault. It has been argued that women novelists of the mid-18th century "defended their own respectability by banishing all hints of sexual desire in their heroines" (Spencer, 118). It is not in fact true that Portia shows no sexual desire for Ferdinand, but the sidelining of sexual desire as a motive is here a necessary strategy to banish emotional excess as woman's dominant characteristic and romantic love as her proper sphere.

The Cry's insistence on the all-importance, to a woman, of love and romance naturally leads them to condemn the concept of female education outside the limited area of domestic skills and social accomplishments. Portia leaves the Cry (and, ostensibly, the reader) in doubt as to the nature and extent of her own education until late in the novel, but she argues forcefully on several occasions in support of a level of education well beyond anything Fielding had outlined in *The Governess*. Portia recounts to the Cry an incident when, on her way to visit a learned female friend,[10] she overheard a conversation between two servants. John and Betty, with all the authority of ignorance, denigrate the lady Portia is to visit and broaden their criticism to include learned ladies in general. John opines that "no gentleman would like to have his family affairs neglected, because his wife . . . because she understood a few *scraps* of *latin*, valued that more than minding her needle, or providing her husband's dinner" (1.147). After impressing Betty with a few scraps of Latin that he himself has picked up, John extends the argument to the ridiculous but logical conclusion that "learning was a fine thing for a man, but 'twas useless and blame-worthy for a woman, either to write or read" (1.151).

Portia effectively ridicules arguments against female education by placing them in the mouth of an ill-informed and ill-educated servant. She goes on to point out that the learned young lady referred to "is remarkably neat in her person, and is uncommonly diligent in every part of useful economy," and that the "leisure" that she found for her studies was certainly not produced "by neglecting anything useful for the family" (1.149). Portia argues forcefully for the rights of such a woman to the education she has attained. And yet the nature of this defense of female learning places strict limitations on the freedoms she claims. She refuses, for example, to put forward the truly radical proposition that such education could provide a valid alternative to skillful performance of domestic duties.

When Portia delivers her own opinion about the value of female education she accepts many of the caveats implicit in John's views:

> That every woman ought to be an oeconomist, and to be thoroughly acquainted with all those things which are call'd female accomplishments, I am so far from contradicting, that I look'd on it as too universally allow'd to need any mention or justification. And, full as distant am I from thinking, that what is call'd a learned education is by any means necessary, or even proper for women in general. But, when added to all the useful knowledge of a woman, without neglecting any of the necessary duties of her station, a young lady employs her leisure hours in acquiring as much learning in languages, as will enable her to have a higher relish both for reading and conversation . . . I see not why she should be stared at as a monster, reviled as a slattern, or ridiculed as an absurd animal, not fit for the company of either men or women. (1.157–58)

Perhaps the strong language of the final sentence reflects Fielding's personal experience of opprobrium leveled at the "learned lady"; but, however strongly Fielding, as an educated woman, might resent the hostility she faces, it does not result in complete rejection of the conventional view of women and education. Later Portia even tries to enlist endorsement of her views from convention itself, asserting that "learning in languages" can itself be regarded as a conventional female accomplishment, since it will enable a woman to be "a real agreeable companion as a wife, to any man of sense" (3.109).

The Cry are generally hostile to the idea of female education, but their particular criticisms are centered on the claims of women to rationality and judgment: women should "not . . . meddle with the philosophers" (2.173); "logic was a man's business" (1.122). Such criticisms constitute encoded, but none too obscure, arguments about whether or not women should be entitled to enter the world of classical learning. It was, after all, through study of the classical authors that the 18th-century gentleman learned philosophical, logical, and rhetorical principles. The conclusions of the novel here are cautious support for women's rights: that Latin and Greek, and the philosophies they embody, should not be male prerogatives. And yet access to the classics is not seen as an unalloyed advantage even for intelligent women with no other calls upon their time. Cylinda is the most learned lady in the book, having been taught the learned languages by her father and having studied deeply and widely among classical authors; but her studies have had an iniquitous effect because she has not learned the ethical principles of a distinctly nonclassical Christian virtue, without which the logic and philosophy of the classical writers is shown to be worthless. Portia, on the other hand, has learned in a more judicious way, and by constantly testing her theoretical learning against her experience she is protected from the ill effects of learning without reasoned judgment.

Portia's other main protection from the worst criticisms of the Cry—as well as from an overweening opinion of her own powers—is the fact that, despite her assertive views, she remains firmly feminine. She is said (although not, of course, by herself) to be as beautiful as a heroine should be. She is modest and submissive in the "real world" of the plot: she plays a largely passive role in the events that take place within Nicanor's family; despite her claims for an enlarged woman's sphere, her own problems focus on the unwelcome attentions of Oliver, and her troubled courtship with Ferdinand; she chooses Ferdinand because she wishes to marry a man to whom she can be submissive ("To marry sensibly let the woman chuse the man she can obey with pleasure" [2.244]); having been disappointed in her choice, she succumbs to a near-fatal fever, in the manner of many another wilting 18th-century heroine.

And yet in the allegorical, intellectual world of the novel—those parts of the text that are most concerned with its central project of exploring the labyrinths of the mind—Portia is the dominant figure. She defers to Una, of course (though on at least one occasion she has to explain the Cry's motivation to Una, who is mystified), but for the most part she is self-confident in her beliefs, determined in her judgment, and forthright in her opinions. She faces up to the Cry, argues with them, defends herself against their criticisms, and occasionally attacks their hypocrisy or malice, "with such a spirit, and real dignity of superior penetration," that the Cry are (temporarily, at least) cowed (2.64).

The opposition between Portia and the Cry, which lies at the heart of the novel, is fundamental and ideological; at its most intense, it is enacted through struggles over the nature of truth, the relationship between words and deeds, and the nature of words themselves. Portia consistently exposes the gap between words as used and their "true" meaning. She would ban the word "friendship" because its meaning has become so debased (1.33); she declares that "whoever has the word obligation continually in his mouth, hath the love of tyranny steadily fixed in his heart" (1.54); she makes a clear distinction between "true maxims of morality" and meaningless tags or quotations.[11] It has been observed, "The extent to which language can reveal reality is one of the basic stylistic and moral problems of the 18th-century novelist."[12] Fielding begins to address the subject in *Volume the Last*, but no other novel before *Tristram Shandy* (1759–67) explores the troubled tensions involved in the relationship between language and reality as thoroughly and openly as *The Cry*.[13]

The Introduction warns that "the puzzling mazes into which we shall throw our heroine, are the perverse interpretations made upon her words; the lions, tigers, and giants, from which we endeavour to rescue her, are the spiteful and malicious tongues of her enemies" (1.13). Portia is indeed beset by the Cry's manipulation of language for their own purposes. "Why, O ye *Cry*," she asks on one occasion, "do you, by leaving out my words, and putting in your own, entirely change my meaning? I said not anything like what you have represented" (1.53). But the Cry are unrepentant: one of their chief delights is to obscure, rather than reveal, meaning. They indulged in "false assertions and malicious representations" (1.46); they "twisted and wrested Portia's words into a thousand different meanings" (1.59); by "absurd inferences" (1.156) or "improper applications" (2.86), they "metamorphose[d]" (2.87), "transform[ed]" (2.88), and "jumbled up" (2.195–96) words until their aim of thoroughly confusing truth and falsehood is achieved. Significantly, the Cry are unable to agree on the definitions of the words they use, squabbling among themselves or being "suddenly struck on a heap into sullen silence" (1.123), if pressed. When, in the course of a particularly frustrating wrangle over what modest female behavior should be, Portia asks the Cry "what idea they had fix'd to the word *romantic*":

> instead of answering her question, they each fell to jogging their next neighbour, and softly whisper'd,—Do you answer her—No, you answer her, says another; and so on to the third, fourth, &c. throughout the whole assembly. (1.59)

And just as their desire is not to clarify by definition, so it is not to listen: they are "not endeavouring to understand [Portia's] words, but to censure them" (2.172–73).

Against this Portia champions "the real purpose of language, the making our ideas clearly understood" (2.19), and the importance of this principle in the moral framework of the novel is endorsed by the connection made between "the real chastity of *Portia's* language" and "the pure images in her honest mind" (1.113). In an essay on the politics of language in the 18th century, John Barrell has described how "the way people spoke was regarded as a matter of social and moral discipline."[14] That the debate here is not simply a matter of semantics—nor indeed of intellectual abstractions—is exemplified in Portia's application of the disciplines of speech to truth, to the general situation of women in society, and to her own moral well-being.

Portia is particularly alert to the dangers for women of believing the euphemisms and falsehoods by which the Cry maintain their ideological impurity. Appropriately drawing her most pointed application from the conventions of courtship, she ridicules the typical lover, who, preparing to make a marriage proposal to his mistress,

> profusely pours forth his angels and his goddesses; makes himself the humblest of her slaves; petitions at the shrine of her altar for some distant hint of her favour. . . . An adulation, which translated into plain *English*, means . . . "Madam, I like you (no matter whether from fortune, person, or any other motive) and it will conduce much to my pleasure and convenience, if you will become my wife: that is, if you will bind yourself before God and man to obey my commands as long as I shall live. And should you after your marriage be forgetful of your duty, you will then have given me a legal power of exacting as rigid a performance of it as I

please." But, as the adulating language is not thus translated 'till the ceremony of marriage is past, and is 'till then perfectly unintelligible; 'tis no wonder that the poor woman, who hath been thus egregiously imposed on, (or rather who hath so egregiously imposed on herself) should find it so difficult a language to learn. (1.69–70)

The novel's urgent central concern with language here merges with the continuing debate on gender politics to argue that accepted linguistic rituals and conventions falsify reality, to the benefit of the male and the cost of the female.[15] In Portia's exemplification of the euphemisms of courtship, "the poor woman" is the victim of her lover's misrepresentation of the offer he is making her; indeed, Portia unmasks such misrepresentation even more brutally later in the novel, when she offers an alternative translation of the male's courtship rhetoric: "that weakness and imperfection is the perfection of a woman; that I am stark mad in love with ignorance, and thus I shall allure her by calling her a fool" (1.152). But Portia, while identifying the power of the male to victimize the female in courtship, is mounting a larger argument: that the ways of the world operate because, in a larger sense, both men and women allow them to do so. Significantly, in Portia's first comment, "the poor woman . . . hath so egregiously imposed on herself"; in her second, the foolishness of a woman who can be allured by being called a fool is so obvious as to require no further emphasis. Woman is victim because she colludes in the process by which she is victimized.

After all, many of the most prominent voices of the Cry—including Duessa, the personification of falsehood (1.196)—are female; if anything, the female members of the Cry are more hostile to Portia and her ideals than are the male (who, albeit for their own reasons, do approve of Portia's vision of the ideal marriage). As in *Volume the Last*, Fielding does not see predator and victim in gendered terms; and in *The Cry* this approach leads Fielding to claim large and radical freedoms for women. The clear implication is that women should not accept either double standards or separate spheres: instead, they should assume—in a moral and ethical sense, at least—the same responsibility as the men in a social world that embraces them all.

Portia does not only demand truth and clarity in language; much more controversially, for her 18th-century audience, she claims the right to invent words. Innovation—in language, as in politics—was regarded with suspicion as potentially subversive. In the 1750s a challenge to the stability of language represented an onslaught on the status quo in general: this was the decade in which Fielding's friend James Harris, in the widely read *Hermes*, argued for the systematization of language[16] and Samuel Johnson's *Dictionary* attempted to control the usage of words by tying them to fixed definitions. Portia's insistence on coining new words is therefore an act of assertion, hardly compromised by her stated intention in so doing, which is to provide a more accurate description of moral and ethical states of mind than existing linguistic forms allow.

Again, however, as so often in this novel, Fielding prescribes strict limitations on the freedom she claims for her heroine. The invented words—"turba" for the state of psychological turbulence that moral and ethical problems or failings produce, "sinistra" for evil, and "dextra" for virtuous tendencies in the mind—are after all hardly new, and in case any ill-educated (female?) reader should be unaware of the Latin derivations, Portia clearly explains sources, precedents, and related usage. Even the potentially radical feminization of language implicit in the feminine nature of the words is diffused under a welter of Latin conventions. Again Portia is claiming only to be free, and not licentious, insisting that as far as words in general are concerned it is the Cry's manipulation, and not her creation, of words that is subversive. She argues not for innovation but rather for a return to linguistic—and with it, she hopes, moral—stability. Her response to the linguistic distortions of the Cry is corrective rather than inventive, stemming from her "sort of detection" (1.45) and her "darting penetration" (1.189); her aim is to recover truth from the snares of "blind and perplexing error" (1.19).

The potential radicalism of Portia's assertiveness in the novel is masked not only by this insistence on precedent and convention, on recovery rather than discovery, but also by the presence of Cylinda as secondary heroine. The strategy of rendering moderate radicalism more acceptable by providing an embodiment of even more extreme views, which can safely be condemned, was often used by later women writers: Harriot Freke in Maria Edgeworth's *Belinda* (1801) and Elinor Joddrell in Fanny Burney's *The Wanderer* (1814), for example, are used in this way. In *The Cry*, if Portia can be regarded as "free," Cylinda is clearly intended to represent the "licentious": where Portia challenges conventional notions of acceptable female behavior and opinion, Cylinda flatly rejects her society's constructions of femininity; where Portia supports the independence of mind that arises from commonsense use of informed judgment, Cylinda's claims to intellectual and social freedom take the concept of independence to what Fielding clearly regarded as disastrous excess.

Cylinda's situation is highly unusual for both a fictional heroine and a real-life woman of the mid-18th century. She is, after her father's premature death, in a position of genuine independence, possessed of health, wealth, and beauty, and unhampered by family commitments. Moreover, she is not only an intelligent but a learned lady, having been provided by her father with a thorough classical education. Eighteenth-century antifeminist narratives often claimed that women sought intellectual knowledge as a form of self-love (Nussbaum, 148). Cylinda certainly exemplifies an unholy alliance between learning and egoism. She regards her own judgment as all-important, refusing to recognize that much of what she considers "judgment" is in fact the operation of her own imagination or desire. Even worse, she does not learn from experience and therefore makes the same mistakes again and again; yet even after a series of contradictory enthusiasms and mounting unhappiness, she still sees herself as "the goddess of wisdom" (2.256). Self-deification—the ultimate result of human pride and vanity—has immense dangers: even her own virtues "were to bow down before my own greatness and profundity" (2.316).

Such egoistic principles are clearly regarded as the logical result of an excess of the female freedoms Portia argues for in a modest degree: independence from conventional norms, and intellectual study. There is, however, another reason for Cylinda's failure to find fulfillment. Her problems stem from the fact that her learning has been in moral philosophy and not in religion. Religion as a theme is unobtrusive in Portia's narrative, but it is Christian principles that underpin her ideas and opinions. Such principles are evidently not to be found in the writings of the classical philosophers, and they were not inculcated separately by Cylinda's father; without them her learning is seen to be worthless.

Cylinda's motivating principle is to gratify herself, and her dominant aim is to maintain her independence. Since she is young, attractive, and wealthy, the most obvious threat to that independence is marriage: "The loss of liberty which must attend being a wife, was of all things the most horrible to my imagination . . . I . . . could not bear the thought of putting myself in any man's power for life" (2.320). Cylinda opts, more than once, to live with a man rather than marry him, audaciously pointing out in her defense that she is libertine from logic rather than from love. In assuming the right to determine the form of her sexual relationships with men, she consciously abandons femininity, claiming to have grown "masculine in my thoughts" (3.21) and to have embraced "the masculine freedom of character" (3.80). She accepts the loss of female respectability that such a course of action might involve—a loss of which the reader is all too aware, since Cylinda was first introduced as "the monster . . . who was the ruin of Nicanor" (3.35). She does not abandon all principles but claims the right to choose her own standards of acceptable behavior.

These standards are not always culpable. They extend, for example, to refusing to marry a respectable young man who does not know of her past: "in my assuming the masculine character, I always resolved to play the part of a man of strict honour" (3.58). But Fielding is adamant that a woman's femininity cannot be flouted. Cylinda eventually, to her own horrified astonishment, finds herself "chain'd down and enslaved to the most rigid of all tyrants, an uncontroulable passion" (3.80), for the very man who would have been her husband, had she accepted his proposals—made in the most conventional of forms, via her father—years before. Her freedom is reduced to "'a frantic ravery for a state of independence on God or man'" (3.88). Shocked at what she has become, Cylinda begins to understand her errors and appreciate that her independence has served her poorly: "a man of true understanding and steady principles . . . might kindly have guided my wandering imagination, and been my protector from the idle and mischievous rovings of my own whimsical brain" (3.104). Having told her story, she stands before Una and Portia as a "poor penitent" (3.278). The Cry wait to claim her as one of their own.

But Fielding clearly believes Cylinda has been punished enough, for she is not abandoned to the clutches of the Cry. Just as Cylinda's sexual transgression has not led—as it surely would have done in a novel by any other author of the time—to social and physical degradation, so her intellectual sins, once acknowledged, are not considered irredeemable. In fact, at the end of the novel Cylinda is described as living happily with Ferdinand and Portia. Her "penances" are mild enough: she must regard her learning as no longer "an instrument of her delusion" but rather "an innocent and delightful amusement" (3.301); and she must live unmarried—a fate that is hardly a penance at all, since it is voluntarily shared by the innocent and virtuous Cordelia, who, having never found a man she wished to join in "so solemn and irrevocable an engagement as marriage" (3.300), is quite happy as she is.

In fact, Cylinda's sexual transgressions are treated with astonishing tolerance both by the author and by the other characters in the novel: her attitude is even to some extent endorsed by the unquestionably virtuous Portia, who declares that, having condemned Ferdinand's morals, if she could not have conquered her passion for him, she would rather have been his mistress than his wife (3.213). The lessons Cylinda must learn are not primarily concerned with sex, or even with gender politics in its wider sense, at all, but with the individual's responsibilities as a member of society: the error she must own is the false belief that she can be intellectually or socially independent, that the way she lives her life concerns no one but herself. The novel has shown that, from intellectual arrogance, Cylinda has come dangerously close to the doctrine of the Cry: "the exalting each themselves, and mortifying all others to the dust" (1.21). Because of her the intellectually weaker Nicanor has wasted his fortune, with near-tragic effects for his family. The lesson is clear: "no creature placed in a social community can injure himself alone" (3.281). Once again, Fielding is arguing not for specifically female areas of autonomy but for equality for women and men in the all-important spheres of ethics and morality.

This most social of Fielding's fictions produces one of her rare optimistic conclusions[17]: Cylinda and Cordelia are happy, while "*Portia* and *Ferdinand* to the end of their lives enjoyed a state of uninterrupted prosperity. They lived to see their childrens children, and possessed every blessing which this world can possibly bestow" (3.303). The equality of moral responsibility for men and women is not only a legitimate freedom but one that is seen to benefit individuals of both sexes, the family, and the wider community.

It was a message that the novel's audience either did not understand or did not welcome. *The Cry* was not widely liked, and sales were poor. Even Elizabeth Carter, who wrote to Catherine Talbot that "on the whole it pleased me mightily," was troubled: "There is sometimes rather too strong a spirit of refining in it," she comments (Pennington 1809, 2.182–83). Many readers were particularly uncomfortable with the nature of Fielding's experimentation; as Clive Probyn suggests, they "took its innovation for eccentricity" (*Correspondence*, xxxiv). Lady Mary Wortley Montagu, independently minded herself, thought the novel's "sentiments generally just . . . a better body of ethics than Bolingbroke's"; yet she judged the "fable . . . just about the most absurd I ever saw" and added that Fielding's "inventing new words that are neither more harmonious or significant than those already in use is intolerable" (Halsband, 266). Samuel Richardson recommended the novel to his protegées Lady Bradshaigh and Sophia Westcomb as "a kind of domestic Piece . . . written by a Lady who has a good Heart as well as

Head."[18] Lady Bradshaigh was honest enough to admit that "I certainly saw my self more than once, amongst the detestable *Cry*," and decided: "Upon the whole I admire the thing and hope to profit by it." Yet she saw defects in the tone of the work—in which she detected a "want of *spirit*" or "a kind of languidness"—and she strongly objected to Fielding's habit of quoting from earlier literary works.[19] Sophia Westcomb, more cautious (or perhaps more confused) in her response, asked Richardson to tell her what to think about the work. Richardson revealed his reservations to her in what is, in modern terms, a distinctly "mixed" review. He began as positively as he could: "I think there are very natural Strokes in the work. . . . The Piece is a new Species of Writing, as I may say. The Plan, the Design at least, is new, and I think it deserves, on the whole, a better reception than it has met with." He added, however, that he strongly disliked the management of the final volume, and quoted his own daughter Nancy's verdict that "she would forgive the Lady [Portia] for forgiving him [Ferdinand], but would not forgive him, for standing in so great Need of her Forgiveness."[20]

When in 1757 Richardson urged Fielding to attempt a reissue of the novel—"I cannot bear that a piece which has so much merit and novelty of design in it, should slide into oblivion," he wrote—it was with the proviso that the plotting of the final section be amended "to make Ferdinand as worthy of his mistress at last, as he was at first" before the issue of a second edition (Barbauld, 2.108–9). But no second edition appeared. Forty years after publication, when *The Cry* was literally a museum piece, Hester Lynch Piozzi wrote that the novel "contains more good Sense and true Knowledge of Life than many a popular Work of its own Sort, but being *odly put together* never had any sale" (Blooms, 249).[21] *The Cry* was not reprinted until 1974.

Chapter Eight

Sex and Sensibility: *The Lives of Cleopatra and Octavia*

"The Lives of *Cleopatra* and *Octavia* form, perhaps, the strongest Contrast of any Ladies celebrated in History." So begins Fielding's dedication to the Countess of Pomfret, which introduces *The Lives of Cleopatra and Octavia*, published by subscription in 1757. Through the stories of the two women, Fielding continues, "the abandoned Consequences, and the fatal Catastrophe, of an haughty, false, and intriguing Woman" can be set beside "an Example of all those Graces and Embellishments, worthy the most refined Female Character." After the formal complexities of *The Cry*, Fielding opts for the technically simple strategy of two personal narratives, told from beyond the grave, each to be considered in light of the other. But by turning for the first time to historical "truth" for the basis of her narratives, and by treating this "truth" as complicit with her own ideas on social and sexual politics, Fielding creates something much more complex—not least in a further destabilizing of the boundaries between the newly developing genre of prose fiction and older literary forms. As one critic has recently written, "Governed by historical events, the *Lives* resists the name *fiction*; told by ghosts, it mocks the name *history*."[1]

Fielding's introduction offers a justification for writing about historical figures rather than fictional characters. She accepts that "Works of Fancy" allow an author greater freedom of invention but argues that the actions of real people "are better suited to inform, and give us juster Notions of ourselves, as they are Originals, and present the Eye with the Prospect of human Nature, taken from Life, and not extended beyond the Limits of Credibility and Truth" (55). History, in the 18th century, was often seen as the vehicle of moral, rather than "factual," truth, and the notion that historical lives should be presented as cautionary tales rather than as "fact" was not radical; an essay in the popular magazine *The Rambler* argued that "no species of writing seems more worthy of cultivation than biography; since none can be more delightful, or more useful, none can more certainly enchain the heart by irresistible interest, or more widely diffuse instruction to every diversity of condition."[2]

Fielding's version of the stories of Cleopatra and Octavia takes its place in a long line of retellings of what was by then a familiar tale. The first and most famous version is Plutarch's *Life of Antony*; most subsequent versions, including Fielding's, depend heavily on his account. It has recently been shown, however, that Fielding consulted an awesome range of other classical sources (in the original as well as in translation) in extensive research for *Cleopatra and Octavia* (Johnson, 1994). She was genuinely concerned about factual accuracy, as Octavia's identification of "a Mistake in *Plutarch*" (126) about her genealogy confirms. Actual political events, such as battles and coups, are not distorted, and the historical circumstances of Cleopatra's position as queen of an Oriental, barbaric, marginal nation negotiating fragile security with the mighty power of classical Rome firmly underpin Fielding's interpretation of her story. The more sources Fielding consulted, however, the more she would have become aware that any concept of factual accuracy was of limited use: the "facts" of the lives of Cleopatra, Antony, and Octavia had been reinterpreted—not to say reinvented—in every version to suit the widely varying political, moral, and ideological intentions of the teller of the tale.

The same was true of the many more or less openly fictional versions current in the 18th century. The most prominent of these were dramatic and well known to the reading public of Fielding's time: the *Monthly Review*, in its review of *Cleopatra and Octavia*, claimed that it could not "suppose our Readers ignorant of characters that have been drawn by Shakespeare, Sidley [sic], and Dryden."[3] These playwrights based their characters, situations, and train of events substantially on Plutarch yet produced very different versions of the story. Shakespeare's *Antony and Cleopatra* (1606–7) is probably the nearest of the three to Fielding's: its concern for the moral implications of passion and the link between lack of self-control in the principal characters and disaster in the state are both themes of *Cleopatra and Octavia*. Sir Charles Sedley's *Antony and Cleopatra* (1677), a formal neoclassical tragedy, presents a quite different Cleopatra: in this version she is victim as well as queen, undermined by the machinations of an evil courtier and therefore largely exonerated from blame. The general line of John Dryden's version—first performed in 1678 and by far the most popular dramatic version in the 18th century[4]—is clearly suggested by his title: *All for Love: Or, the World Well Lost*; Dryden openly admitted in his Preface to the play that in the creation of his love-tragedy he had drawn the characters of both Antony and Cleopatra "as favourably as Plutarch, Appian, and Dion Cassius would give me leave."[5]

The story of Antony, Cleopatra, and Octavia, then, was familiar to the 18th-century public from both classical and modern, "factual" and dramatic sources, and it was a story from which political, moral, and ideological messages, of various kinds, had already been drawn. There are several respects, however, in which Fielding's is unlike any previous version. She was the first to concentrate not on the love affair between Cleopatra and Antony but on the contrasting characters and fortunes of Cleopatra and Octavia, thus locating the chief point of interest in the two women rather than in issues of romantic love or moral struggle in the mind of the male. Dryden had distorted history in *All for Love* to engineer a meeting between Cleopatra and Octavia (an event that never occurred in fact and does not occur in Fielding's[6]), and increasing interest in the moral contrast between the two women is a feature of late-17th- and early-18th-century versions of the story; no one, however, had given it first prominence before Sarah Fielding.

More importantly still—and a fact closely related to this shift in emphasis—Fielding's *Cleopatra and Octavia* is the first version of this highly gender-conscious story to be written by a woman and from a perspective of avowedly feminine morality.[7] The lives of the great femme fatale and the pattern wife can thus be read for the first time in doubly feminine terms, as an account of woman's lot by a woman.[8] In several of her earlier fictions, Fielding's criticism of constructions of femininity formed part of a wider condemnation of the customs of society as a whole. Now, however, she specifically addresses issues central to woman's place in the world—the negotiation between private and public spheres, the struggle between dependence and autonomy, the nature of relationships possible between woman and man—to reveal a truth behind the ideologies of femininity, which, her argument suggests, have not changed much in the centuries between Cleopatra's lifetime and her own.

The form of Fielding's narrative, although technically simple, was also original. Scholars have had difficulty finding precedents for the precise strategy of the recounting of personal histories from beyond the grave. Fielding herself argued, as she often did elsewhere when she wished to disclaim her own innovations, that she was merely following classical examples (55), but those she cites provide a model only for the movement of literary and historical figures between this world and the next. It has been argued that narratives in the style of the 16th-century *Mirrour for Magistrates* provide closer precedents,[9] but there is no evidence that Fielding was familiar with this tradition. Links have also been suggested with "dialogues of the dead," or narratives of religious conversion. The very reference to religion, however, acts as a reminder that one of the startling omissions from the narratives of the two women is any indication of the effect of their lives in this world on their fate in the next. Indeed, this absence troubled the seriously minded Catherine Talbot, who wished that Fielding had presented Cleopatra "like Hamlet's ghost, concealing the secrets of the great deep . . . but intimating that they were very dreadful, and the consequence *to her* of that life" (Pennington 1809, 2.251).

In fact, the single directly comparable personal narrative of the life of a historical figure, told from beyond the grave, is the chapter in Henry Fielding's "A Journey from This World to the Next," published in his *Miscellanies* (1743), "*Wherein* Anna Boleyn *relates the History of her Life.*"[10] This chapter is quite different in tone from the rest of "A Journey," a fact that Henry acknowledges in a footnote: Anna Boleyn's narrative, he declares, "is in the Original writ in a Woman's Hand," and so he is "inclined to fancy it was really written by one of that Sex" (*Miscellanies*, xxxv). Since Anna Boleyn's narrative is closely concerned with the fictional and didactic interests prominent elsewhere in Sarah Fielding's work—the negative effects of female ambition, the destructive results of "inconsistent Behaviour, which must always be the Consequence of violent Passions" (*Miscellanies*, 116), the ease with which men can be manipulated by a woman's "Words of Cottages and Love" (*Miscellanies*, 123)—it seems almost certain that the narrative is by Sarah.[11] She might well have been working on *Cleopatra and Octavia* shortly after *Miscellanies* were published; certainly the project was well enough advanced for 600 subscription receipts for it to be printed in 1748 (*Correspondence*, 30).[12] For some reason, however—perhaps subscribers could not be tempted to support Fielding again so soon after the publication of *Familiar Letters*—the project was deferred. Frequent references in *The Cry* to Cleopatra and Octavia, and the themes of their story, suggest that Fielding had taken up the manuscript again by 1754.

In *The Cry*, when the heroine, Portia, wishes to explain the feelings of the villainess Melantha, she uses the method by which she can "in the most lively and intelligible manner . . . paint the real history of *Melantha*'s mind" and actually assumes Melantha's identity so effectively that many of her audience are convinced by the deception (*The Cry*, 2.144). Portia—and Fielding—evidently relished the opportunity both to play devil's advocate and to appropriate the sexual and moral freedom denied respectable women of their time. One can only speculate on the novelty for Fielding, a genteel old maid of the 18th century, of assuming the identity of Cleopatra, Queen of Egypt, the most prominent icon of the destructive sexual allure of woman, in history. The results of Fielding's telling the Cleopatra story out of Cleopatra's own mouth, however, measured against earlier versions of Cleopatra's story, are devastating.

It has been suggestively declared that Cleopatra is "'a woman and a queenly queen . . . to whom the poets have been able to add nothing, and whom dreamers find always at the end of their dreams'"[13] (the dreamers, in the French original of the quotation, are clearly male) and that "'Before the thought of Cleopatra every man is an Antony.'"[14] Before *Cleopatra and Octavia* Cleopatra had always been described by men and regarded primarily as an object of male desire. Now, for the first time, Cleopatra speaks for herself as a woman through the creative intelligence of a woman writer alert to the strategies of sexual politics. Cleopatra's narrative is unexpectedly reasoned, practical, and witty. Her motivation, equally surprisingly, is revealed to be neither instinct nor passion but shrewd logic, the development of which she traces in detail. No longer is she the magnetic "other," the mystical object of man's love who could inspire from an unwilling admirer the tributes that turn her faults to virtues—"she did make defect perfection"—and deny her very mortality: "Age cannot wither her, nor custom stale / Her infinite variety" (Shakespeare, *Antony and Cleopatra*, 2.2.231, 235–36). The difference can clearly be seen in a comparison of perhaps the most famous lines of Shakespeare's play with the same scene in Fielding's novel. Shakespeare's Enobarbus describes Cleopatra's arrival for her first meeting with Antony:

> The barge she sat in, like a burnish'd throne
> Burn'd on the water: the poop was beaten gold;
> Purple the sails, and so perfumed that
> The winds were love-sick with them; the oars were silver,
> Which to the tune of flutes kept stroke, and made
> The water which they beat to follow faster,
> As amorous of their strokes. For her own person,
> It beggar'd all description: she did lie
> In her pavilion—cloth of gold, of tissue—
> O'er-picturing that Venus where we see
> The fancy outwork nature. On each side her,

> Stood pretty dimpled boys, like smiling Cupids,
> With divers-colour'd fans, whose wind did seem
> To glow the delicate cheeks which they did cool,
> And what they undid did. (2.2.191–204)

Fielding's Cleopatra describes the scene as follows:

> I embarked on the River *Cydnus* in a small Galley; the Head of which
> shined with inlaid Gold. The Sails were of purple Silk: The Oars were
> Silver, which beat Time to the Flutes and Hautboys. I lay under a
> Canopy of Cloth of Gold, curiously embroidered; and I was dressed as the
> Goddess *Venus* is usually represented. Beautiful young Boys, like Cupids,
> stood on each Side to fan me. My maids were attired like Sea-nymphs and
> Graces; some steering the Rudder; some working at the Ropes. The
> Perfumes diffused their Fragrancy from the Vessel to the Shore. (61)

The difference is not simply that between poetry and prose, or between
an old soldier's romanticized memories and the personal recollections of
a more active participant (although the flatness of Cleopatra's tone in
Fielding is marked even in relation to the rest of her narrative and is
surely a deliberate deflation of Shakespeare). It is more that Cleopatra's
account leaves little or nothing to the imagination; it lays bare the con-
trivance behind the mystery, suggesting the work that went into the
choosing of the boys and maids and perfumes and the precise effect they
would make; it is as if the movie star coolly and carelessly reveals the
secrets of lighting, make-up, and stunts that have given reality the illusion of enchantment. Such revelations already begin to make the successfully deceived observer look more than a little foolish: and indeed,
the chief interest of the early part of Cleopatra's story, as told by
Fielding, is in witnessing how Cleopatra's ambition and skillful management combine to produce positive results for her at the expense of the
judgment, understanding, and even the personal dignity of the all-pow-
erful but sexually impressionable Anthony.[15]
     Already, by the time she meets Anthony, Cleopatra has successfully
managed her relationship with Julius Caesar to fortify her tenuous hold
on her throne; later she will try to seduce Herod and Octavius. But now
she sees an opportunity to rule the world through Anthony, "the
amorous triumvir." Her methodology, as always, depends on conscious
manipulation of gender relations. She plans her meeting with Anthony
in as great detail as she did her barge journey; when all is ready, she

assumes "a pensive Posture" and waits for the scene to begin. The metaphorical link with stage performance is an apt one: Cleopatra is quite consciously acting out her victim's fantasy.

> The first Moment it was apparent that I saw him, I rose with an Air of such Alertness, to meet and welcome my Guest, that my Foot slipped, as it were by Accident, and I fell on my Knees. *Anthony* flew to raise me; and as soon as it might be thought I could recover the Fright, which I affected to be in at my Fall, I thanked him, and said, I hoped this Accident, at our first Interview, was a good Omen, that by his Strength he would support a Woman's Weakness, and defend a Queen who resigned herself to his Power. (62)

Cleopatra's stratagem here depends entirely on fulfilling Anthony's expectations of the weakness and vulnerability of women. It offers an equally conscious comment on 18th-century constructions of femininity: "If to be feeble was both charming and commendable, then the strong, independent woman must of necessity conceal her true nature" (Hughes-Hallett, 166). Cleopatra succeeds: Anthony sees what he expects to see and is completely taken in. In fact, Cleopatra has measured the precise impact of each move in the scene she has devised for Anthony's benefit: "My Fall and Fright moved his Pity; whilst the Turn I gave it raised his Admiration, and at the same time reminded him of his own Greatness" (62). And while she is flattering Anthony's vanity and pride by fulfilling his expectations of female vulnerability, she is already beginning to despise the man she can so easily manipulate: "It is scarcely to be credited how good an Effect this little Trick (trifling as it may appear) had on the Mind of Anthony. I read my Success in his Eyes, and inwardly applauded my own Wisdom."

Cleopatra manipulates Anthony, here and throughout their relationship, because she has "Experience in the Ways of Men" (62). She is sexually experienced—coolly concluding a comparison of Anthony and Caesar with the comment that Anthony must be her favorite because he has more to offer her, but "if I gave a Preference to the Person of either, it was to that of *Caesar*" (63). However, "Person" is clearly unimportant here, since for Cleopatra the sexual relationship represents not mutual love but competition; her liaison with Anthony is frequently described in terms of a military campaign. This is the woman's route to power and control: indeed, Cleopatra ascribes part of her success with Anthony to the fact that "as I had no Passion for him, my Judgment was cool, and enabled me to turn his Passions to my own Advantage as I pleased." She observes his character and opinions solely in order to use them to her advantage: "*Anthony* was very apt to place a full Confidence in the Integrity of Others: A Fine Disposition to be managed by a Woman he liked!" (63).

While Anthony is entranced by the female mystique of which earlier writers had made so much, Cleopatra continues to outwit him. Far from being the passive object of male desire, she is actively manipulative, deceitful, and untrustworthy. She offers Anthony a bewildering series of hedonistic pleasures in order to keep his mind and senses fully occupied with her and to ensure that he remains intent on finding new ways to please her. Her very changefulness—that famous "infinite Variety"—is a conscious ploy, not only to keep Anthony guessing about her (and therefore "enslaved" to her will) but also to destabilize his sense of right and wrong: Cleopatra records, with undisguised contempt, that he "sooth[ed] my Humour, at the Expence of his Friendship, his Honour, his Justice, and his Understanding" (65). His judgment turned inside out by Cleopatra's influence, Anthony reneges on his duty as triumvir, abandons the peace-making marriage with Octavia, loses the trust of his own men, and fights on his weakest ground against Octavius. When he is told (on Cleopatra's instructions) that Cleopatra is dead, he kills himself.

Cleopatra, of course, loses everything, too; but Fielding, true to her stated intention of making Cleopatra the epitome of a "haughty, false, and intriguing Woman" (41), offers no sympathy. Cleopatra is prompted throughout by motives of vanity, pride, avarice, and ambition: she cares for nothing and no one but herself; she has no thought for the sufferings of others—whether Octavia as a deserted wife or the Romans as a war-ring nation; she is relentless in the pursuit of self-interest through the strategy of sexual domination. In the climactic scene at the Monument, even Plutarch—whose account of Cleopatra had been written to please her enemies—had allowed Cleopatra an outburst of genuine grief at Antony's death: "she dried up his blood that had berayed his face, and called him her Lord, her husband, and Emperour, forgetting her owne miserie and calamity, for the pitie and compassion she tooke of him."[16] Fielding's Cleopatra comments that "[a] little Compassion for *Anthony*, and a good deal for myself, overwhelmed my Eyes with Tears of Sorrow" (122); the "Passion" that overwhelms her on this rare occasion results less from grief than from the frustration of defeat and the fear—justified, as it turns out—that she will not be able to allure the coldhearted and calculating Octavius as she had done the warm-blooded and passionate Anthony.

In introducing Cleopatra and Octavia as "perhaps, the strongest Contrast of any Ladies celebrated in History," Fielding probably intended her Queen of Egypt to have no redeeming features at all. Cleopatra's cruelty, her self-centeredness, her deceit, her greed, her willful subordination of every interest to the gratification of her own vanity and ambition—all these qualities and more are clearly irredeemable. No reader can condone Cleopatra's murder of real or fancied rivals, or her careless condemnation of whole nations to war, in the hope of gaining personal advantage out of the conflict. At one level, Fielding offers through Cleopatra simply a new perspective on the theme of feminine wiles, familiar in didactic literature since the tempting of Adam in the Garden of Eden.

And yet the message of Fielding's narrative is not so simple. Cleopatra's, after all, is a non-Christian world. Her contemporary environment is one of violence and barbarity; it is the rule, rather than the exception, to dispose of rivals and competitors by murderous means. And Cleopatra is Queen of Egypt in her own right, which means that she has inherited personal power, in the public world of politics and strategy, and the responsibility to maintain it or be destroyed herself (a responsibility subtly different from that which Octavia, as Caesar's sister rather than a figure of authority in her own right, possesses). Cleopatra survives—even, for a time, flourishes—by using the propensity of men of a certain type (including Caesar, as well as Anthony) to think of women in a certain way. In *The Cry* Fielding had shown how women collude with men in the demeaning rituals of 18th-century courtship to their own disadvantage. In *Cleopatra and Octavia* Caesar and Anthony, and others like them, collude in a view of women that is responsible for their own victimization. In this context Cleopatra's story is that of an intelligent and capable woman of any era who negotiates an alien, male-dominated world by pretending to be the kind of woman the patriarchal male finds irresistible. Her narrative lacerates the foolishness of men who compartmentalize "women," as Anthony does, whether as an inferior race or as a mystical "other." As a demolition of male constructions of femininity—constructions that were at least as valid for the 18th century as for the classical world—Cleopatra's narrative is supreme. In this respect, Fielding's dissection of sexual politics is quite as ruthless as Cleopatra's recorded behavior. It is hard to imagine the author of *The Cry* remaining unaware of the ironies involved in acknowledging the intellectual awareness, the humor, the delight in invention, and the sheer vitality of her symbol of all that is bad about women.

Cleopatra's is the dominant voice of the book. Hers is the first of the two personal histories (reflecting, albeit only as a "Shadow . . . of her former Royalty" [55], the fact that she holds a higher position in the social hierarchy than Octavia), and her narrative occupies more than three-quarters of the total text; her scope ranges geographically from Egypt to Rome to Palestine and covers a multiplicity of political as well as amatory matters; the strength of her personality imposes control on the story she tells. As Octavia's life is completely ruined by Cleopatra's beguiling of Anthony, so her story is completely overshadowed by her rival's more forceful and vivid version of events. Octavia's narrative—much of which has been told before she even begins to speak—seems largely to exist in relation to Cleopatra's.

The opening of Octavia's story, for example, proceeds in a series of point-by-point contrasts with Cleopatra's narrative of her early life. The education of the two women is brought into direct comparison: Cleopatra is brought up to believe "the Notion, that to please myself was the sole Business of my Life, and that every one around me was born to be my Slave" (56); Octavia is taught "that to contract my Desires, to command my Passions, and to share my Pleasures with others, was the only Conduct which could promise me Happiness" (126). Cleopatra declares herself ruled by vanity, pride, and ambition; Octavia's "predominant Passion was Love." Cleopatra willingly embraces the manipulations and machinations inherent in playing the political game for herself; Octavia seeks "a private Life, with a Husband who was agreeable to my Inclinations, and capable of a reciprocal Affection," and dreads becoming involved in politics in the only way that is likely for her—by being given away in a politically motivated marriage. Cleopatra's life is based on strategies of art and artifice; Octavia loathes the very thought of "artful Behaviour" (127). Cleopatra consistently subordinates others to self and cares nothing for the fates of nations in comparison to her own well-being; Octavia declares that she would willingly subordinate private inclination to public duty, "had my Uncle *Julius Caesar* continued in the Opinion that, in order to prevent the spilling of much *Roman* Blood, it was necessary to make me a Sacrifice."

Fielding had some latitude in her presentation of Octavia, since relatively little is recorded about her in the classical versions of the story. For example, although the name of Octavia's first husband, Marcellus, appears in some of Fielding's source material, his character and the details of his relationship with Octavia are almost entirely Fielding's own invention. Proceeding again on the principle of contrast, Fielding draws Marcellus as the opposite of Anthony; and the relationship between Octavia and Marcellus is presented as an ideal, against which Octavia's second marriage, to Anthony, and Anthony's extramarital relationship with Cleopatra, are both found wanting. Marcellus "had an excellent Understanding, a lively Imagination, a penetrating Judgment, and so acute in the Discernment of Things, as not to be imposed on by outward Appearances" (127–28)—capacities (especially the last) that Anthony signally lacks. Marcellus does not judge Octavia by the standards of "many . . . Women in the World" (129) but appreciates her as an individual. "We lived together with the utmost Simplicity," Octavia recalls. "Artifice and Cunning were banished [from] our Bosoms" (129).

Against this description of an ideal relationship between a man and a woman—one of equality, simplicity, and true happiness—the shortcomings of Anthony's affair with Cleopatra are rendered even more apparent than Cleopatra's narrative has admitted. Furthermore, the reader—who is already well aware of the unsatisfactory nature of the marriage between Octavia and Anthony, from Cleopatra's own informed account of it—begins to guess at the impact of other contrasts, which are horribly confirmed when Octavia recounts the experience of her second marriage. What Fielding demonstrates in Octavia's account of her life with Anthony is that a woman, however well endowed with desirable feminine virtues, can live a happy and fulfilled married life only if her husband appreciates those qualities; if her husband fails to do this, her life becomes a torment.

Octavia knows, before she marries Anthony, that he has been ruled "by Stratagem and double Designs" (133) by two devious women: his first wife, Fulvia, and Cleopatra. She marries Anthony to save bloodshed, by cementing the relationship between Octavius and Anthony; throughout her marriage she tries to hide her woes from her brother, fearful not only of aggravating the rivalry between the two men but of causing war in the Roman Empire. But her efforts are doomed to failure because, as far as relationships with Anthony are concerned, love and duty are no substitute for skill in sexual politics. While Cleopatra comments that "it seems almost incredible how easily I could impose on *Anthony*, to misconstrue my affected Behaviour as an Instance of Love" (75), Octavia finds that her own genuine love and care for Anthony are considered by him affectation and deceit.

It has to be said that in Octavia's story, as in Cleopatra's, Anthony himself cuts a poor figure. In Fielding's representation, this powerful

Roman general—whose achievements and potential are the central point of interest for many other versions of the story—is seen only through the eyes of his mistress and his wife; and he is deluded in his opinion of them both, entirely at the mercy of the artifices and deceit of his mistress, and rejecting the possibility of moral and political redemption offered by the virtues of his wife. Motivated throughout by the indulgence of his senses and his passions, at the expense of his reason and judgment, he is not even allowed true nobility in his suicide, since Cleopatra describes it as one more example of his entirely erroneous belief in her love for him. He dies as blindly as he lived, believing in the woman who has boasted of "having it in my Power thus to make a Man, a *Roman General*, one of the Three Lords of the Universe, a Monkey for my sake" (98).

Octavia believes that the role of a wife in marriage is to protect and enhance the interests of her husband, but the very qualities in Octavia that lead to successful marriage with Marcellus fail completely with Anthony. Accustomed to thinking of "women" and their behavior in a certain light through his experience of Fulvia and Cleopatra, he cannot believe that Octavia's care for him is genuine, and he is deeply suspicious of her attempts to protect him from his own failings. When he discovers that Octavia has heard rash criticism of him from his exasperated friends, "he looked on my attempt to conceal it as an Instance of Dissimulation" (135). Octavia's attempts to behave as she believes a wife should—and in a way consistent with the recommendations of 18th-century books of advice on female conduct—are consistently misinterpreted by Anthony, who has come to expect the stimulation of artifice as a necessary component of a relationship with a woman.

"The deluded Triumvir," as Cleopatra dismissively calls him, has also come to expect open acknowledgment of himself as a being superior to all women, even to Cleopatra, the queen among them. Cleopatra consistently flatters Anthony's opinion of himself and his belief in the superiority of the male over the female sex: she makes him think any of her good ideas are his own, convinces him that his military defeats are victories, and praises his judgment and authority especially when he is deficient in both qualities. Her principle is straightforward enough, and she articulates it only too clearly: "To govern a Man by continually putting him in mind that one is too weak to govern him" (71).[17]

Octavia, who is aware of the nature of Cleopatra's power over Anthony, rejects the deceit such a strategy requires for success, but she is astonished to find that Anthony resents her for it:

It entered not into my Head, that a Man of *Anthony*'s Understanding
could live with a Woman as a Rival, and be angry with her, because her
whole Mind, employed on him, sometimes proposed a Scheme for his
Emolument, which had not happened first to come from himself. (135)

When Anthony's childish sulking is accompanied by complaints of "the
Contempt he had for all Women of Sense" (136), the intelligent and
articulate Octavia is driven to the stupefying conclusion that, since she
cannot pretend to be intellectually inferior to her husband, her marriage
to Anthony would have more chance of success if she were stupid in reality: "So little did I value myself on my Understanding, that I would willingly have parted with it, to have gained my Husband's Love."

The element of masochism inherent in Octavia's previously expressed
willingness to be a "Sacrifice" is strengthened by this extraordinary statement, which reinforces the impression that Octavia's story is as equivocal in its moral effects as is that of Cleopatra. In fact, Octavia's
limitations are as prominent as her virtues. She is intelligent, thoughtful,
reflective, and resourceful, yet her belief in the submissive and devoted
behavior she is convinced is required of a wife leads to a willing assumption of powerlessness. As a result, she actually destroys the very peace
and stability—not only of her personal relationship with Anthony but of
the nation and empire, which depend upon continued harmony between
Octavius and Anthony—which she holds so dear. She would willingly
part with her understanding to gain Anthony's love; she is incapable of
actively trying to outwit her rival for his affections and for the much
larger prize of international peace. Moreover, she fails to recognize that
her own stance toward Anthony, as much as Cleopatra's, is predicated on
a basis of deceit: she praises honesty highly but does not tell her husband
the truth if she judges it not to be in his interests.

Is Fielding suggesting that such limitations are inevitable in the feminine ideal that "the accomplished Character of *Octavia*" (41) is intended
to represent, or is it simply that a late-20th-century sensibility finds
Octavia's form of negative virtue unconvincing? The historical Octavia
was often presented in the 18th century as "a touchstone of feminine
virtue" (Hughes-Hallett, 168), and certainly Fielding gives her many of
the qualities the 18th century prized in a woman—modesty, submissiveness, grace, delicacy, sensibility—while omitting to mention more equivocal anecdotes in the sources Fielding consulted. Octavia is shown as
capable of participating in, and being fulfilled by, an ideal marriage with
Marcellus. Most notably of all, perhaps, she is a tender and caring moth-

er, not only to her own children but to the neglected offspring of Fulvia, and even, finally, the equally neglected offspring of Cleopatra herself.

But when Octavia is described as a "refined female Character" (41), the reader recalls that "Refinement" was, in *The Cry*, an ambivalent quality. Surely there is at least an implication here that the constructions of femininity that Octavia embodies carry their own flaws, which come to the surface on the frequent occasions when the ideal marriage does not occur—that a woman as "a sincere Friend, an affectionate Sister, a faithful Wife, and both a tender and instructive Parent" (41) may inevitably self-destruct if the father, brother, husband, or son who has authority over her does not, like Marcellus, recognize and celebrate her virtues. Octavia survives both Cleopatra and Anthony; she rears their children with her own, follows her studies, and dies with her loving family around her. But while her narrative has argued for reason and resignation as a cogent basis for personal contentment, it has also shown that the qualities praised so highly in Octavia comprehensively lose the argument in the real world when placed in competition with the uncontrolled passion of an Anthony or the conscious deceit of a Cleopatra.

Cleopatra and Octavia was praised by its first reviewers, and a second edition was published within a year of the first. Its success, however, was short-lived; no other edition was published until 1928. By that time the power of this pair of fictional autobiographies as an anatomy of 18th-century, rather than Roman, femininity was beginning to be recognized: a reviewer of the new edition saw the chief interest of the book in the fact that in it "Fielding is exhibiting the first flickerings of revolt at the subsidiary place allotted to women by a society which has since changed its mind, thanks to her and others like her."[18] This remark now seems more startling in its optimism about 20th-century society than about Fielding. Certainly, out of this simplest of Fielding's experiments with form comes one of the most complex of her statements about history, truth, and gender relations.

Chapter Nine

Histories of a Young Lady's Entrance into the World: *The History of the Countess of Dellwyn* and *The History of Ophelia*

Sarah Fielding's last two novels, *The History of the Countess of Dellwyn* (1759) and *The History of Ophelia* (1760), seem, on first consideration, to be much more conventional than her earlier works: at least one critic has dismissed them as mere "potboilers" (Foster, 75). Undoubtedly one of Fielding's main aims in writing both novels was to add to her income, but that had been the case throughout her writing career. In fact, Fielding was continuing to experiment with fictional form in both these novels, but she chose to make more subtle use of the conventions that formed part of the mainstream development of the modern novel rather than developing allegorical or moral-exemplum alternatives.

A number of features of *The Countess of Dellwyn* and *Ophelia* are particularly relevant in this context. One notable change from Fielding's earlier style is the move away from type names (such as Jenny Peace and Mrs. Teachum in *The Governess*), or romance names (such as Cylinda and Nicanor in *The Cry*): main protagonists are no longer David Simple or Portia but Charlotte Lucum, who soon becomes the Countess of Dellwyn, and Ophelia Lenox, later the Countess of Dorchester.[1] Another is the move toward a univocal narrative recounting a broadly linear plot: there are few digressions, or inset stories, to disturb the main narrative voice—an ironically detached third-person narrator in *The Countess of Dellwyn* and the heroine herself in *Ophelia*. Yet another is Fielding's direct engagement, in both novels, with the social world of the middle and upper classes in mid-18th-century England. In *David Simple* "the world" is largely an object of (occasionally bitter) satire; in *Volume the Last* individual situations symbolize the large sweep of social and ethical forces; in *The Cry* the emphasis is on the allegorical representation of philosophical dilemmas. But in *The Countess of Dellwyn* and *Ophelia* the main characters exist as part of a realistically depicted, recognizably contemporary social world—an urban society based on materialism and personal indulgence, with a very real capacity to corrupt innocent young women who stray unwarily into its orbit.

London as the center of social corruption was a familiar preoccupation of 18th-century fiction: Fielding herself had touched on it in *David Simple*, and her brother had dealt with it in detail in the tales of Wilson in *Joseph Andrews* and the Man of the Hill in *Tom Jones*. Much of the action of *The Countess of Dellwyn* and *Ophelia* takes place in London; but, perhaps informed by her own observations as a resident of Bath, Fielding also follows the upper classes to their newer centers of leisure and pleasure, the spas, Bristol in *The Countess of Dellwyn* and Tunbridge in *Ophelia*. Moreover, she is an acute observer of social trends: she identifies and dissects the growing appetites of consumerism among the wealthy and would-be wealthy, which reached what have recently been described as "revolutionary proportions" in the third quarter of the 18th century.[2]

Many previous accounts of the corruption of innocence by the social world had concentrated on the young, unattached male. Fielding turns the focus on the young, unattached, and unprotected gentlewoman and in so doing provides two highly significant versions of a narrative that quickly became a popular subgenre of women's fiction: "the history of a young lady's entrance into the world."[3] Both *The Countess of Dellwyn* and *Ophelia* concern a young woman who has been brought up in a sheltered, rural environment but who finds herself materially and socially adrift in a metropolitan society that is, in essence, hostile to natural behavior, innocence, and truth. In both novels the chief forces of corruption are those very males—fathers, lovers, and husbands—who, in a social structure dominated by patriarchy and patronage, should be the prime protectors of the vulnerable female. The different ways in which Charlotte Lucum fails, and Ophelia Lenox succeeds, in dealing with the dangers and difficulties of maintaining personal integrity in such circumstances represent the crux of their personal histories and the focal point of Fielding's narratives.

J. Paul Hunter has pointed out that "[m]ost eighteenth-century novels center on the life of an individual and become essentially the telling of that person's story . . . whether the force is exemplary or cautionary, the question of being in the protagonist's place is a real one" (Hunter, 328–29). Hunter nicely catches the coexistence in 18th-century novels of the didactic impulse and of a presentational realism that encourages readers to place themselves in the protagonist's position, but he fails to convey any sense of the tension that inevitably arises between moral and theoretical certitudes on the one hand and the ambiguities and ambivalences of experience on the other. It is a tension that makes Fielding's two late novels, in their different ways, problematic as texts. Certainly the force of *Ophelia* is broadly exemplary and that of *The Countess of Dellwyn* broadly cautionary. On a superficial level, at least, Fielding's moral judgments, in both cases, are uncompromising. Yet, in both instances, the reader's sense of personal identification with a realistic protagonist in realistic circumstances produces a nagging dissatisfaction with any suggestion that a neat moral verdict can satisfactorily account for her fate.

Although the element of moral compromise seems carefully controlled by Fielding in *Ophelia*, it is less certain how far she consciously encourages an ambivalent response on the part of the reader of *The Countess of Dellwyn*: of all Fielding's protagonists, Charlotte Lucum seems to have attracted the most divergent reactions from readers.[4] And yet Fielding presented Charlotte's story in light of extensive thinking about the nature and purpose of fiction as a literary genre. In a lengthy Preface to *The Countess of Dellwyn* Fielding demonstrates a thoughtful interest in the theory of fiction. She resists any idea of realism as an end in itself. Her main interest continues to be in portraying "Pictures of human Nature."[5] But at the same time her attempt to understand and convey a sense of "the Labyrinths of the human Mind" (xvii) requires her, as writer, to be "thoroughly acquainted with the Bent of the Dispositions" of those whose characters and actions she intends to portray (xiii) and to ensure that, in recounting situations in which her fictional characters are involved, "the Fact will appear to the Reader not only as a Probability, but also will carry with it an Air of real Truth" (xi).

Fielding goes on to illustrate her argument with a practical example: if characters are to be shown in a blazing house, "the Fire must not walk to the House, and burn it . . . but natural Circumstances must combine for that Purpose" (xi).[6] It is a strong and reasoned plea for circumstantial realism in fiction and one that many other 18th-century writers would have done well to heed. But when the same theory is applied to individual characters, the careful explanations of why people behave as they do inevitably complicate simple judgments of good and evil, virtue and vice. As a result, both Fielding's late novels hover ambiguously between the certitudes of moral exempla and the circumstantiality of realistic fiction. Just as the cautionary conclusion of *The Countess of Dellwyn* is compromised by the reader's sympathy for the faulty Charlotte, so the exemplary fate of Ophelia is undercut by awareness of the compromises she has had to make to find happiness in an imperfect world.

The Countess of Dellwyn

In deliberate defiance of the already well-known obsession of prose fiction with courtship, *The Countess of Dellwyn* begins with a wedding—a wedding, the narrator tells us, "which if Truth did not prompt me to reveal, its Improbability would never suffer me to invent" (1.2–3). The elderly groom, Lord Dellwyn, is wheeled to the ceremony in a "Machine, invented for the Assistance of Imbecility" (1.4); his bride, 17-year-old Charlotte Lucum, "preserved an unalterable Steadiness, rather inclined to the gay" (7); the bride's father is eager to assist in any way he can—including picking up the ring, which the groom drops on three ominous occasions.

This opening scene not only is a tour de force in itself but establishes one of the major themes of the novel—the nature of marriage in upper-class society—and introduces the three characters who will dominate the action. The early chapters are then devoted to explaining how this ludicrous Hogarthian tableau came about. Charlotte originally rejects the earl's proposals: she is happy living quietly in the country, with her books for company. But her father, a failed politician dazzled by the thought of resurrecting his career by the favors of an aristocratic son-in-law, is as determined as the earl to make Charlotte Lady Dellwyn. Together they concoct a plot. Mr. Lucum brings Charlotte to London and provides her *"First Introduction into the gay World"* (1.34), with the deliberate aim of tempting her to succumb to the allure of worldly vanity. When it appears that Charlotte is able to resist the most seductive blandishments this latter-day Vanity Fair has to offer, her father makes her home so disagreeable that she is driven to seek refuge in social gatherings. And so Charlotte is gradually corrupted: "Force of Custom rendered that Manner of Life tolerable, to which at first she had been so averse" (1.39). The revolution in her thinking is completed when she loses self-control, overcome with jealousy at the sight of her cousin Fanny's superior diamonds.

Much is made throughout the novel of the destructive force of Charlotte's envy of the diamonds: all her subsequent actions can be traced to "that unreasonable Vanity with which she was first infected by the dazzling Glare of Lady *Fanny*'s Diamonds . . . which, like deadly Poison, seemed to have taken so deep a Root, as to admit of no Antidote to expel its Venom" (2.115–16). Charlotte's mind does indeed seem to be poisoned. Her previous tranquillity is replaced by the turbulence of warring passions; her habits of reflection are lost in the ceaseless activity of the social round. When her father suddenly declares they must return to the country and hints that Lord Dellwyn is to marry Fanny, Charlotte, distraught, throws herself at Lord Dellwyn; and so the men have their way, and the wedding takes place.

Charlotte had originally called the match "Prostitution" (1.30); Lord Dellwyn and Mr. Lucum had agreed it was a "Bargain" (1.28). This marriage is quite openly a matter of trade between the husband and the bride's father. Charlotte has been coerced into participation but, inexperienced in "this Sort of Commerce" (1.94), is constantly at a disadvantage in dealing with her new situation. She refuses to admit that she has acceded to an arrangement that has reduced her very self to a commodity. But she has been encouraged to privilege commodities—things—over human relationships and even over her own sense of self: to "accept of a Coronet," together with the concomitant advantages of equipage, house in town, and jewels (1.57), and to subsume her personal identity in the generic title Countess of Dellwyn. It is a logical corollary (and possibly a subliminal act of revenge) that her chief activity, when she is taken as a bride to the earl's castle, is in "reversing every thing . . . as totally as her own Mind had been changed" (1.90), replacing anything useful with the icons of current fashion: "*China* Images, and all manner of *Chinese* Figures . . . trifling Gew-gaws" (1.90–91).

After her marriage, Charlotte continues to degenerate morally, in defined stages. First she falls into a mood of deep depression: aware that she is living a lie, she blames herself but is unwilling to consider any change of personal behavior that might alleviate the situation. Her moral position worsens when she discovers the truth about events leading to her marriage: now she shifts all responsibility for her situation on to her father and husband. Another downward step is taken when she begins to allow her contempt for the earl to reveal itself in public rather than struggling to contain her feelings. The situation described at the end of the novel's First Book forms a companion piece to the opening scene and the equivalent of a second plate in a Hogarthian series of "Marriage à la Mode": husband and wife have now become "Two unamiable Figures; for on the one hand might be seen (to speak plainly) a haughty, discontented, extravagant Wife, and on the other, a morose, covetous, and disappointed Husband" (1.153).

But Charlotte can fall further yet. Reduced to a position where she "had lost the Niceness of examining the Merit of her Admirers" (2.123), she is tempted into adultery by the worldly Lord Clermont. It is not that she is overwhelmed by the passion of love—indeed, she does not care for Clermont and has successfully repulsed him earlier in the novel—but rather that Clermont has now understood how to manipulate the motivating power of her vanity. The process that led to her marriage to Lord Dellwyn is repeated as Lord Clermont first flatters her, then keeps her passions in turmoil, and finally arouses her fears of rejection. For a second time she is tricked into an action that her judgment rejects, with equally serious results. Captain Drumond, an impecunious man who seeks preferment from Lord Dellwyn, delivers written proof of her adultery to her husband.

According to the historian Roy Porter, the "cardinal functions" of a married lady in polite society in the 18th century were clear. "The first duty was to obey her husband. Second, she was an heir-producing machine."[7] Charlotte has failed on both counts, and Lord Dellwyn, whose own vanity (which is quite as powerful as hers) has been tormented by his wayward wife, has had enough of the marriage. At first Charlotte is relieved: she is willing to submit even to a private separation as an escape from an intolerable union.[8] But once again she finds she is not in control of her situation. She has not taken account of the importance of an heir to an earl, nor of the lengths to which a vain and self-indulgent man will go to satisfy his desires, nor of the sheer power of an aristocratic male in a patriarchal society. Lord Dellwyn wishes to marry again; and, to do that, he needs to divorce Charlotte. Her adultery has provided the evidence he needs.

The Countess of Dellwyn is one of the very few novels of this period to deal with formal divorce; indeed, formal divorce was a very rare event.[9] It involved a cumbersome and expensive legal procedure, culminating in the passing of a law by the House of Lords; as a result, it was available to very few. Those few were of high rank and overwhelmingly male: of all the petitions submitted in the 18th century, only one was made by a woman, and that was rejected (Stone 1990, 432). If women were unable to benefit from legislative means of divorcing themselves from a cruel or adulterous husband, the situation of a woman against whom a divorce was sought was even worse—especially where the grounds were her adultery. As the situation in *The Countess of Dellwyn* amply shows, Lord Dellwyn, despite his many and manifest failures as a suitor and husband, is able to divorce his wife and emerge without a stain on his character as far as the social world is concerned. For Charlotte, once Lord Dellwyn has divorced her, no extenuating circumstances are allowed: she becomes a social outcast, pursued by gossip and innuendo wherever she goes. Charlotte is further unfortunate that there is no refuge to be found with her father, who, in a vain attempt to retain Dellwyn's favor, casts her off with an ostentatious display of "virtue."

Lady Dellwyn does what she can to rectify the situation, and for a moment it seems she might outwit society. Traveling to Paris before rumor has had time to cross the Channel, she attracts the love of a rich young man and very nearly manages to slough off her past and her title (to which, in any case, she has now no legal claim) in a second marriage. But the young man is successfully outmaneuvered by his father, and Charlotte is relegated permanently to the most distant fringes of the social world in which, for a short time, she had shone.

Charlotte's story forms the main narrative of *The Countess of Dellwyn*, but as in her other fictions, Fielding creates structures and rhythms of comparison and contrast, exploring moral principles by presenting them in a number of variations. Throughout the novel, Charlotte's behavior and attitudes are contrasted with those of other characters. The quietly virtuous Miss Cummins,[10] Charlotte's childhood friend, shows what Charlotte might have become, had she retained her tranquillity and love of books. Both Mrs. Saunders and Mrs. Bilson, social acquaintances of the Dellwyns at Bristol, provide more positive examples of wifely behavior to emphasize Charlotte's deficiencies.

The story of Mrs. Bilson provides the novel's chief subplot and offers a lengthy alternative view of marriage to set beside that of the Dellwyn household. Mrs. Bilson triumphs over marital adversities much more formidable than those that face the countess, and her story provides a strong comment on Charlotte's deficiencies as a wife. Like Charlotte, Mrs. Bilson has been married off, at a very young age, by her father, to a man who soon develops into an unsatisfactory husband; her conception of what marriage involves is, however, very different from that of Miss Lucum. Charlotte regards marriage as a gateway to liberty and privilege, a platform for social self-indulgence. Mrs. Bilson, in contrast, "knew so little of the World, that she imagined a Wife's Scene of Action ought to be in her own House, that there she should spend her Time, and there, or no-where, find her Happiness" (1.163). Unlike Charlotte, Mrs. Bilson studies to please her husband rather than herself. And, for her, adultery is out of the question.

Her principles do not immediately lead to happiness. Men in this novel are almost invariably deficient in true virtue, and Mr. Bilson is no exception. He fails in his duty to provide for his family and spends his small fortune on himself; the day he is imprisoned for debt, Mrs. Bilson discovers that he has been supporting a natural child born within weeks of her own eldest daughter. She is shocked and sickened at his behavior, but she does not desert him even in this extremity. A stroke of luck occurs when she rejects the sexual advances of her predatory landlord: in gratitude, his wife offers Mrs. Bilson practical help in saving her family from destitution. Whereas Charlotte pinned all her hopes on selling herself into marriage, Mrs. Bilson determines to enter the world of trade and commerce in a more direct—and infinitely more honest—way: by making and selling "a Variety of Female Ornaments in which her Rank in Life had given her a Taste and Elegance, that made them greatly surpass what most Shops could exhibit" (1.186).

It is an ironic touch that honest livings can be made by providing the commodities that the rich—including, notably, the Countess of Dellwyn—so recklessly consume. In fact Mrs. Bilson makes not merely a living but a real success of business—and all without compromising her essential femininity. She conducts her trade on private visits to the houses of rich ladies rather than opening a shop;[11] she uses her profits to benefit those around her. Living with her husband in debtors' prison, she employs her family and an increasing number of other unfortunates in income-earning schemes. When the family finally does come into a substantial inheritance—appropriately through a relative of Mrs. Bilson who has identified her merits because of her industry—they free all those inhabitants of the Fleet prison who (on a not overstrict scrutiny) deserve it, and then devote their lives to "communicating [their] Happiness to as many as possible" on their country estate (1.203). They establish seminaries for young people and almshouses for the elderly; they assist young couples getting married and provide nursing for the sick; they hire a large house as "a Receptacle for Gentlewomen, who either had no Fortunes, or so little that it would not support them" (2.207), complete with library, musical instruments, and "Implements for various Works" (2.208). But in all their charitable activities "the utmost Oeconomy was preserved" (1.206); their main aim is not to give ostentatiously, but to help people to help one another. The reader is irresistibly reminded that one of Charlotte Lucum's least attractive characteristics is her lack of interest in anyone but herself.

Mrs. Bilson's story has a greater significance even than providing a contrast and corrective to Charlotte's refusal to fulfill a proper wifely function, to take responsibility for her own moral and physical health, or to offer benevolence to others. In a larger sense, the Bilson narrative provides a completely different model of a community from anything portrayed in the wider world that is the scene of the rest of *The Countess of Dellwyn* and a reminder to the reader that all the aristocrats and would-be aristocrats dallying in London and Bristol could be carrying out many more useful activities on their own country estates. Crucially, the narrative links this alternative vision of society with an assurance (lacking elsewhere in the novel) that there is a place for women's moral and physical strength in 18th-century society and that women can fulfill themselves by taking responsibility for a destiny not irreparably compromised by society's constrictions, including that of marriage.

In so doing, Mrs. Bilson's story rewrites the most famous fictional portrayal of an ideally dutiful wife in the 1750s, Henry Fielding's *Amelia* (1751). There are many similarities between the Bilsons and the Booths. Booth and Bilson are both attractive men who squander their family's security by their fecklessness and self-indulgence and are unfaithful to their wives. Amelia Booth and Mrs. Bilson are both faithful and virtuous wives and mothers who never falter in their love and loyalty to their wayward men. Both have virtue enough to reject, and ingenuity enough to escape, the attentions of sexual predators. But Mrs. Bilson exhibits a toughness and capability for action that Amelia never possesses. While Amelia bravely declares to Booth, "'I have a heart, my Billy, which is capable of undergoing any thing for your sake; and I hope my hands are as able to work, as those which have been more inured to it,'"[12] her actual exertions remain resolutely domestic: making meals go further, mending items of clothing, and so on. Mrs. Bilson takes charge of the whole situation, makes a success in the public world of business, and supports her husband as well as her children. Her later activities, in using her wealth to establish a community of mutual benevolence based on her country estate, has no parallel in *Amelia*.

Fielding is exploring new terrain for female activities. The ideal community portrayed in *The Countess of Dellwyn* predates, and presages, a similar community—also established by enlightened women rather than men—in Sarah Scott's *Millenium Hall* (1762). Both novelists were searching for a realistic way of solving contemporary social problems[13] and clearly saw new possibilities for enlarging women's sphere.[14] Mrs. Bilson's narrative ends happily, and her philosophy is held up as a positive example; her story is told with sympathy, understanding, and approval.

By contrast, the narrator has little sympathy for any of the protagonists in her main plot. The narrative conveys some understanding of why these characters think and behave as they do, but it retains considerable detachment from the worries and fears of Lord Dellwyn and his countess as individual human beings, involving them, rather, in broader criticism of the world they choose to inhabit. The narrator's stance is distanced, generalized, and heavily ironic: in describing Lord Dellwyn's growing dependence on the parasitical Drumond, for example, the narrator remarks: "It is observable, that every Man (however wrong he may be in his own Conduct), is desirous of a virtuous Friend" (2.108). The quotations from plays and poems that punctuate the text are often similarly two-edged. There is no more sympathy for Charlotte than for the earl. The narrator has maintained stoutly throughout the novel that, in stark contrast to the great majority of other 18th-century heroines, Charlotte has in effect seduced herself, or, rather, that "Vanity [was] her first and last Seducer" (2.205) and that her fate is therefore no one's fault but her own.

Fielding's insistence throughout her fictions that women must be held accountable for their own actions is usually one of her strengths as a writer; it requires women to be considered—and to consider themselves—morally responsible human beings. But in this instance the narrator's declared judgment is at the very least an oversimplification of the story she has told. It is certainly true that Charlotte is often at the mercy of her own destructive passions—not only vanity but other faults related to vanity, such as pride and envy. But it is also true that "[w]hen Lady Dellwyn has an affair with the practised seducer Lord Clermont, she is cast off by her husband, her father, and fashionable society—all of them to blame for her situation" (Spencer, 120). There is a real question as to how far Charlotte can genuinely be held responsible for her actions.

Charlotte is, for example, like all of Fielding's characters, a product of her education, and the education provided by her father has been both superficial and inadequate. The one positive moral principle she has thoroughly internalized—a regard for truth—is a reaction *against* her father in his role as a party political hack (where he had "some plausible Reason ever ready to account for his sudden Alteration of Opinion" [1.20]). Once Lord Dellwyn makes his proposal, Mr. Lucum's behavior crucially compromises Charlotte's choices. It was, after all, axiomatic for a young lady in the 18th century to obey her father; however, the axiom recognizably broke down when parental demands were wholly unreasonable. Mr. Lucum not only demands that his daughter marry Lord Dellwyn but actually enters into a conspiracy with the potential bridegroom to overcome her natural, and instinctively sound, reluctance. His only concern throughout is himself, including the benefits to him of being an earl's father-in-law; as for Charlotte, "if his Daughter would not be a Countess, it was very reasonable that she should be abandoned to any Misfortunes or Miseries whatsoever" (1.31). He follows this point of principle in the crisis over the Dellwyns' divorce, during which even the narrator calls his letter repudiating Charlotte an "outrageous Epistle" (2.152) and during which his sole strategy is to retain his son-in-law's favor, even if it means destroying his daughter.

Lord Dellwyn himself is no less coercive of Charlotte than is her father. In relating the story of his life of dissipation before he met Charlotte, the narrator remarks that he has had "free Choice" (1.13) in all his actions; he is therefore the more blameworthy in tricking Charlotte—described at the outset as "his destined Prey" (1.4)—into marriage. Once married, he is as remiss in fulfilling his marriage vows as is Charlotte. The husband should guide and protect his young wife; instead Lord Dellwyn first indulges and then condemns her. At the end of the novel he is punished by a termagent second wife, but it is hardly a fate of commensurate misery to Charlotte's. Lord Clermont's abandonment, and Captain Drumond's hatred, of Charlotte equally close off other possible courses of action.

And if the contrast with Mrs. Bilson's actions and attitudes is clearly to Charlotte's disadvantage, other characters and situations in the novel provide more problematic comparisons. Just as Lady Fanny's diamonds are superior to Charlotte's at the beginning of the novel, so her hardness and brilliance outshine Charlotte throughout. It is a dubious superiority. "In true Wit Lady *Dellwyn* had greatly the Advantage; but Lady *Fanny* could turn the comic, or rather the farcical, Side of any Subject to a much fuller View. Her Power of Ridicule was superior"; in comparison with Lady Fanny, "Lady *Dellwyn* laboured under the Disadvantage of yet retaining some Degrees of Bashfulness; Pertness, and Self-Sufficiency could at any time put her out of Countenance" (2.17). Charlotte never does become expert in the hypocrisies and impertinencies in which Lady Fanny sparkles. Furthermore, Charlotte never loses her power to condemn herself: she is "no Proficient in the Art of imposing Falsehood on herself. . . . She could not film over the Odium of her own Actions, by applying to them the Words Gallantry, Intriguing, Coquetting, with many other softening Terms" (2.50–51). Yet, although an infinitely more unpleasant and less virtuous woman than Charlotte, Lady Fanny has a kinder fate. When her behavior becomes too outrageous for her husband to tolerate, he quietly removes himself from her and her social milieu, leaving her reputation intact and her sphere of social activity, if anything, enlarged. The moral seems to be that Charlotte must suffer either because she is not wicked enough to lose her conscience or because she is not lucky enough to be married to an accommodating husband.[15]

Another subplot offers an equally complex comparison. Sir Harry Cleveland becomes, for a short time, one in the circle of Charlotte's admirers. He has been ill, and at Bristol he is encouraged to abandon his own natural tendency to reflection and study. After a few initial qualms, he plunges into social dissipation and is soon behaving as hypocritically and as rudely as his companions. In many respects, therefore, he is the male equivalent of Charlotte—although he far exceeds her in cruelty to the socially awkward (as well, it has to be said, as in benevolence to the truly disadvantaged). But when he falls in love with Miss Bilson, he comes under the auspices of the Bilson family and begins to reform, in much the same way that Mr. Bilson himself reformed with the encouragement of his wife. It is hard to escape the conclusion that virtue, once again, is largely a matter of luck—this time, in finding suitable mentors.

Charlotte is isolated in this respect. With the exception of brief strictures from Miss Cummyns, Charlotte receives no advice or guidance to lead her back to virtue. Mrs. Bilson makes no attempt to help her; other female friends are lacking; and the acknowledged authority figures of father and husband actively conspire her downfall. As a picture of the destructive nature of a hypocritical and heartless patriarchal society this is highly effective, but as a justification to blame Charlotte for her fate it is inadequate.

In fact, by the end of the novel, the reader is beginning to resist the narrative closure that the moralist-narrator seems to be insisting upon. Accepting the individual's responsibility—male or female—for his or her own actions is all very well, but, given the powers ranged against the individual in the world Fielding describes, individual virtue stands little chance of survival.

The actual ending of the novel, however, springs a further surprise. Lady Dellwyn has paid for her sin of adultery by the punishment of public disgrace. This is bad enough, of course; but, interestingly, there is no further descent to prostitution or degradation or death. Charlotte even maintains a certain amount of integrity in her fallen state: still fleeing from reflection on her own actions, she turns to gambling, but only moderately, since "the Love of Play was not natural to her" (2.180). At the end of the novel, while wedding bells ring out for Sir Harry Cleveland and Miss Bilson (whose family "continued a Blessing to the

World from Generation to Generation" [2.191]), Charlotte survives, living a dreary existence certainly but defying both narrative closure and
the moral certitude that would have killed her.

In this context, the final tragedy of this ultimately rather strange
novel is, surely, not that Charlotte prostituted her own good sense to
vanity but that neither her father nor her husband nor a single member
of the wealthy and privileged world she entered has the moral principle
to recall her to her natural virtues.[16]

Ophelia

Like Charlotte Lucum, Ophelia Lenox is a beautiful and lively teenage
girl, an only child, brought up and educated in a tranquil rural environment, by a lone relative who has withdrawn from the world in disillu-
sionment at its ways. But whereas Charlotte's father has turned his back
on society largely because society has turned its back on his political
ambitions, Ophelia's aunt has lost her good name, and most of her small
fortune, through a rash marriage to a "young Nobleman" who proved to
be already married to someone else. Thus are established, at the outset,
two of the major themes of *Ophelia*: the vulnerability of a young woman
to betrayal by worldly deceit and the particular problem of marriage in
a society based on that deceit. Ophelia's aunt—she is never named—
retreats to a remote cottage in the depths of the Welsh countryside and
ensures that Ophelia has no knowledge either of the trappings of the
social world or of men. Ophelia is content with her aunt, her books, an
elegant cottage, and picturesque scenery.

Into this idyll stumbles—literally—young Lord Dorchester, who has
rambled out of his way in enjoyment of the natural beauties of the land-
scape. Dorchester is dazzled by the innocent, intelligent, and beautiful
young girl; after her aunt has warned him away, he abducts Ophelia.
With no means of returning to her aunt and no knowledge of the conventional formalities of male-female relationships, Ophelia makes the
best of her situation and gradually becomes fond of Lord Dorchester. He
takes her with him to his country estate for the summer and then to
London for the winter season, where he passes her off as his rich ward.
His plan is to convince Ophelia that she should become his mistress
rather than his wife; to this end he tries to ensure that she learn social
behavior without either finding out too much about the less salubrious
ways of the world or becoming aware of the rumors that soon begin to
circulate about her.

With the assistance of the unscrupulous society hostess Lady Palestine he succeeds for a surprisingly long time. However, in London and later in Tunbridge Wells, Ophelia attracts new suitors; eventually one of them, Lord Larborough, tells her the truth about the man she has by this time learned to love. Disappointed and disillusioned, in her turn, at the standards acceptable in the social world, she flees Dorchester's protection. But he is not prepared to lose her, and eventually—though with considerable reluctance—she accepts his proposal of marriage.

In its broad outline, this is the most conventional of all Fielding's fictional plots; moreover, it is told using conventional—not to say hackneyed—techniques. An Advertisement informs the reader that the author of *David Simple* discovered the story in the form of papers in a recently purchased "old Buroe"; the "papers" consist of Ophelia's narrative of her own story, told in a serial letter to a female correspondent.[17] The claim to be "editor," rather than author, of letters had become popular at least as early as 1740, when Samuel Richardson used it to introduce *Pamela*.[18] Fielding's use of these conventions, however, differs considerably from that of Richardson and his many imitators. It has been pointed out that, though *Ophelia* is Fielding's "attempt at a truly 'popular' novel," she subverts conventional forms even as she uses them;[19] her deployment of epistolary conventions provides a significant example of this strategy.

Richardson had developed the art of correspondence into a mechanism for providing multivocal narratives of considerable complexity, and he had made a particular strength of the letter's capacity of "writing to the moment"; furthermore, he had introduced a wide variety of naturalistic devices concerning letters as artifacts, including the possibility of their going astray, being forged, or simply being misread. Fielding takes up hardly any of these opportunities in the main narrative of *Ophelia* (although their presence in some inset letters demonstrates that she could have followed Richardson more closely, had she chosen to do so). Instead, she uses the letter form for two very simple purposes.

The first is to establish that Ophelia has a particular audience for her narrative. She is not simply telling her story but telling it to someone who has asked to hear it—a someone Ophelia refers to as "your Ladyship," who is connected to the "civilized" world rather than to a rural utopia and who has imposed certain specific criteria for the tale: "You expressly desire to know the Impressions I received from the first View of Customs, so unlike what I had ever seen," Ophelia reminds her (Introduction). The second is to produce an effect that is, ironically, the very reverse of "writing to the moment." Ophelia is recalling her story a long time after the event, and her letter is therefore an effort of memory rather than a description of events as they occur. She frequently comments on the actions and attitudes of her younger self, and the narrative develops a double-layered tone and rhythm: emotion recollected in tranquillity, age recalling youth, experience reflecting on innocence. It is peculiarly appropriate for Fielding's purposes, enabling her for the first time in her fictions to enact, rather than describe, the habits of reflection and thoughtfulness, which she praises so highly as virtues.[20] In so doing, she—perhaps inevitably—humanizes her earlier didacticism. The overall tone of the novel is elegiac: to take one small but significant example, the older Ophelia is only too well aware of the transitory attractions of her own, now lost, beauty: "I have seen the Observation [of the World] lessen as my Complexion has decayed" (1.59).

This elegiac tone is enhanced by the fact that Ophelia, relatively early in the narrative, makes clear to the reader what the recipient of her letter already knows: that she will, ultimately, marry Lord Dorchester. Subsequent interest in her story, therefore, focuses not on suspense at the outcome but rather on how Ophelia comes to embrace a fate that, as it conflicts with her declared moral principles, acquires the problematic force of predestination.

Ophelia diligently satisfies her correspondent's request to give her impressions of experiences and attitudes that are new to her, and much of the novel is concerned with descriptions of the ways of the world as they would appear to a complete stranger. Often this is presented as comedy, markedly lighthearted in comparison with the harsh tone that dominated *The Countess of Dellwyn* (*Ophelia* is, at times, very funny indeed). For example, shortly after her abduction Ophelia finds herself in "a small Hut . . . neat and pretty, but . . . better calculated for Beauty than Convenience; for there was but just Room for us to sit." She is astonished when the "Hut" begins to move, and she refuses to be pacified until Dorchester explains not only the concept of a carriage but also "the Structure and Design of such Vehicles, as well as their Safety" (1.33).

Ophelia soon becomes "perfectly well reconciled to this most agreeable Invention of the Luxurious"; many of her subsequent encounters with the world, both on Dorchester's country estate and in London drawing rooms, continue to reflect a newcomer's uncritical sense of wonder. Often, however, her response is refracted through the impatience of the older Ophelia with what she sees as gullibility in her younger self: on her first sight of London, for example, "every Gewgaw charmed me, every tawdry Shop amazed me. . . . The Vivacity of my Sentiments made my Folly the more conspicuous" (1.127). And so the idea of urban society as a focus of worldly folly begins to be introduced.

Later, when Ophelia is taken to Tunbridge Wells for her health, she commits a social faux pas by rejecting a dancing partner and then dancing with Lord Dorchester. This innocent transgression of social boundaries causes mayhem: the rejected gentleman is furious, and he and Dorchester quarrel. When Fanny Burney used exactly the same situation in *Evelina* (1778), the humor revolved around the social embarrassment of a well-meaning but naive heroine mortified by awareness of her social ineptitude and terrified at the way the men use the situation as an excuse for exercising aggression.[21] Fielding's Ophelia is equally concerned that she might unwittingly have caused harm to others by her lack of knowledge of social forms, but she also criticizes the social forms themselves. She refuses the gentleman, to his face, on the honest and reasonable grounds that "I had determined not to dance, and saw nothing in this Stranger, that should conquer my Resolution" (2.138); she later tells him openly that Dorchester must be a preferable partner because "my Intimacy with him must make him more agreeable to me" (2.139). When, in recalling the scene, Ophelia acknowledges that social difficulties were caused by her own "Simplicity," she refers not only to her previous ignorance of the ways of the world but also to her honest and straightforward approach to human relationships. In such incidents the chief effect is to highlight the stultifying formalities of social convention.

Ophelia soon becomes aware that social formality is at its most constricting when it focuses on male-female relationships. Looking with fresh eyes on society, Ophelia asks highly pertinent questions. Why must she lodge in a different house from that of a man she likes, just because he is unmarried? Why is any friendly conversation between a man and a woman interpreted as a sign of passion? Why does a man feel he must bombard a reasonable woman with hyperbolic compliments? And, most importantly of all, why must a woman be so dishonest as to hide her liking for a man? Ophelia is astonished that

> the World would have allowed me to have grieved for the Loss of a Parrot, to have been wretched at missing a Masquerade, miserable at being deprived of the Sight of a new Opera, or distressed to the last Degree at being disappointed of the principal Part of the Company at an approaching Drum; but would never have forgiven me for declaring my Regret for the Loss of the most agreeable Companion that Society could afford me, if that Companion happened not to be of my own Sex. (1.139)

Other features of civilized society seem equally unnatural to Ophelia and provide equally complex challenges to her natural morality. Ophelia never quite becomes accustomed to the concept of money as anything other than a means of benefiting the unfortunate; the commercialization of virtue constitutes some of her most troubling perceptions of the world. She is nonplussed at her first encounter with an innkeeper and his wife and the discovery that "their Hospitality was a mere Trade, by which they gained a Subsistence" (1.39); she is more critical of doctors who refuse to exercise their ability to heal the sick unless they are paid for it. Ophelia's reflections on such matters occasionally bring her close to political radicalism, as in her concern that, even in a country church-yard, "the Rich and the Poor do *not* lie down together" (1.58). But Ophelia's state of nature is never presented as an argument for political democracy; rather, she focuses on the discrepancy between the ways of the world and the Christian principles that have formed the basis of her "natural" education.

The opposition between nature and artifice—and related oppositions between truth and deceit, honesty and dishonesty, virtue and vice—forms the central argument of this novel, in which contemporary society is clearly regarded as a degenerate, rather than a civilized, state of nature. One of Ophelia's earliest lessons of the great world is that even the language of virtue and vice has no meaning for the social elite who determine society's forms and customs. Attending her first large party in London, Ophelia is horrified to find that the extravagant declarations of friendship that the guests make to one another are nothing more than "Falsehood," and she is even more horrified to find that such falsehoods are universally tolerated, as "Expressions used by every one, but believed by no body, meer Words of Course" (1.147). The lesson of social inter-course, Ophelia learns, is that "to be impatient was civil, and thorough-ly troublesome was being perfectly well-bred" (1.205).

Thus Ophelia's clear-eyed commentary exposes the hypocrisies, lies, and deceits that underpin the glittering surface of "polite Society." Ophelia is never taken in by the allure of wealth and luxury, which had proved so irresistible to Charlotte Lucum. Where Charlotte Lucum adopted the standards of society in place of her own moral values, Ophelia never becomes convinced that society offers a viable alternative to her own natural sense of virtue and vice. She herself remains at one remove from society's concerns. "I liked better to be an Observer, than the Subject of Observation" (1.59), she comments at one point. But the irony of this stance is that, unknown to her, she is the object of

Dorchester's own worldly deceit and will, if he gets his way, become one of society's victims herself—while the men and women of Dorchester's social circle who claim friendship for Ophelia, like those members of society who surrounded Lady Dellwyn, stand by and do nothing to warn her of her danger.

Moreover, although Ophelia is never corrupted by society as Charlotte Lucum is, she is undeniably affected by its requirements. Symbolically, as she travels from Wales into England at the beginning of the novel, her first concern is to conform to the demands of fashion, if only to avoid being stared at as an alien. She refuses to wear stays, "which seemed to me invented in perverse Opposition to Nature" (1.49), but she has to don a hoop because her dress would otherwise be too long, and immediately her freedom of movement is constricted. This kind of compromise faces her throughout her experiences on Dorchester's country estate and in London and Tunbridge. Always the tendency is to constrict and confine natural freedom. Eventually Ophelia becomes less open in her own behavior, for fear of misinterpretation or censure, and less confident of the good intentions of others as she learns from experience not to trust the people among whom she lives. She comes reluctantly to accept that truth and innocence are not enough, in themselves, to defend her from the cruelty and thoughtlessness of the world.

One manifestation of natural behavior that she retains throughout, however, is genuine emotional responses to joy or misery. Here again Fielding makes use of popular literary conventions of the time—in this instance, the vogue for sentiment—and manipulates them for her own purposes. If "sentimentalism in the novel derives from the attempt to conceive of an uncorrupted social being," as John Mullan suggests (Mullan, 15), then it is not surprising to find that *Ophelia* equates sentiment with a natural virtue at odds with the artificial formality of social conventions; and certainly sentiment is organically connected to Fielding's moral and thematic concerns in an unusually direct way. Ophelia's particular capacity for sentiment displays itself not in verbal language, which is seen to be easily compromised by hypocrisy and deceit, but in the natural responses of the body, which are not to be disguised. Ophelia depends on the natural language of the body above words even in her judgments of others: "The most obstinate Incredulity could not stand before the Tenderness so visible in his expressive Countenance," she remarks (judging correctly, in this particular instance) of Dorchester (1.138).

Mullan has pointed out that the "vocabulary" of sensibility is "that of gestures and palpitations, sighs and tears" (Mullan, 61). Ophelia

responds to joy and sorrow by tears, an instinctive response to an instinctive emotion. If her exposure to grief is more prolonged, her tears turn to
illness—fever, general debility, even emaciation—despite her "natural"
good health.[22] The connection between psychological and physical health
is clearly demonstrated. Moreover, "to cure a Distemper by Medicine,
which proceeds from Anxiety of Mind is a vain Attempt" (1.188);
Ophelia declares a genuine conviction that only restoration of mental
tranquillity or emotional confidence can prevent her actually dying from
despair. Significantly, the older Ophelia does not criticize her younger
self for this; but, also significantly, Ophelia's sentimental despair is a dis-
criminating emotion, reaching its height only in the case of misunderstandings with Dorchester.

    In this context, it forms unconscious evidence of Ophelia's growing
love for her protector. In fact, a capacity for sentiment acts as a strong
link between Ophelia and Dorchester, who is as ready as she to weep in
the face of depression or distress. Sentiment, despite its tendency to
tears, sighs, and fevers, is not necessarily a passive state. It can also offer
an important index of more active qualities of moral virtue, leading to
action to assist others, and Dorchester's capacity for this kind of sentiment is a major point in his favor. Just as Sir Harry Cleveland, in *The
Countess of Dellwyn*, revealed his fundamental good nature by his instinctive willingness to be benevolent to a worthy family in distress, so
Dorchester's good qualities manifest themselves in his care over helping
Traverse, a soldier down on his luck after being overlooked for promo-
tion by those whose interests are in power politics rather than personal
worth. "Compassion, and a Desire to Assist" are motives to justify trans-
gressing the social code that would leave an unfortunate person well
alone. There is certainly an element in Dorchester's attitude toward
Traverse and his family that borders on cultivating the luxury of sentiment for its own sake—including what seems to the reader a quite
unnecessary tormenting of Traverse with bogus proposals to send him to
the West Indies before revealing that his fortune has been made at
home—but even here the dominant argument is in favor of good nature
and benevolence rather than of self-indulgence.

    Ophelia's own capacity for tears, illness, and identification with oth-
ers' joys and sorrows is also balanced by tougher physical and intellectual characteristics. Unlike most other sentimental fictional heroines of the
period, she is not—or not for long—entirely debilitated by shock at
becoming involved in events beyond her control; and this toughness
manifests itself most clearly when she finds herself in the situation

beloved by sentimental novelists for its capacity to emphasize the physical vulnerability of the victimized female: abduction. Ophelia is actually abducted three times during the course of the novel. We see at length how she accommodates herself to being in Dorchester's power. Equally impressive is her composure when she finds herself accidentally eloped with in the place of another young woman at an inn. At first only mildly suspicious—she imagines Dorchester is teasing her—Ophelia gradually begins to work out for herself what must have happened. By the time the scene has developed into a Mozartian tangle of voluble landladies, enthusiastic lovers, and enraged parents, Ophelia has, with politic caution, sought refuge in a cupboard; but through its glass door she continues to observe, and "as I became convinced of the Error which occasioned this Bustle, I began to find some Entertainment in the Fray" (1.110). At an opportune moment she extricates herself with an admirable combination of elegance and common sense. The fact that Ophelia's fearlessness stems, at least in part, from ignorance—lack of awareness of the danger she might be in, even lack of understanding of the worldly events in which she has become entangled—underlines the fact that fear is one aspect of the feminine character that society has insisted upon as part of a woman's social role.

Ophelia's third abduction provides an even clearer example of her refusal to subside into the inactivity of sentimental despair—and yet another instance of Fielding's sensitivity to, and subversion of, fictional trends. Four years before the publication of Horace Walpole's *The Castle of Otranto*, commonly regarded as the first Gothic novel, Fielding actually immures her heroine in a full-blown gothic castle. Indeed, Ophelia's first vision of the castle, whose crumbling contours are rendered even more awesome by the dim light of a late afternoon, strongly prefigures a paradigmic gothic scene in Ann Radcliffe's *The Mysteries of Udolpho* (1794).[23] Unlike Mrs. Radcliffe's heroine, however, Ophelia is by no means overcome by the experience: she comments dryly that "the View did not conduce to my Satisfaction" (2.18). She proceeds to describe the moldering bridge, oak-paneled rooms, leaded casements, overgrown walks, and "all the Modulations of a bleak Winter's Wind" (2.21). But she is entirely undaunted by the romantic power of the place; the massive old furniture is notable only for its discomforts, and the most obtrusive feature of the house itself is the reverse of awe-inspiring: "had all the 'Perfumes of *Arabia*' been dispersed about the House, they could not have got the better of the Stench arising from the Moat" (2.20). As Ann Marilyn Parrish has pointed out, "one can scarcely believe there was no

Gothic novel for Miss Fielding to be satirizing" (Parrish, 221). Ophelia makes the best of her period of imprisonment, bides her time, and in due course organizes her escape.

Free to choose, she returns not to Wales but to Lord Dorchester. Throughout the novel Ophelia has been falling in love with Dorchester, although Dorchester himself has remained something of a cipher. He is the outsider who destroys Ophelia's utopia; Ophelia admits that his abduction of her was "my first Acquaintance with Deceit" (1.30), but she remains unaware of his full villainy—which in any case remains a matter of intention rather than of achievement. In fact, apart from his nefarious plans for Ophelia, Dorchester proves to be an above-average representative of the polite world to which he introduces her. He has many good qualities, which are made manifest as the novel progresses and which genuinely impress Ophelia: he is a man of benevolent impulses, a conscientious estate holder, a good landlord, a thoughtful teacher of facts and philosophy, an affectionate lover. But he is also a man of worldly experience, tolerant of the hypocrisies upon which society's standards turn; moreover, he is dominated by self-indulgence, ruled by emotions rather than reflective thought. Natural virtue and worldly vice, therefore, fight their battle within him. His sudden passion for Ophelia stems from his appreciation of her beauty and her merits; his abduction of her arises from his indulgence of his desires without thought of the consequences.

Although Ophelia's love for Dorchester grows gradually, nurtured by her appreciation of his practical virtues, Dorchester's passion for Ophelia proceeds by fits and starts, reflecting his worldly lack of confidence and trust in others. Never secure in his feelings, he is periodically overcome with jealousy of other men. On one occasion, having created a narrative of betrayal in his own mind, he accuses Ophelia of deceiving him. Ophelia is bewildered: "this Man accuses me of what he must know is a Stranger to my Heart" (1.186). Why, she reasonably argues, does he not simply ask her to tell him the truth? As the relationship between Dorchester and Ophelia progresses, it becomes clear that he has as many lessons to learn as she. Whereas Ophelia is ignorant of the way society organizes itself, and the conventions of contemporary life, Dorchester— the representative of that life—is equally ignorant of the implications of true feeling. Misunderstandings between them, in which Dorchester is the prey—and Ophelia the innocent victim—of his own fears, enact the novel's central conflict between the natural morality of the individual "untainted" by the world and the destructive artificiality of polite society.

Like his famous fictional predecessor, Richardson's Lovelace, Dorchester has set himself a self-defeating task: he loves Ophelia for her natural moral virtues but can only fulfill his idea of love by destroying the virtues he admires so highly. It is not easy to see how any resolution of such a basic incompatibility between hero and heroine can, even in the terms of fictional conventions of the period, appear other than facile. Richardson had recognized that the logic of the situation between Clarissa and Lovelace allowed no compromise, and Fielding had defended the tragic ending of their story. In *Ophelia*, however, Fielding deals with the problem in a different way.

First, she brings out into the open the main focus of Dorchester's fears as Lord Larborough encourages Dorchester to rehearse the reasons for his desire of living with Ophelia without benefit of matrimony. Dorchester's reasoning is unexpectedly eloquent, even idealistic. He is not simply a rake in rather dilatory pursuit of another seduction but a well-meaning young man reacting in distaste to worldly deceit. Marriage, he argues, is a human invention rather than a natural state of affairs between a man and a woman. It is entered into for all sorts of interested motives and often proves disastrous for both partners. Ophelia " 'might give herself to me in Marriage out of Prudence and Interest' " (2.176). He would prefer her to choose him, as he would choose her, from love.

> "We will love to the End of our Lives, always assured of each other's Affections, by unabated Assiduity and Tenderness. Necessity shall have no Hand in our Union, for I will make a Settlement on her, which shall render her perfectly independent of me. We shall be linked only by Love, and therefore cannot doubt of the Strength of the Chain while neither breaks it." (2.175)

Ophelia, who has been placed to overhear the conversation (and who has refused to believe Dorchester a villain until she hears it from his own mouth), is unconvinced. Although by now she knows that she loves him, she flees his presence. So far Ophelia has followed the same pattern of behavior as Portia in *The Cry*; Fielding, however, allows Ophelia to take her independence further than Portia. Even when Dorchester finds Ophelia, repudiates his whole scheme, and asks her to marry him, she stoutly refuses to return to him. Her choice is to withdraw once more from the world of disillusion.

> "I have lost all my Confidence in you, and detest the rest of your Nation. I will go where I shall be secluded from Mankind, where Virtue makes

every Action open and intelligible; there I am capable of living happily, without learning the Arts that here hide every real Thought." (2.237)

Ophelia's declared intention here does offer a possible resolution to the novel: indeed, some critics have seen it as more satisfying, or more true to the spirit of the text, than what eventually occurs.[24] But it is not the resolution Fielding chooses.

Having tried every other means to convince Ophelia that her love has reformed him, Dorchester seeks out her aunt and once more rehearses his arguments against marriage. This time he is challenged by a forceful counterargument. Ophelia's aunt is scathing:

> "You talk of Freedom and Equality, in a Situation which entirely abolish-es both. What can render a Woman so much your Slave, as having given up her fair Fame, and *that sweet Peace that Goodness bosoms over*, to gratify your mean Passions? Where then is the Equality between you? You have in your Power every Pleasure but Self-Approbation, and, perhaps, the hardened do not want that, while the Woman has nothing left her but your Love, which it is . . . her Interest to keep, even by little despicable Arts." (2.272)

She speaks, of course, from personal experience. Her searing analysis of the double standard that society has established for the relationships between men and women, and the full implications for Ophelia of his designs, convinces Dorchester of his error. Ophelia's aunt is touched by his remorse and by his evident love for Ophelia, and she agrees to plead for him with her niece.

Ophelia is now beset on all sides. Her aunt, whose own experience of male deceit had led her to withdraw from the world, counsels Ophelia to accept Dorchester's expressions of repentance and marry him. Miss Baden, the only representative of polite society the novel has produced who could remotely be described as virtuous, advises Ophelia on differ-ent grounds to make the best of it: she "ought not to expect consum-mate Virtue among a degenerate People" but "ought to allow for the Force of Custom and Education" (2.246–47). Ophelia is still doubtful: why should she trust that her lover has indeed repented of his wish to seduce her? And why should she compromise with a degenerate world? But the encouragement of both rural and urban female mentors, allied to Ophelia's love for Dorchester, leads her to yield. It is, after all, impos-sible to return to a prelapsarian world, and in the real world compromis-es are unavoidable. "I may repent, but I find, I must comply!" (2.280).

Because Ophelia is telling her story years after the event, she is able to confirm that Dorchester was sincere and that she has been happy in her marriage. She acknowledges, however, that she owes her happiness more to luck than to judgment. She took a chance, as all must who inhabit an imperfect world, and luckily, on this occasion, it paid off.

Both *The Countess of Dellwyn* and *Ophelia* attracted mixed reviews. *Critical Review*[25] thought that the author of *The Countess of Dellwyn* showed some taste but with (probably unconscious) cruelty advised her to cultivate more of what she did best: imitating Henry Fielding. *Monthly Review*,[26] however, gave the novel high praise, and both reviewers singled out her skill in depicting "the bustle of high life, and the futility of publick amusements."[27] But despite such encouragement the novel did not achieve popularity, and no reprint was called for.[28] The unexpected success of the story of Mrs. Bilson, which was reproduced at least twice in magazines as a self-contained tale in the year following the publication of *The Countess of Dellwyn*, would not have compensated Fielding for the failure of the novel as a whole—nor for loss of the extra 40 guineas she had been promised if the work went into a second edition.

Ophelia was given little attention by the critics but nevertheless became immediately popular with readers: Catherine Talbot recorded in April 1760 that "we are deep in and amused with Ophelia" (Pennington 1809, 2.323). A second edition was published in 1763 (and a German edition in 1764); in 1785 the novel was republished (bound with Smollett's *The Expedition of Humphry Clinker* and Francis Coventry's *Pompey the Little*) in the *Novelist's Magazine* series of outstanding novels. By the end of the century editions had appeared in France and Germany as well as in Ireland. It is impossible to know whether the success of *Ophelia* owed more to its conformity with, or its subversion of, current fictional conventions; it is at the very least an ironic comment on Fielding's long career as an innovator that she achieved most success, in the years following her death, with what was, on the surface at least, her most conventional work.

Chapter Ten

From "Fielding's Sister" to Sarah Fielding

At the time of her death, Sarah Fielding's reputation as a writer was vulnerable. She had not written anything new for some years; she had been living in increasing seclusion because of ill health; and her closest literary friends—Henry Fielding, Samuel Richardson, the publisher Andrew Millar—had all died before her. To add to what Jane Spencer has aptly described as "the continuing tendency to disparage or forget" women writers (Spencer, ix), recognition of Fielding's literary achievement was threatened in a very specific way: she was in the unique situation, in her time, of being a famous female writer with an only too famous male writer for a brother.

Increasingly, as the 18th century progressed, "Fielding" meant Henry Fielding: confusion between the two writers was nearly always at Sarah's expense. At the outset of her literary career, readers had been uncertain whether *David Simple* was written by Henry or Sarah; publishers and advertisers ever afterward were only too willing to obfuscate the question of authorship of Sarah's works in Henry's favor. *The Lives of Cleopatra and Octavia* was advertised in 1758 as by "Mr. Fielding"; the successful German translation of *The History of Ophelia* was designated "By Henry Fielding"; a reprint of "Fielding's *Governess*" in the 1790s clearly implied Henry's authorship. Sarah's own habit of signing herself "the Author of *David Simple*" allowed ample scope for confusion.

For a few years after her death, however, a small number of writers and commentators, mostly female, recalled her work with admiration. In 1774 Mary Scott's verse poem praised Fielding among notable 18th-century women, in language that reflected familiarity with Fielding's work:

> 'Twas FIELDING's talent, with ingenious Art
>
> To trace the secret mazes of the Heart,
>
> In language tun'd to please its infant thought,
>
> The tender breast with prudent care SHE taught.
>
> Nature to HER, her boldest pencil lent,

And blest HER with a mind of vast extent;

A mind, that nobly scorn'd each low desire,

And glow'd with pure Religion's warmest fire.[1]

Eleven years later Clara Reeve, in her influential history of prose fiction, *The Progress of Romance*, praised Fielding's achievement even more highly. Sarah is discussed third in the order of 18th-century writers, after Richardson and Henry Fielding, and her champion, Euphrasia, asserts that in some "material merits" Sarah Fielding's work excels even that of her brother. But, ominously, Hortensius confesses he is not acquainted with all "this lady's works," and when the list is rehearsed for his benefit, both *The Cry* and *Volume the Last* are missing (Reeve, 142–43).

Although several of her books—notably *David Simple* and *Ophelia*—achieved renewed popularity in the closing decades of the 18th century, Fielding's name and literary achievements were becoming forgotten. She influenced Fanny Burney's *Evelina* (1778) and *Cecilia* (1782), but there is no evidence that she was read by Jane Austen; for the new radical women writers, such as Mary Wollstonecraft and Mary Hays, Fielding must have seemed unacceptably conformist, far too willing to compromise with the outdated conventions of an earlier generation.

Victorians occasionally recalled Fielding as one of a group of 18th-century women writers whose work achieved passing fame; but since she was neither a notorious figure, like Eliza Haywood or Mary Wollstonecraft, nor an undeniably formidable intellectual, like Elizabeth Carter or Catherine Macaulay, little attention was given to the individual aims and objectives of her work. Fielding's literary persona, "the Author of *David Simple*," ironically achieved validity, as she was now remembered only for that first novel.

Charlotte Yonge had *The Governess* reprinted in 1870, but when Clementina Black wrote a revisionist article on Fielding in *Gentleman's Magazine*, in 1888, she began with the assertion that Fielding was "probably not known at this moment to a dozen readers."[2] Black discusses *David Simple*, *Familiar Letters*, and *Ophelia*. She praises the quality of the first and the last and begins to establish Fielding's place in a specifically feminine tradition of writing by pointing out the influence of *Ophelia* on *Evelina*. But the highest praise she can find for Sarah Fielding is that Sarah's best work is indistinguishable from that of Henry (488).

By the end of the 19th century, scholarly examination of the roots of the modern realist novel was focusing on Henry Fielding and Samuel Richardson as the two "great" exponents of the new genre in the 18th century. In this context there was a slight resurgence of interest in Sarah, as the sister of one and the friend of the other. This perspective led to some bizarre critical judgments: when Arnold Needham identified the similarities between the plots of *David Simple* (1744) and *Tom Jones* (1748), he declared, with no supporting evidence, "It is more reasonable to suppose that Sarah got her plot from Henry than that Henry got it from Sarah" (Needham, 73).

In the past 30 years or so, however, critical approaches to 18th-century fiction, and to the role of women writers, have changed dramatically. And, in fact, as this study has shown, detailed analysis of Sarah Fielding's fiction reveals a high degree of originality in both content and technique. *David Simple* can now be recognized as not merely a pale imitation of *Pamela* and *Joseph Andrews* but an innovative and influential attempt to establish fiction as an appropriate vehicle for the presentation of morality in action; moreover, in 1744 it represented a new model for women writers, mapping an area—didactic fiction—through which they might respectably and profitably enter the literary marketplace. *The Governess* introduces a whole literary subgenre in the form of the school story for girls while at the same time providing a template for the presentation of educational material in an entertaining form. *The Lives of Cleopatra and Octavia* devastatingly deconstructs Cleopatra as an icon of femininity and develops the emerging topos of fictionalized history. *The Cry*, *The Countess of Dellwyn*, and *Ophelia* all experiment in different ways with the conventions and taboos of prose fiction. The translation of Xenophon is a landmark of 18th-century female scholarship.

But more significant than the achievements of her individual texts is the moral and intellectual vision that informs Sarah Fielding's body of work as a coherent whole. Her philosophical principles were developed in response to her own experiences and to the writers and thinkers whose work she studied. Her ethics directly address the tensions and inequalities of the society within which she lived. While (sometimes reluctantly) accepting the conventions of patronage and deference that governed that society—there were few who argued for political reform in an era when the greatest political threat arose from the exiled Stuarts—she urges the humanization of the system into a network of benevolence and gratitude, with the aim of minimizing the everyday social and personal injustices that outrage her sense of fair play and common human decency. She exposes the myriad ways in which the powerful manipulate the language of morality for immoral purposes and consistently reasserts the need to reconnect the link between word and deed.

Most importantly, she argues that women should be treated as more than male chattels: they should be given a better education, taught the truths about a world that too often deceived them about their place in it, given a genuine opportunity to make honest and affectionate marriages. And in return she requires much of women themselves. Again, Fielding is no overt revolutionary: she accepts the importance of women fulfilling their duties as daughters, sisters, wives, and mothers, with wisdom and honor. But she also demands that, above and beyond these duties, women—whether fictional heroines, or Fielding's real-life contemporaries—accept a preeminent responsibility to themselves as mature human beings responsible for their own actions. It is in such demands that Sarah Fielding's true radicalism lies.

Notes and References

Chapter One

1. R. E. M. Peach, *Historic Houses in Bath: And Their Associations*, 2nd series (1884), 32; hereafter cited in the text.

2. Clive Probyn's recent biographical account brings together most of what is currently known about her life. See *The Correspondence of Henry and Sarah Fielding*, eds. Martin C. Battestin and Clive T. Probyn (Oxford: Oxford University Press, 1993); hereafter cited in the text as *Correspondence*.

3. Martin C. Battestin, with Ruthe R. Battestin, *Henry Fielding: A Life* (London: Routledge, 1989, reprinted 1993), 11; hereafter cited in text as Battestins.

4. Statement of Frances Barber, servant at East Stour, PRO C24.1396.Pt1.No29.

5. There is another possible candidate in the form of a friend of Elizabeth Carter also called Rooke or Rookes.

6. Colonel Fielding did not lose touch completely with his children. In 1729, after Anne Rapha's death, he married for a third time: his new wife was a well-to-do Salisbury widow, and he may well have been visiting his family in Salisbury around this period.

7. Isobel Grundy, quoting a letter from Henry Hele, in "Inoculation in Salisbury," *Scriblerian* 26: 1 (1993), 63–65. Grundy suggests that, on the basis of the ages of the children inoculated, the two missing children are Ursula and Sarah and speculates that they might have had smallpox already.

8. Daniel Defoe, *A Tour Through the Whole Island of Great Britain, 1724–26*, abridged and edited by Pat Rogers (Harmondsworth: Penguin Books, 1971, reprinted 1983), 194.

9. Hester Lynch Salusbury Thrale, *Thraliana*, ed. Katharine C. Balderston (1942), 78; hereafter cited in the text.

10. Edmund seems to have played no significant part in Sarah Fielding's life after the East Stour estate was sold, and little is known about him. He became a soldier in his father's regiment, married in London in 1753, and was at Madras early in 1755 —Battestins, 652.

11. It is unlikely that this declaration was true. With no other visible income, General Fielding's widow lived comfortably for many years after his death.

12. This could have been Sarah's most serious miscalculation. The conditions of the will are complicated, but annuities amounting to £100 a year were allocated to the five named Fieldings as a group (Edmund, for some rea-

son, was excluded), to be divided equally among those still living. By 1754, Sarah was the only named sibling still alive. If the annuities had not been sold, she would therefore have been the beneficiary of £100 a year for the last 14 years of her life, which would have made a vast difference to her financial situation. For the original will, see PRO.PCC.1738.

13. The letter was glossed by Henry Fielding: "This letter was written by a young lady on reading the former" (that is, Horatio's letter to Leonora). See Henry Fielding, *The History of the Adventures of Joseph Andrews* (1742), ed. R. F. Brissenden (Harmondsworth: Penguin, 1977, reprinted 1988), 114. There is no proof that the "young lady" was Sarah Fielding, but no other likely author has been suggested.

14. Advertisement to the first edition of *The Adventures of David Simple* (1744), quoted here in its entirety. Astonishingly, it is not reproduced in the most widely available contemporary edition of *David Simple*, ed. Malcolm Kelsall (Oxford: Oxford University Press, 1969); hereafter cited in the text.

15. These figures are taken from Cheryl Turner, *Living by the Pen: Women Writers in the Eighteenth Century* (London: Routledge, 1992), 38; hereafter cited in the text. Turner's figures do not take account of anonymous fictions, which might be written by women.

16. Turner's figures may reflect an increasing choice of anonymity among women writers rather than a decrease in their numbers; this would still endorse the argument that respectable women were unwilling to acknowledge authorship.

17. Battestins describe Eliza Haywood as "loose of life and pen" (Battestins, 84). Henry Fielding and Haywood knew and disliked each other. He lampooned her as Mrs. Novel in his play *The Author's Farce* (1730, 1734); she ridiculed him in her novel *The History of Miss Betsy Thoughtless* (1751).

18. Lady Mary Wortley Montagu to Lady Bute, 1 March 1752, *The Complete Letters of Lady Mary Wortley Montagu*, ed. Robert Halsband (Oxford: Clarendon Press, 1967), 3.67; hereafter cited in the text.

19. Leicestershire County Record Office, ref. DG7 D2(ii). I am grateful to Isobel Grundy for pointing out this reference.

20. J. Wooll, *Biographical Memoirs of the Late Rev. Joseph Warton* (1806), 215.

21. See Battestin, Martin C., "Henry Fielding, Sarah Fielding, and 'The dreadful sin of incest,'" *Novel* 1979, 6–18, hereafter cited in the text, and Battestins, 411–12. Battestin draws strong inferences from evidence that Henry, as a child, committed some unspeakable act with one of his sisters (not Sarah), that both Henry and Sarah are concerned in their fiction with incest, and that Henry was unusually interested in sexual deviation in the 1744–47 period. However, the theme of incest is not nearly as uncommon in early 18th-century fiction as Battestin suggests. Moreover, the Camilla-Valentine episode in *David Simple*, which he cites, was written before Sarah went to live with Henry.

22. In *Familiar Letters* (1747), 2.222–24; hereafter cited in the text.

23.   *The Correspondence of Samuel Richardson*, ed. Anna Laetitia Barbauld (London, 1804), 2.62; hereafter cited in the text.

24.   Collier and Fielding evidently participated in Richardson's literary discussions too. On 15 November 1751 Richardson wrote to Charlotte Lennox that he had recommended her novel *The Female Quixote* to Andrew Millar (who published the work in 1752) "in the same sincere manner that you heard me Speak of it to Miss Collier and Miss Fielding." The letter is quoted in Duncan Isles, "The Lennox Collection," *Harvard Library Bulletin*, vol. 18 no. 4 (October 1970), 336.

25.   Richardson's friend Lady Bradshaigh took a similar view. Having read *The Cry* in 1754, she wrote to Richardson: "I think she seems to favour the author of Joseph Andrews. That is the thing I least like in her." Lady Bradshaigh to Samuel Richardson 2–22 March 1754, Forster collection, reel 15, F.48.E.5.28, Victoria and Albert Museum, London.

26.   See *The Jacobite's Journal and Related Writings*, ed. W. B. Coley (Oxford: Clarendon Press, 1975), 317.

27.   Andrew Millar ordered subscription slips for the work by June 1748.

28.   There is evidence of at least one other friendship, probably from this period. Among the poems included in Esther Lewis's *Poems Moral and Entertaining* (1789) is one written "long since," "To Miss Fielding, in London, the Writer of *David Simple* and other Publications." Lewis writes, as she often did in the 1740s and 1750s, as "Sylvia"; she addresses Sarah as "Melissa" and refers to a snuffbox that "Melissa" gave her. The poem is constructed as a conventional address from Sylvia in the country to Melissa in the town. Although the idea of Sarah Fielding's residing "in the joyous town, / Where circling pleasures circling pleasures drown" (lines 3–4) is slightly incongruous, the later reflection that Melissa "wishes me by reason still to move" rings true—Esther Lewis, *Poems Moral and Entertaining* (1789), 298–300.

29.   In fact, her writings were particularly lucrative during this period. Andrew Millar paid a total of £266.1.0 from his account at Coutts Bank to Sarah Fielding between October 1750 and October 1762.

30.   Jane Collier, *The Art of Ingeniously Tormenting* (1753), 1.43. The text has been reprinted, with an introduction by Judith Hawley, by Thoemmes Press (1994).

31.   Richardson consistently praised Sarah Fielding in the context of the human heart. On 14 February 1754 he described her to Lady Bradshaigh as "a Lady who has a good Heart as well as Head" and on 9 August 1754 he wrote to Sophia Westcomb that "the Authoress [of *The Cry*] shows a great Knowledge of the Human Heart." Forster collection, reel 15, F.48.E.5.24 and reel 16, F.48.E.8.143, Victoria and Albert Museum, London.

32.   Peach, 35; Alicia Lefanu, *Memoirs of the Life and Writings of Mrs. Frances Sheridan* (1824), 95.

33. Barry Cunliffe, *The City of Bath* (Gloucester: Alan Sutton, 1986), 115.

34. Tobias Smollett, *The Expedition of Humphry Clinker* (1771), ed. Angus Ross (Harmondsworth: Penguin, 1967, reprinted 1985), 62.

35. The publisher, Andrew Millar, suggested that Sarah should herself write a longer memoir of Henry and append Harris's memoir to it but Sarah rejected this proposal out of hand.

36. See particularly Mrs. Bennet in *Amelia* (1751).

37. Hester Thrale wrote that Sarah had expressed, through Collier, a lively interest in her own progress in the classics during the late 1750s. Aware of the friendship between Sarah and Collier, Thrale "perswaded myself" that Fielding was the author of an anonymous poem sent to her in 1760: "These Verses are nothing extraordinary God knows, but I dare say they are hers" (Balderston, 77–78). Thrale's literary judgment is accurate; if the verses are by Sarah—which seems unlikely—they would do nothing for her reputation as a poet. The poem begins "No weed in Nature's Garden grows / Botanick Writers say; / To whom the Bryar puts forth a Rose / The Thorn a Flow'r of May" and continues in the same vein for seven more stanzas.

38. *The Ladies' Library* (1714), 1.20.

39. Quoted in Felicity Nussbaum, *The Brink of All We Hate: English Satires on Women, 1660–1750* (Lexington: University Press of Kentucky, 1984), 148.

40. Janet Todd, *The Sign of Angellica: Women, Writing and Fiction, 1660–1800* (London: Virago, 1989), 32; hereafter cited in the text.

41. Quoted in Sylvia Harckstark Myers, *The Bluestocking Circle: Women, Friendship, and the Life of the Mind in Eighteenth-Century England* (Oxford: Clarendon, 1990), 158.

42. Robin Waterfield, Introduction to *Xenophon: Conversations of Socrates*, including *Memoirs of Socrates* (Harmondsworth: Penguin, 1990), 61.

43. MO 5787, from the Montagu Collection, Huntington Library, California; letters hereafter cited in the text by identification number.

44. *Monthly Review* 27 (September 1762), 171. Fielding's translation was included in *The Minor Works of Xenophon* (1813) and *The Whole Works of Xenophon* (New York, 1855). The *Defence of Socrates* was reprinted in *Socratic Discourses by Plato and Xenophon* (Dent, 1910); this edition was itself reprinted in 1913, 1915, 1918, 1923, 1925, 1927, 1929, 1933, 1937, and possibly later. I am grateful to Clive T. Probyn for this information.

45. The academic ambitions of the work are emphasized by the fact that subscriptions were sought by advertisement in Oxford and Cambridge.

46. Carter (1717–1806) was 7, Montagu (1720–1800) 10, and Scott (1723–95) 13 years younger than Sarah Fielding.

47. There is an interesting discussion of Fielding and "the Bath community" of intellectual women in Betty Rizzo, *Companions Without Vows: Relationships Among Eighteenth-Century British Women* (Athens: University of Georgia Press, 1994), 304–27; hereafter cited in the text.

48.   Talbot to Carter, *A Series of Letters Between Mrs. Carter and Miss Talbot, 1741–1776*, ed. Montagu Pennington (1809), 2.188; hereafter cited in the text.

49.   Quoted in Reginald Blunt, ed., *Mrs. Montagu, "Queen of the Blues": Her Letters and Friendships from 1762 to 1800* (Constable, n.d. [1923]), 2.144.

50.   Sir John Fielding's account at Coutts Bank records payment of £10 to Sarah Fielding in October–November from 1763, when the account was opened, to 1767, the last autumn of Sarah's life.

51.   This bequest, together with the inclusion of gardening in the curriculum at Mrs. Teachum's academy in *The Governess*, and David Simple's predilection for cultivating his garden in *Volume the Last*, suggests that gardening was a hobby of Fielding's.

52.   The second (1767) edition of the Xenophon translation shows no sign of further authorial input.

53.   The most critical comment that has survived about Sarah Fielding comes from Thrale: "I have . . . heard from Mr Johnson that she was accused of drinking, but it was new to me, and I never from Dr Collier heard anything but good of her" (Balderston, 79). It is surely impossible that Scott would have used the "sober"/"intoxicating" analogy had the accusation been true.

54.   *Mrs. Elizabeth Carter: Letters . . . to Mrs. Montagu Between 1755 and 1800*, ed. Montagu Pennington (1817), 1.371; hereafter cited in the text.

Chapter Two

1.   Quoted in Jerry C. Beasley, *Novels of the 1740s* (Athens: University of Georgia Press, 1982), 4.

2.   Clara Reeve, *The Progress of Romance* (1785), 1.111; hereafter cited in the text.

3.   Arthur Blackamore, Preface to *Luck at Last, or the Happy Unfortunate* (1723), reprinted in *Four Before Richardson: Selected English Novels, 1720–27*, ed. William McBurney (Lincoln: University of Nebraska Press, 1963), 4; Preface to *Leonora, or Characters Drawn from Real Life: A Novel* (1745).

4.   Horace, *On the Art of Poetry*, in Aristotle/Horace/Longinus, trans. T. S. Dorsch, *Classical Literary Criticism* (Harmondsworth: Penguin, 1965), 90.

5.   See J. Paul Hunter, *Before Novels: The Cultural Contexts of Eighteenth-Century English Fiction* (New York: Norton, 1990), esp. 227–42, for an interesting discussion on the appeal of didacticism—what Hunter calls a "spontaneous overflow of righteous indignation and moral concern" (233)—to 18th-century readers; hereafter cited in the text.

6.   By the late 1770s even a respectable female novelist no longer needed to assert her didactic purpose. Fanny Burney, in the Preface to *Evelina*, claims, "To draw characters from nature, though not from life, and to mark the manners of the time." See *Evelina, or The History of a Young Lady's Entrance into the World* (1778), eds. Edward A. and Lillian D. Bloom (Oxford: Oxford University Press, 1968, reprinted 1985), 7; hereafter cited in the text as *Evelina*.

7. Sarah Fielding, *The Adventures of David Simple, Containing an Account of His Travels Through the Cities of London and Westminster in the Search of a Real Friend* (1744), ed. Malcolm Kelsall (Oxford: Oxford University Press, 1969, reprinted 1987), 7; hereafter cited in the text.

8. Ian Watt, *The Rise of the Novel: Studies in Defoe, Richardson and Fielding* (London: Chatto & Windus, 1957; reprinted Hogarth Press, 1987), 15.

9. Critics have differed as to whether Fielding treats David's simplicity ironically. My own feeling is that irony is only rarely evident in *The Adventures of David Simple*, but its latent potential is developed in *Familiar Letters* and *Volume the Last*.

10. Henry Fielding, *The History of the Adventures of Joseph Andrews, and of His Friend Mr. Abraham Adams* (1742), ed. Douglas Brooks-Davies (Oxford: Oxford University Press, 1966, reprinted 1980), 9; hereafter cited in the text.

11. This novel is reprinted in McBurney.

12. See by contrast Charlotte Lennox's variation on Cervantes, *The Female Quixote* (1752), in which the quixotic notions of the heroine, Arabella, exist in strong tension with her lack of freedom as a woman.

13. See also Mr. Wilson in *Joseph Andrews* (1742) and the Man of the Hill in *Tom Jones* (1748). As the son of a tradesman David Simple is of a lower class than these "gentlemen," but his assumption of a gentleman's leisure and his travels in "high life" as well as in other spheres of activity make the comparisons valid.

14. This description of Orgeuil's character is given by Spatter, but it is clear from Orgeuil's behavior in *Volume the Last* that, in this instance at least, Spatter has not maligned the object of his criticism.

15. The cult of sensibility, an extraordinary 18th-century phenomenon, is well described in John Mullan's *Sentiment and Sociability: The Language of Feeling in the Eighteenth Century* (Oxford: Oxford University Press, 1988) and Janet Todd's *Sensibility: An Introduction* (London: Methuen, 1986); both hereafter cited in the text. The movement grew in literary terms to a culmination in Henry Mackenzie's *The Man of Feeling* (1770) before subsiding by the early 19th century.

16. The importance of David's social status is discussed by Gillian Skinner in "'The Price of a Tear': Economic Sense and Sensibility in Sarah Fielding's *David Simple*," *Literature and History*, 3rd series, vol. 1, no. 1, Spring 1992, 16–28.

17. The only obviously comparable heroines to Camilla and Cynthia are Clarissa Harlowe and Anna Howe in Richardson's *Clarissa*, written chiefly in the years of *David Simple*'s early popularity; Clarissa and Anna are similarly both "good" young women with differing personalities. But while Richardson keeps the more spirited of his heroines in the background as a foil (Anna is never able actively to assist Clarissa), Fielding allows Cynthia a central role in *David Simple* and *Familiar Letters* whereas in *Volume the Last* tragedy strikes the Simple community only when Cynthia has been dispatched to the West Indies.

18.   "Wit" was a dubious advantage for a woman at this time. Elizabeth Montagu, a lively and intelligent woman, wrote: "Wit in woman is apt to have bad consequences; like a sword without a scabbard it wounds the wearer and provokes assailants. I am sorry to say the generality of women who have excelled in wit have failed in chastity." Quoted in Todd 1989, 131.

19.   Lady Mary Chudleigh, "To the Ladies" lines 1–2, quoted in *Poetry by English Women, Elizabethan to Victorian*, ed. R. E. Pritchard (Manchester: Carcanet, 1990), 87.

20.   Bridget Hill, ed., *The First English Feminist: "Reflections upon Marriage" and Other Writings: By Mary Astell* (Aldershot: Gower/Maurice Temple Smith, 1986), 100.

21.   Daniel Defoe, *Roxana, The Fortunate Mistress* (1724), ed. Jane Jack (Oxford: Oxford University Press, 1964, reprinted 1986), 132.

22.   *Gentleman's Magazine* 17 (April 1747), 178. Ironically, T. Single saw the solution to such problems in a "traditional" female upbringing, to ensure that young women *did* have husbands before their fathers left them alone in the world.

23.   Dale Spender has provided a witty commentary on this incident— *Mothers of the Novel* (London: Pandora, 1986), 187–89; hereafter cited in the text.

24.   In *The Governess* Jenny Peace recalls that "my good Mamma bid me to remember how much my Brother's superior Strength might assist me in his being my Protector; and that I ought in return to use my utmost Endeavours to oblige him; and that then we should be mutual Assistants to each other throughout Life" (15).

25.   I have explored this question in more detail in "'Cits and Traders': Commerce and Industry in the British Novel, 1760–1832" (Ph.D. thesis, University of London, 1990), 336–57.

26.   Arnold Needham, "The Life and works of Sarah Fielding" (Ph.D. Diss., University of California, 1943), 75; hereafter cited in the text.

27.   Needham declares that the episode "has no other connection with the novel" than the fact that Isabelle once met Cynthia in Paris, and he refuses to comment upon it further (Needham, 115).

28.   See, for example, Roderick Random, who is showered with the fruits of his father's trading activities, and Sidney Bidulph, who receives a princely mansion and £3,000 a year from her long-lost uncle Warner—Tobias Smollett, *The Adventures of Roderick Random* (1748); Frances Sheridan, *Memoirs of Miss Sidney Bidulph* (1761).

29.   Lady Grey is using "Mrs." in its 18th-century sense, as the courtesy title of a mature adult woman, married or not.

Chapter Three

1.   Named literary sources include Shakespeare, Milton, Ovid, and Aesop. Unnamed sources include an "Acquaintance of mine [who] has turned the Fable I allude to into Verse" (1.210).

2. Sarah Fielding, *David Simple: Volume the Last* (1753), reprinted in *The Adventures of David Simple*, ed. Malcolm Kelsall (Oxford: Oxford University Press, 1969, reprinted 1987), 307–432; hereafter cited in the text. The "first two volumes" mentioned in the Preface (309–11) clearly refer to the two volumes of *David Simple* and not to *David Simple* and *Familiar Letters*.

3. In the story itself Fielding subverts contemporary conventions of the "novel" as "a small tale, generally of love": the heroine, Belinda, deliberately refuses to act like a typical heroine.

4. For example, Cynthia, when describing the company at Bath, is forcibly reminded of the opinions of "Mr Bickerstaff," the main "character" of *The Tatler* (87). In *David Simple* the difference between Livia's fair features and unpleasant personality is described by reference to "the Goddess of Justice's Mirror of Truth, as it is described in that beautiful Vision in *The Tatler*" (143).

5. J. R. Foster, *History of the Pre-Romantic Novel in England* (Oxford: Oxford University Press, 1949), 74; hereafter cited in the text.

6. Cynthia's irritated comment that "I am forbid to read with the Bath waters" is such an exception to the rule that it is tempting to guess that Fielding herself endured this penance.

7. It has been plausibly suggested by Needham (142) that Isabinda is a prototype for the heroine of Eliza Haywood's *History of Miss Betsy Thoughtless* (1751). Haywood's novel elicited the comment from a contemporary reviewer (reproduced in Todd 1989, 146–47) that "the history of a young inconsiderate girl, whose little foibles, without any natural vices of the mind, involve her in difficulties and distresses, which, by correcting, make her wiser, and deservedly happy in the end" was "a barren foundation" for a novel. The reviewer was of course mistaken: this plot is an apt description not only of the stories of Isabinda and Betsy but also of Jane Austen's Emma Woodhouse and Elizabeth Bennet.

8. For example, in the story of Cælia and Chloe in *The Governess*.

9. "Within a comparatively short time after its appearance *The Pilgrim's Progress* became the peculiar possession of the English people, of all classes, to an extent beyond any other work except the Bible"—Walter Allen, *The English Novel: From "The Pilgrim's Progress" to "Sons and Lovers"* (Harmondsworth: Penguin, 1954, reprinted 1986), 32. The idea of a dream allegory was taken up by Steele and Addison. *The Tatler*, No. 81 contains "The Tables of Fame: A Vision," which begins, "I dreamed that I was conveyed into a wide and boundless Plain, that was covered with prodigious Multitudes of People, which no Man could number." Fielding's tale opens in a similar way, but the nature of the visions soon varies; *The Tatler* provides a satiric survey of historical figures who sought fame. See Richard Steele and Joseph Addison, *Selections from The Tatler and The Spectator*, ed. Angus Ross (Harmondsworth: Penguin, 1982, reprinted 1988), 113–19; hereafter cited in the text.

10. I have assumed that the narrator is female, but since Fielding perceives men and women as being equally interested in morality and ethics, the gender of the narrator is of less importance than it is in the work of other writers of the period.

11.   See, for example, Cynthia's criticism of "*'fine Ladies'*" who "spend their whole Lives in affecting a Superiority, which it would not cost them so much really to attain" (1.85).

12.   The others were *The Lives of Cleopatra and Octavia* and the translation of Xenophon's *Memoirs of Socrates*.

13.   See Pat Rogers, "The Writer and Society," in *The Context of English Literature: The Eighteenth Century*, ed. Pat Rogers (London: Longman, 1978), 16.

14.   Cheryl Turner, *Living by the Pen: Women Writers in the Eighteenth Century* (London: Routledge, 1992), 111; hereafter cited in the text.

15.   Turner cites a 1975 study of subscription lists identifying 71 works by women published by subscription between 1700 and 1800 (Turner, 112).

16.   Advertisement to *David Simple*.

Chapter Four

1.   Lawrence Stone has identified "major changes in child-rearing practice among the squirearchy and bourgeoisie" between 1660 and 1800, involving "a kindlier attitude towards children" and a more permissive approach to child development—*The Family, Sex and Marriage in England 1500–1800* (Harmondsworth: Penguin, 1979, reprinted 1988), 284, 278.

2.   John Locke, *Some Thoughts Concerning Education* (1693), ed. John W. and Jean S. Yolton (Oxford: Oxford University Press, 1989), section 1, 83; hereafter cited in the text as *Thoughts*, with section and page numbers.

3.   Advertisement in the *Penny London Morning Advertiser*, 18 June 1744, quoted in F. J. Harvey Darton, *Children's Books in England: Five Centuries of Social Life* (Cambridge: Cambridge University Press, 1932, 3rd ed., revised by Brian Alderson, 1982), 1; hereafter cited in the text.

4.   Julia Briggs, "Women Writers and Writing for Children: From Sarah Fielding to E. Nesbit," *Children and Their Books: A Celebration of the Work of Iona and Peter Opie*, eds. Gillian Avery and Julia Briggs (Oxford: Clarendon Press, 1989), 224; hereafter cited in the text.

5.   Quoted from the title page of the first edition of *The Governess* (1749), facsimile edition, ed. Jill E. Grey (Oxford: Oxford University Press, 1968). Quotations from *The Governess* are taken from this edition, hereafter cited in the text. Any consideration of *The Governess* owes much to Grey's full and informative introduction to the text, hereafter cited in the text as Grey.

6.   Henry's eldest daughter, Charlotte (born 1736), died in 1741/2. His son, also Henry, was born in 1741/2 and his daughter Harriet in 1743. There may have been two other daughters, born between 1737 and 1740 (see Battestins, 191, 234). There is not enough evidence from this to infer, as some critics have, that Sarah Fielding wrote *The Governess* specifically for her niece(s). In 1749 Harriet would have been about the age of the youngest girl in the school, little Polly Suckling.

7.   Cited in Josephine Kamm, *Hope Deferred: Girls' Education in English History* (London: Methuen, 1965), 75–76.

8. The extract from *A Midsummer Night's Dream* quoted on the title page of *The Governess* also endorses the idea that Fielding had pleasant memories of school:

> Shall we forget the Counsel we have shar'd,
>
> The Sisters Vows, the Hours that we have spent,
>
> When we have chid the hasty-footed Time
>
> For parting Us? O! and is all forgot?
>
> All School-Days Friendship, childish Innocence?

9. For Locke, dancing is "that which gives *graceful Motions* all the Life, and above all things Manliness, and a becoming Confidence to young Children, I think it cannot be learn'd too early"—*Thoughts*, 196.252. Steele describes how dancing lessons could become exercises in torture for a girl: "with a Collar round her Neck, the pretty wild Thing is taught a fantastical Gravity of Behaviour, and forced to a particular Way of holding her Head, heaving her Breast, and moving with her whole Body; and all this under Pain of never having an Husband, if she steps, looks, or moves awry"—Ross, 256.

10. Mrs. Teachum "knew, that the Faculties of the Mind grow languid and useless, when the Health of the Body is lost" (114). The six-mile round-trip visit to the dairy would require considerable stamina from children as young as six years old.

11. I am indebted to Sarah Prescott for the observation that in the long and illustrious history of girls' school stories there has been a consistent lack of interest in what took place *during* lessons.

12. Symbols of an apple as the source of temptation are clearly related to Eve in the biblical Garden of Eden; but the apple also brings echoes of the story of the Apple of Discord, the cause of the quarrel among Hera, Pallas Athene, and Aphrodite, which eventually led to the Trojan War.

13. It is also significant that the verses describing the claims of the dove are reproduced from Edward Moore's *Fables for the Female Sex* (1744), a volume of verse tales concentrating on qualities perceived to be peculiarly relevant to the female character. They seem distinctly at variance with Fielding's style of writing.

14. The story has recently been reprinted as the first tale in *The Oxford Book of Modern Fairy Tales*, ed. Alison Lurie (Oxford: Oxford University Press, 1993). Its theme of female friendship's surviving the rivalry induced by romantic attachment to a man echoes one of the stories in Fielding's *Familiar Letters* and is in some respects one of the main themes of Richardson's *Clarissa*, which appeared in 1747–48.

15. See, for example, Geoffrey Summerfield, *Fantasy and Reason* (London: Methuen, 1984), 92.

16. See Hunter, 141–59, for an account of the repression of fantasy and folk tale in the 17th and 18th centuries.

17. Servants, probably because of their country origins and their lack of formal education, were often seen as the repository of fantasy, whether folk or fairy tales, and more generally as a bad influence on children in their care. Locke warned that children "frequently learn from unbred or debauched Servants such Language, untowardly Tricks and Vices, as otherwise they would possibly be ignorant of all their Lives" (*Thoughts*, 68.127). In *The Governess* Sukey Jennett, for example, remembers that an old servant had encouraged her willfulness: "I was a favourite of hers, and in every-thing had my own way" (76).

18. In terms of political subtext, this story endorses the restoration of a rightful but exiled ruler—but only if that ruler is capable of ruling wisely.

19. It has been suggested that the feminocentricity of many fairy tales makes them far more radical than they may at first appear. See, for example, Jack Zipes, "The Origins of the Fairy Tale for Children, or, How Script Was Used to Tame the Beast in Us," Avery and Briggs, 123.

20. There were 126 performances of it between 1722 and 1762, and references in *The Spectator* suggest the characters and situations in the play were widely known. See Introduction to Richard Steele, *The Funeral, or Grief à la Mode: A Comedy* (1702), in *The Plays of Richard Steele*, ed. Shirley Strum Kenny (Oxford: Oxford University Press, 1971), 6–7.

21. "Vice, for vice is necessary to be shewn, should always disgust; nor should the graces of gaiety, or the dignity of courage, be so united with it, as to reconcile it to the mind; wherever it appears, it should raise hatred by the malignity of its practices, and contempt by the meanness of its strategems; for while it is supported by either parts or spirit, it will be seldom heartily abhorred"—Samuel Johnson, *Rambler* 4, 31 March 1750.

22. To give one example: Lady Eleanor Fenn, b. 1743, used the pseudonym Mrs. Teachwell in her own educational writings later in the century and included *The Governess* among "Mrs. Teachwell's library for her young ladies"—Grey, 63.

23. See Grey, 353–60, for a detailed publishing history.

24. Erasmus Darwin's lengthy list of advised reading for girls in boarding schools includes only one work of Fielding's: her translation of Xenophon's *Memoirs of Socrates*—*A Plan for the Conduct of Female Education in Boarding Schools* (1797), 123.

25. M. Nancy Cutt, *Mrs. Sherwood and Her Books for Children* (Oxford: Oxford University Press, 1974), 39; hereafter cited in the text.

26. The only mention of Fielding in Sherwood's version is a passing comment in the introduction that the earlier *Governess* was "'said to have been written by a sister of the celebrated Fielding'"—Grey, 74.

Chapter Five

1. Tom Keymer, *Richardson's "Clarissa" and the Eighteenth-Century Reader* (Cambridge: Cambridge University Press, 1992), 58; hereafter cited in the text.

2. Fielding wrote to Richardson on 8 January 1749 that "when I read of [Clarissa] I am all sensation; my heart glows; I am overwhelmed; my only vent is in tears; and unless tears could mark my thoughts as legibly as ink, I cannot speak half I feel"—*Correspondence*, 123.

3. *Remarks on Clarissa*, ed. Peter Sabor (Augustan Reprint Society, nos. 231–32, Los Angeles: William Andrews Clark Memorial Library, 1985); hereafter cited in the text.

4. See *Oxford English Dictionary*, definition 2.

5. *Critical Remarks on Sir Charles Grandison, Clarissa, and Pamela*, by "A lover of virtue" (1754, reprinted Augustan Reprint Society, no. 21 [Series 4, no. 3], Los Angeles: William Andrews Clark Memorial Library, 1950), 18.

6. Henry Fielding wrote to Richardson that Clarissa's letter to Lovelace, after the rape, was "beyond any thing I have ever read. God forbid that the Man who reads this with dry Eyes should be alone with my Daughter when she hath no Assistance within Call. Here my Terror ends and my Grief begins"—*Correspondence*, 70. The extravagance of Henry's language renders Bellario's contribution a model of moderation.

7. Possibly as early as 1744—T. C. Duncan Eaves and Ben D. Kimpel, *Samuel Richardson: A Biography* (Oxford: Oxford University Press, 1971), 206–7; hereafter cited in the text.

8. Richardson to Aaron Hill, 12 July 1749, in *Selected Letters of Samuel Richardson*, ed. John Carroll (Oxford: Oxford University Press, 1964), 125.

9. Richardson later wrote that he had not seen the pamphlet before it was printed. See Richardson to Stinstra, 6 December 1752, in *The Richardson-Stinstra Correspondence and Stinstra's prefaces to "Clarissa,"* ed. William C. Slattery (Carbondale and Edwardsville: Southern Illinois University Press, 1969), 6; hereafter cited in the text.

10. There is no evidence that *Remarks* was ever translated.

11. William Beatty Warner, *Reading "Clarissa": The Struggles of Interpretation* (New York and London: Yale University Press, 1979), 233. Warner does not approve of Fielding's views: his deconstructionist approach regards Richardson's moral didacticism, and Fielding's endorsement of it, as "bullying."

Chapter Six

1. *David Simple: Volume the Last*, ed. Malcolm Kelsall (Harmondsworth: Penguin, 1969, reprinted 1987), 309; hereafter cited in the text.

2. See particularly Carolyn Woodward, "Sarah Fielding's Self-Destructing Utopia: The Adventures of David Simple," in *Living by the Pen: Early British Women Writers*, ed. Dale Spender (New York: Teachers College Press, 1992), 65–81; hereafter cited in the text. Woodward treats *David Simple* and *Volume the Last* as a single work, an approach that informs her opinion of both novels.

3. In this, Mrs. Orgeuil bears a strong resemblance to Brunetta, the wicked fairy in the story of Hebe in *The Governess*.

4. See, for example, Woodward, Skinner, and Todd (1989).

Chapter Seven

1. The editor of Dodsley's letters records the transaction as one of only two "deviations from the usual modes of payment" in Dodsley's publishing dealings but does not assume multiple authorship as a cause—*The Correspondence of Robert Dodsley, 1733–1764*, ed. James E. Tierney (Cambridge: Cambridge University Press, 1988), 31.

2. Authorship may have extended beyond Fielding and Collier. The occasional appearance of the "hath" grammatical construction associated with Henry Fielding suggests that he might have contributed. Collier's brother Arthur later claimed to have written the section concerning the philosophy of Lord Shaftesbury—*The Piozzi Letters: Correspondence of Hester Lynch Piozzi, 1784–1821, Volume 2, 1792–1798*, eds. Edward A. Bloom and Lillian D. Bloom (Newark: University of Delaware Press, 1991), 249; hereafter cited in the text.

3. See, for example, *Correspondence*, 124–25.

4. In *The Art of Ingeniously Tormenting*, Collier refers to Orgeuil, in *Volume the Last*, and to *Familiar Letters* (142–43). Much of Fielding's writing, including, for example, Lady ———'s treatment of Cynthia in *David Simple* and Mrs. Orgeuil's treatment of little Cynthia in *Volume the Last*, concerns "the art of ingeniously tormenting," as explicated by Collier.

5. *The Cry* (1754), a facsimile reproduction of the first London edition (New York: Scholars Facsimiles and Reprints, Delmar, 1986), 1.1; hereafter cited in the text. Mary Anne Schofield's introduction hereafter cited in the text as Schofield 1986.

6. Lady Mary Wortley Montagu ascribed the work to Fielding, but since she also believed that Fielding was the author of Charlotte Lennox's *The Female Quixote* (1752)—and that Henry Fielding wrote Tobias Smolett's *Roderick Random* (1748)—her evidence is not conclusive.

7. Quoted in Deborah Downs-Miers, "Labyrinths of the Mind: A Study of Sarah Fielding," Ph.D. dissertation (University of Missouri-Columbia, 1975), 72.

8. The *Oxford English Dictionary* defines "licentious" as "disregarding accepted rules" and as "unrestrained by law, decorum, or morality." Both definitions are directly relevant to Fielding's concerns in *The Cry*.

9. This is one of several aspects in which *The Cry* threatens to subvert Richardson's narrative of a loving young woman and an ideal son of a faulty father, which forms the basis of *Sir Charles Grandison*.

10. Fielding asserts in a footnote that the anecdote is true and the friend "too well known to need any further description." Catherine Talbot assumed

(probably correctly) that the reference was to Elizabeth Carter and was offended by Fielding's "sign-post painting" (Pennington, 2.188).

11. Portia's attitude here irresistibly recalls Mrs. Orgeuil in *Volume the Last*: when she hears of her husband's recovery from illness, "Mrs. *Orgeuil*'s Joy now appeared as violent as her Sorrow had before, and she began to repeat all the Poetry she could remember" (423).

12. W. Austin Flanders: *Structures of Experience: History, Society, and Personal Life in the Eighteenth-Century British Novel* (Columbia: University of South Carolina Press, 1984), 44.

13. The distinction between "free" and "licentious" is again directly relevant; the *Oxford English Dictionary* definition of "licentious" as "disregarding accepted rules" offers a specifically linguistic dimension by adding "especially in matters of grammar or style."

14. John Barrell, "The Language Properly So-Called: The Authority of Common Usage," in *English Literature in History: 1730–1780: An Equal, Wide Survey* (London: Hutchinson, 1983), 138; hereafter cited in the text.

15. See Schofield 1986, 8, for an interesting discussion on this point.

16. See Clive T. Probyn, *The Sociable Humanist: The Life and Works of James Harris, 1709–80: Provincial and Metropolitan Culture in Eighteenth-Century England* (Oxford: Oxford University Press, 1991).

17. It is only matched by the fate of the Bilson family in *The History of Ophelia*.

18. Samuel Richardson to Lady Bradshaigh, 14 February 1754, Forster collection, reel 15, F.48.E.5.24, Victoria and Albert Museum, London.

19. Lady Bradshaigh to Samuel Richardson, 2–22 March 1754, Forster collection, reel 15, F.48.E.5.28, Victoria and Albert Museum, London.

20. Samuel Richardson to Sophia Westcomb, 9 August 1754, Forster collection, reel 16, F.48.E.8.143, Victoria and Albert Museum, London.

21. It seems that in the late 18th century a copy of *The Cry* was acquired by the British Museum. Piozzi's letter was a reply to the British Museum librarian, who had written to her seeking information about the work.

Chapter Eight

1. Sarah Fielding, *The Lives of Cleopatra and Octavia*, ed. Christopher D. Johnson (London and Toronto: Associated University Presses, 1994), 16. Johnson's text is based on the first edition. His introduction contains comprehensive information about text, sources, and variants between editions; hereafter cited in the text as Johnson 1994.

2. *Rambler* 60, 13 October 1750 (4 vols., 1753), 2.54.

3. *Monthly Review* 17 (7 July 1757), 39.

4. Shakespeare's *Antony and Cleopatra* was known in the 18th century as a written text rather than as a stage performance; it was not performed on the London stage between 1700 and 1750—Rogers, 70.

5. John Dryden, *All for Love: Or, the World Well Lost* (London: A. & C. Black, 1975), ed. N. J. Andrew, 10.

6. The fact that Henry Fielding burlesqued Dryden's confrontation scene between Cleopatra and Octavia in his play *The Tragedy of Tragedies* (1730–31) suggests a possible early interest in the subject—Battestins 107.

7. Lucy Hughes-Hallett identifies Fielding as "the first woman to relate her own version of the story of Cleopatra"—*Cleopatra: Histories, Dreams and Distortions* (London: Bloomsbury, 1990), 165; hereafter cited in the text.

8. Compare the traditional view of 18th-century fiction and culture: "the English novel . . . is middle class from the start, and the middle class code and imagination exclude the Cleopatra type as beyond its pale and beyond its comprehension"—Robert Palfrey Utter and Gwendolyn Bridges Needham, *Pamela's Daughters* (London: Lovat Dickson, 1937), 9.

9. Ann Marilyn Parrish, "Eight Experiments in Fiction: A Critical Analysis of the Works of Sarah Fielding" (Ph.D. dissertation, Boston University Graduate School, 1973), 144; hereafter cited in the text.

10. *Miscellanies by Henry Fielding, Esq.; Volume Two*, ed. Hugh Amory with commentary by Bertrand A. Goldgar (Oxford: Clarendon Press, 1993), 113–28; hereafter cited in the text as *Miscellanies*.

11. Bertrand Goldgar writes in his introduction to *Miscellanies* (xxxiv–xxxv) that "there is enough circumstantial and internal evidence to make most scholars take the attribution seriously." A computer analysis has also suggested Sarah's authorship—J. F. Burrows and A. J. Hassall, "*Anna Boleyn* and the Authenticity of Fielding's Feminine Narratives," *Eighteenth-Century Studies* 21 (1988), 444.

12. It has been suggested that a draft of *Cleopatra and Octavia* was complete by July 1744, on the basis of a letter from Edward Young to Samuel Richardson: "I particularly insist that, when you go to North End, you let Cleopatra and Octavia know, that by their favour I was so happy, that in their company, and so sweet a retirement, I thought, with Antony, the world well lost" (Barbauld, 2.3). A footnote suggests this comment refers to "The Lives of Cleopatra and Octavia, Written by Miss Fielding," but the connection seems slender. In 1757, Catherine Talbot wrote that her mother had two hens called Cleopatra and Octavia (Pennington 1809, 2.251).

13. Hughes-Hallett, 1, quoting Théophile Gautier.

14. Hughes-Hallett, 5, quoting Arthur Symons.

15. Fielding spells "Anthony" rather than "Antony" throughout.

16. Sir Thomas North translation, cited in William Shakespeare, *Antony and Cleopatra*, ed. M. R. Ridley (Oxford: Oxford University Press, 9th ed., 1954, reprinted 1972), 273.

17. This is an astounding reversal of the claim in *The Cry* that men dominate women by pandering to their foolishness.

18. "Fielding's sister," review of *The Lives of Cleopatra and Octavia*, ed. R. Brimley-Johnson, *Times Literary Supplement*, 4 April 1929, 273.

Chapter Nine

1. There was a real-life Lord Dorchester, a distant relative of Fielding herself; the title was held, successively, by Lady Mary Wortley Montagu's father and nephew.

2. Neil McKendrick, John Brewer, and J. H. Plumb, eds., *The Birth of a Consumer Society: The Commercialization of Eighteenth-Century England* (London: Europa, 1982), 9.

3. Earlier examples include Eliza Haywood's *The History of Miss Betsy Thoughtless* (1751). Later examples range from Maria Edgeworth's *Belinda* (1801) to Jane Austen's *Northanger Abbey* (1818). The actual phrase "The history of a young lady's entrance into the world" is the subtitle of Fanny Burney's *Evelina* (1778). Burney may have taken the name of the hero of *Evelina* from the idealistic young French nobleman D'Orville in *The Countess of Dellwyn*; the more extensive influence on *Evelina* of *Ophelia* is described below.

4. Ann Marilyn Parrish, for example, argues that the reader is intended to feel some sympathy with the countess at the end of her story; and yet Parrish herself records the verdict of William Werner that Fielding would have been appalled at the thought of the reader's sympathizing with the countess—Parrish, 173.

5. Sarah Fielding, *The History of the Countess of Dellwyn* (London: A. Millar, 1759), vi; hereafter cited in the text. The novel was reproduced in facsimile by Garland Press in 1974.

6. Fielding's example is drawn, in essence, from her own writing: in *Volume the Last*, the fire that destroys David's house is carefully and comprehensively accounted for.

7. Roy Porter, *English Society in the Eighteenth Century* (Harmondsworth: Penguin, 1982, reprinted 1988), 41.

8. Early in her marriage Charlotte actually falls ill with distaste for Lord Dellwyn. The narrator comments that, had Charlotte been able to tell Lord Dellwyn the truth about her poor health, she would have had to admit, "'My lord, you are my Disease'" (1.111–12).

9. It was, however, more prevalent in the 1750s than in earlier decades of the century. There were 16 divorces in the period 1751–60, compared with 14 in the period 1701–1750—Lawrence Stone, *Road to Divorce: England 1530–1987* (Oxford: Oxford University Press, 1990), 432; hereafter cited in the text.

10. Spelled "Cummyns" in Volume 2.

11. Opening a shop was seen as a conclusive loss of respectability for a fictional gentlewoman—see Charlotte Smith's radical challenge to this concept in *Marchmont* (1795).

12. Henry Fielding, *Amelia* (1751), ed. David Blewett (Harmondsworth: Penguin, 1987), 441.

13. Moreover, they acted on their theories. In the late 1760s Scott and her sister Elizabeth Montagu participated in the establishment of a small-scale

community on the lines suggested by *The Countess of Dellwyn* and *Millenium Hall*. The community was not, however, a success: see Rizzo, 306–19.

14.   There was a vogue for "ideal-community" novels in the 1770s and 1780s, but the prominence Fielding and Scott gave to women was not always maintained; in *Munster Village* (1778) Lady Mary Hamilton describes a community led by a woman, but Courtney Melmoth's *Shenstone-Green* (1779) and Robert Bage's *Mount Henneth* (1781) both give women subordinate roles.

15.   In this respect there are similarities between Charlotte Lucum and one of Fielding's earliest faulty female characters, Nanny Johnson in *David Simple*, who married for money and status, but who "if she had not met with this Temptation . . . would have made a very affectionate Wife to the Man who loved her" (38).

16.   I do not support Mary Anne Schofield's interpretation of Charlotte as "one of the most magnificent dissemblers of feminine eighteenth-century literature"—Mary Anne Schofield, *Masking and Unmasking the Female Mind* (1990), 120; hereafter cited in the text.

17.   Sarah Fielding, *The History of Ophelia* (London, 1760); hereafter cited in the text. The novel was reproduced in facsimile by Garland Press in 1974.

18.   One generally unimpressed reviewer of *The History of Ophelia* suggested that "for any great Instruction or Amusement a Reader of Taste and discernment will meet with in the perusal, the manuscript might as well have still remained within the buroe"—*Monthly Review* 22 (April 1760), 328.

19.   Deborah Downs-Miers, "Spring the Trap: Subtexts and Subversions," in *Fetter'd or Free? British Women Novelists, 1670–1815*, eds. Mary Anne Schofield and Cecilia Macheski (Athens: Ohio University Press, 1986), 318.

20.   Her technique builds on the narrative mode of *Cleopatra and Octavia* but is more complex, showing the narrator and a younger self as the same living person at different stages of experience.

21.   *The History of Ophelia* provided a model for Fanny Burney's novel. Similarities extend far beyond the basic situation of "a young lady's entrance into the world" and the parallels in this scene: for example, Burney's Evelina, like Fielding's Ophelia, visits the opera and the theater and records similar impressions. The experiences of Burney's later heroine Cecilia at a masquerade are similar to those of Ophelia.

22.   Mullan (16) describes illness as "the last retreat of the morally pure."

23.   "Emily gazed with melancholy awe upon the castle . . . for, though it was now lighted up by the setting sun, the gothic greatness of its features, and its mouldering walls of dark grey stone, rendered it a gloomy and sublime object. . . . As the twilight deepened, its features became more awful in obscurity, and Emily continued to gaze, till its clustering towers were alone seen, rising over the tops of the woods, beneath whose thick shade the carriages soon after began to ascend"—Ann Radcliffe, *The Mysteries of Udolpho* (1794), ed. Bonamy Dobrée (Oxford: Oxford University Press, 1966, reprinted 1986), 226–27.

24. See, for example, Schofield 1990, 127.

25. *Critical Review* 7 (April 1759), 378–79.

26. *Monthly Review* 20 (April 1759), 380–81.

27. *Monthly Review* 20 (April 1759), 380.

28. A Dublin edition was issued in 1759 and German editions in 1761 and 1771.

Chapter Ten

1. Mary Scott, *The Female Advocate: A Poem. Occasioned by Reading Dr. Duncombe's Feminead* (1774), lines 256–64.

2. *Gentleman's Magazine* 265 (1888), 485–92; hereafter cited in the text.

Bibliography

Place of publication is London unless otherwise stated.

PRIMARY SOURCES

The Adventures of David Simple (1744), ed. Malcolm Kelsall (Oxford: Oxford University Press, 1969).

Familiar Letters Between the Characters of David Simple and Others (1747).

The Governess, or Little Female Academy (1749), ed. Jill E. Grey (Oxford: Oxford University Press, 1968).

Remarks on Clarissa (1749), ed. Peter Sabor (Augustan Reprint Society, nos. 231–32, Los Angeles: William Andrews Clark Memorial Library, 1985).

David Simple: Volume the Last (1753), ed. Malcolm Kelsall (Oxford: Oxford University Press, 1969).

The Cry (1754; reprinted Delmar, New York: Scholars Facsimiles and Reprints, 1986).

The Lives of Cleopatra and Octavia (1757), ed. Christopher D. Johnson (London and Toronto: Associated University Presses, 1994).

The History of the Countess of Dellwyn (1759).

The History of Ophelia (1760).

(trans.), *Xenophon's Memoirs of Socrates, with the Defence of Socrates Before his Judges* (Bath and London, 1762).

SECONDARY SOURCES

Battestin, Martin C. and Clive T. Probyn, eds., *The Correspondence of Henry and Sarah Fielding* (Oxford: Oxford University Press, 1993). Contains Sarah Fielding's complete correspondence, much of it previously unknown; includes biographical introduction and comprehensive footnotes.

Battestin, Martin C., with Ruthe R. Battestin, *Henry Fielding: A Life* (London: Routledge, 1989). Detailed account of the shared childhood of the Fieldings, Henry's life, and the society he and Sarah inhabited.

Beasley, Jerry C., *Novels of the 1740s* (Athens: University of Georgia Press, 1982). Survey of the literary scene in the 1740s, including (though not very prominently) *David Simple*.

Burrows, J. F. and A. J. Hassall, eds., "Anna Boleyn and the Authenticity of Fielding's Feminine Narratives," *Eighteenth-Century Studies* 21 (1988), 427–53. Discusses computer analysis of narrative style of Henry and Sarah Fielding.

Carpenter, Lissette Ferlet, "Sarah Fielding: A Mid-Century Link in Eighteenth-Century Feminist Views," (Ph.D. Diss., Texas A&M University, 1989). Feminist view of Fielding, with some interesting commentary on her work from this perspective. Claims that Fielding stands in line between Astell and Wollstonecraft less convincing.

Collier, Jane, *The Art of Ingeniously Tormenting* (1753), ed. Judith Hawley (Bristol: Thoemmes Press, 1994). Written while Collier and Fielding were lodging together. Shares principles and techniques with Fielding's work.

Davys, Mary, *The Accomplished Rake, or Modern Fine Gentleman* (1727), repro-duced in William McBurney, ed., *Four Before Richardson: Selected English Novels, 1720–27* (Lincoln: University of Nebraska Press, 1963). Provides interesting contrast with *David Simple* and example of female fiction before Fielding.

Downs-Miers, Deborah, "Labyrinths of the Mind: A Study of Sarah Fielding" (Ph.D. Diss., University of Missouri-Columbia, 1975). Detailed consider-ation of Sarah Fielding's work, from a broadly feminist perspective.

✓ ———, "Spring the Trap: Subtexts and Subversions," in Mary Anne Schofield and Cecilia Macheski, eds., *Fetter'd or Free?: British Women Novelists, 1670–1815* (Athens: Ohio University Press, 1986), 308–23. Overview of Fielding's fiction, concentrating on language and feminism.

Eaves, T. C. Duncan and Ben D. Kimpel, *Samuel Richardson: A Biography* (Oxford: Oxford University Press, 1971). Standard biography of Richardson, containing information about his circle, including Fielding.

Fielding Henry, *Amelia* (1751), ed. David Blewett (Harmondsworth: Penguin, 1987). Contains themes reworked in *The History of Ophelia*.

Hunter, J. Paul, *Before Novels: The Cultural Contexts of Eighteenth-Century English Fiction* (New York: Norton, 1990). Explores the culture and conditions of writers (including Fielding) in the early 18th century.

Johnson, Christopher D., Introduction to *The Lives of Cleopatra and Octavia* (London and Toronto: Associated University Presses, 1994). One of the first explorations of *The Lives of Cleopatra and Octavia*; see especially its conclusions concerning the depth and extent of Sarah Fielding's reading.

MacCarthy, B. G., *Women Writers: Their Contribution to the English Novel 1621–1744* (Cork: Cork University Press, 1946). Regards Fielding as a literary figure at the end of a prenovel tradition rather than as a pioneer. Informed traditional view of early 18th-century fiction.

Mullan, John, *Sentiment and Sociability: The Language of Feeling in the Eighteenth Century* (Oxford: Oxford University Press, 1988). Occasionally dense, but always fascinating, exploration of the reasons for the cult of sensibility.

Myers, Sylvia Harckstark, *The Bluestocking Circle: Women, Friendship, and the Life of the Mind in Eighteenth-Century England* (Oxford: Clarendon Press, 1990). Little on Fielding but much on Elizabeth Carter, Catherine Talbot, Sarah Scott, Elizabeth Montagu, among others.

Needham, Arnold, "The Life and Works of Sarah Fielding" (Ph.D. Diss., University of California, 1943). Primarily interested in Sarah Fielding as

"Fielding's sister," but contains some incisive traditional scholarship on her work.

Parrish, Ann Marilyn, "Eight Experiments in Fiction: A Critical Analysis of the Works of Sarah Fielding" (Ph.D. Diss., Boston University Graduate School, 1973). Pioneering, if occasionally superficial, study of innovations in Sarah Fielding's writing.

Rizzo, Betty, *Companions Without Vows: Relationships Among Eighteenth-Century British Women* (Athens: University of Georgia Press, 1994). Explores a number of relationships, including that of the "Bath circle" of women writers. See especially "Satires of Tyrants and Toadeaters: Fielding and Collier," 41–60, and "Reformers," 306–19.

Schofield, Mary Anne, Introduction to *The Cry* (New York: Scholars Facsimiles and Reprints: Delmar, 1986). First modern attempt to discuss *The Cry* as a serious work of fiction.

———, *Masking and Unmasking the Female Mind* (1990). See especially 108–27 on Sarah Fielding; discusses most of Fielding's writing.

Scott, Sarah, *A Description of Millenium Hall* (1762). Important novel by friend of Fielding's, influenced by ideas of a female community presented in *The History of the Countess of Dellwyn*.

Skinner, Gillian, "'The Price of a Tear': Economic Sense and Sensibility in Sarah Fielding's *David Simple*," *Literature and History* 3rd. series, vol. 1, no. 1, Spring 1992, 16–28. Sets *David Simple* in the context of economic and sentimental conventions of the time.

Spencer, Jane, *The Rise of the Woman Novelist: From Aphra Behn to Jane Austen* (Oxford: Basil Blackwell, 1986, reprinted 1989). Important account of 18th-century female fiction. See especially "Masculine Approval and Sarah Fielding," 91–95. Spencer sees Fielding as compromised by her need for acceptance within a masculine-dominated world.

Spender, Dale, *Mothers of the Novel* (London: Pandora, 1986). Enthusiastic view of 18th-century women writers, though not always reliable in detail. See especially "Sarah Fielding and Misrepresentation" (180–93).

Todd, Janet, *Sensibility: An Introduction* (Methuen, 1986). Accessible overview of the cult of sensibility in the 18th-century.

———, *The Sign of Angellica: Women, Writing and Fiction, 1660–1800* (1989). Important exploration of women and fiction in the 18th century. See especially "Novelists of Sentiment: Sarah Fielding and Frances Sheridan," 161–75, which compares *David Simple* with *The Memoirs of Miss Sidney Bidulph*.

Turner, Cheryl, *Living by the Pen: Women Writers in the Eighteenth Century* (Routledge, 1992). Provides useful information especially about why women wrote and how much they might expect to earn from different kinds of writing.

Woodward, Carolyn, "Sarah Fielding's Self-Destructing Utopia: The Adventures of David Simple," in *Living by the Pen: Early British Women Writers*, ed. Dale Spender (New York: Teachers College Press, 1992).

Index

The Author

Linda Bree obtained her Ph.D. from the University of London in 1992. She is an editor in literature at Cambridge University Press and teaches in the Department of Continuing Education at the University of Essex. She has written on the 18th- and early 19th-century novel and has developed a particular interest in the literature and culture of women novelists of the mid-18th century. She is currently working on a new edition of Sarah Fielding's *The History of Ophelia*.